STUDIES
OF
INDIAN LIFE
AND
SENTIMENT

BAMPFYLDE FULLER

ISBN : 978-93-5324-529-0 (HB)

First Published, London, 1910

Published, 2020

Published by

Facsimile Publisher
12 Pragati Market
Ashok Vihar, Ph-2
Delhi-110052
E-mail: books@facsimilepublisher.com

Printed at: G. Print Process, Delhi.

Studies of Indian Life and Sentiment

Author:Bampfylde Fuller

STUDIES OF INDIAN LIFE AND SENTIMENT

By SIR BAMPFYLDE FULLER

K.C.S.I., C.I.E.

LONDON

JOHN MURRAY, ALBEMARLE STREET

1910

To the Memory of my Mother,
to whose influence I owe it if my life
has been of any service to others.

Preface.

THIS book will not contribute much that is new to the stores which Indian experience and study have collected. But it may be of service in diffusing information which these stores seclude. Of recent years the British democracy has begun to realise more insistently its responsibilities towards India; and Indian affairs excite increasing interest. My object has been to use an intimate acquaintance with the country to give such an account of it, of its people and of its government, as may assist others to understand the problems that are offered by the development of a vast population for whom the British nation is trustee.

I am indebted for kind advice to Sir Charles Lyall; and I acknowledge assistance derived from Sir Herbert Risley's *People of India*, Mr. Vincent Smith's *Early History of India*, and from the *Imperial Gazetteer of India*. My thanks are also due to the Editor of the *Nineteenth Century and After* for permission to extract some passages from articles that I have contributed to that review.

BAMPFYLDE FULLER.

April 1910.

Contents.

i.—The Indian Monsoon.

The dramatic character of the Indian rainfall.

THERE are clefts in the desert, such as Egypt, Mesopotamia, and Sindh, which have been filled with rich soil and are carpeted with verdure by the action of mighty rivers that spread over them the rainfall of far-off lands. For them there is little question of weather, and any unaccustomed rain-storms are for a threat and not a promise. Elsewhere the ultimate hopes of mankind are in the clouds above them. This is so in Europe not less than in India. But in India the dependence of man upon the weather is driven home to him with dramatic intensity. Where rain falls more or less all the year round, it is accepted as a matter of course, like the rising and setting of the sun. But where, for months at a time, the path of the rain-clouds is turned altogether aside, and the winds gain each day in heat and dryness till they become as the breath of a furnace, man realises that it is only the return of the clouds that can save his fields from being scorched into a desert; and in the burning discomfort of the Indian June he watches the sky as anxiously as did the prophet on Carmel. One day the crackling dryness of the air is softened by a current of moisture: swarms of insects take courage to begin life above ground: on the roadsides one sees streams of winged ants spouting up like little geysers from their underground nests: clouds appear on the horizon: they grow into a dark bank illumined by frequent lightning: a wind comes, chilly in comparison with the breathless heat it disturbs: there follows the rushing of the rain, distant at first, then engulfing the country with a deluge. The earth smells of life again. The monsoon has set in.

Alternations of drought and of moisture.

Thenceforward for three months heavy clouds drift over the land, giving frequent showers. Sometimes they form a thick canopy which drenches the country unceasingly for several days at a time. Then again they break up, and here and there heavy masses move across a deep-blue sky in slow procession, touching the earth with inky rain-blurs. There are days when the sky is altogether clear—when the sun blazes down through the well-washed sky with a concentrated brilliance that draws vegetation upwards in its crudest colours. There is the oppression of breathless, dazzling heat, than which the hot weather dust haze seems more endurable. Gradually these breaks become more frequent, and in northern India by the end of September the monsoon is at an end. Some storms are expected in October to moisten the ground for the sowing of the cold-weather crops. They are capricious; but more precious than two-thirds of the deluge which has preceded them. Indeed, with their assistance, two bumper harvests have been gathered from a rainfall which in the aggregate was only a third of the average. So greatly does the value of the rain depend upon its distribution. From the middle of October all cloud canopy is again withdrawn for two months: the cold weather sets in with a sky of lighter blue, air as clear as crystal, dry, cool, and exhilarating: the country dressed out in the tender green of sprouting wheat and barley. Towards the middle of December clouds should again appear, coming this time not from seawards, but from the steppes of central Asia. They give the cold-weather rain—two or three inches—which, were it not for chances of blight, would secure the excellence of the spring harvest. These showers over, the country relapses into five months' drought, tempered only by the hail-storms of April, which not unfrequently ruin the wheat harvest, or by the dust-storms of May and June which, whirled upwards from the desert, descend upon the country in raging wind, enveloped in a darkness that can literally be felt.

Given water, the Indian climate is suitable for plant-growth all the year round. Even in the north, outside the tropics, the cold weather is not sufficiently cold to compel hibernation; it merely changes the character of the crops from tropical to temperate. There are two harvests, the autumn and the spring, the former of tropical crops such as cotton and millet, which are sown on the setting-in of the monsoon; the latter of temperate crops, such as wheat, barley and linseed, which are sown in October in reliance upon the moisture that the ground retains from the monsoon rain or that is given by the longed-for October showers.

The seasons.

The cold-weather rain, which sweeps down from central Asia, does not extend far down the peninsula. On the other hand, southern India profits by the withdrawal of the monsoon current, which in its retreat seawards lets heavy showers fall during November and December. Indeed the eastern coast districts of Madras receive during these months the heaviest rain of the year.

Origin of the monsoon.

This monsoon, without which India would be as burnt and desolate as Arabia, is a current of moist air that during the summer months flows northward from the seas on the Equator, drawn, we are told—or at all events started, —by the necessity of replenishing the air which is heated and driven upwards by the surface of Asia. According to this theory, Asia may be regarded as a furnace from which land-air ascends like smoke, the monsoon being a draught of sea-air which rushes to the fire-bars. Its initial direction is from south to north. But the current suffers some remarkable deflections. The eastward motion of the earth gives it an eastward twist so that its general direction upon Ceylon is from the south-west. North of the latitude of Ceylon it is split up by the Indian continent into two branches, one running up the Bay of Bengal and the other up the Arabian Sea, between the Bombay coast and Africa. Both of these branches curve inwards towards India, the Bengal current arriving from the south-east, and the Bombay current from the west-south-west, or even from the west. So that the monsoon may be said to embrace India as with a pair of arms, which clasp it from almost opposite directions. The deflection of the Bombay current from south-west to west is very great, and it has a very remarkable result. The current, losing practically the whole of its drift from the south, is unable to reach Arabia, Persia, and Baluchistan: it flows parallel to and south of their coast-line and leaves them unwatered. Karachi, three

Its two currents.

hundred miles north of Bombay, is beyond the rain-track. But before losing its impulse from the south the stream of clouds has flung itself upon the high-lands of Abyssinia, and, dissolving upon them in heavy rainfall, has replenished the fertilising waters of the Nile. The curve of the western (or Bombay) branch of the monsoon is extraordinarily abrupt: the current reaches Abyssinia flowing south to north, it then sweeps eastward, and passing south of Socotra directs itself upon the coast of India, flowing west to east. The Bengal branch also follows an inward curve, but to nothing like the same extent, or it would leave Burma unwatered. These curious deflections, with their prodigious consequences in the history of mankind, are ascribed to a trough of low pressure which appears each year in the deserts of Sindh and Rajputána. But the atmospheric trough which can exert so tremendous an attraction upon distant currents of sea-air is unable to draw them home to itself: its locality remains an un-watered desert.

Moreover, the ocean wind-current that arises from the Equator meets with considerable opposition on its way northwards. Normally the winds blow towards the Equator from both north and south of it, and the monsoon has to overpower the north wind before it can find a clear run towards the coasts of Abyssinia and India. The causes that assist or retard its victory in this conflict are obscure, but are probably connected with synchronous oscillations in atmospheric pressure. Upon those mysterious waverings depend the amount of rainfall that reaches India, and the happiness or misery of millions of mankind.

The monsoon is then far from being a steady, resistless flood of moisture-laden air. It is a thing of turns and twists: a force the strength and direction of which depends upon barometric conditions that are themselves unstable, and which is liable to annual variations that may cause disastrous floods, or still more disastrous famines. And we may perhaps be permitted to speculate whether within comparatively recent times there may not have been a swing in its general direction—whether, for instance, there may not have been a time when it did not leave Arabia and central Asia unvisited. We realise that within the ages which geology unfolds there have been immense changes in the earth's surface: dry land and the sea bed have risen and fallen as if set upon a see-saw: plains have been thrust up into mountains, and mountains have been worn down into plains. But we are accustomed to think that, during the times that are linked to us by tradition or history, the existing features of the earth's surface have remained unchanged. Speculations as to the causes of the great migrations of mankind have seldom attributed them to physical changes of surface or climate. Yet it is by no means certain that the earth herself might not have caused them by cutting off the rainfall that afforded subsistence. It may be that the monsoon current in days long past penetrated much further into Asia than it does at present, and that to its withdrawal is due the gradual drying up of central Asia, and the vast migrations which for ages have been forcing strains of fresh blood into Europe, into India, and into the Far East. Not only westwards, towards

Variability of the monsoon: possible secular changes.

Europe, or southwards towards India, did the hordes of Turkestan press their way: they pressed eastwards and, crossing the icy valleys of Tibet, poured down upon the eastern limits of India, and onwards into the hills and valleys of Burma. The tribes of eastern India and Burma are akin to the Tibetans, and there are similarities of language which show their kinship, distant though it may be, with the Turks. That central Asia has been drying up during historical times there is no doubt. The borders of the Caspian testify to a very extraordinary fall in the water-level. Tracts in south-eastern Persia, that are now quite rainless, contain numerous tanks, long since dry, for the impounding of rainfall. And, in close proximity to India, the recent explorations of Dr. Stein have disclosed a civilisation which, within comparatively recent times, has literally been dried out of existence. In Chinese Tartary, beyond the Himalayas that lie north of Kashmir, there is a barren valley of shifting sand, now utterly deserted by mankind. Here and there through the sand vestiges of human habitation appear, and excavation has revealed the deserted houses of a large population, possessing an advanced civilisation and using a script which is closely related to those of India, and was in use not more than two thousand years ago. There is everything to show that rivers which now can hardly trickle beyond the Himalayan hill-foot once had a current that forced its way across this valley and irrigated it. Their springs have failed, and the hill-ranges from which they flow must have been deserted by rain-clouds that formerly watered them. It may seem impossible that the influence of the Indian seas should have extended across the high glaciers which lie between this range and the plains of the Panjáb. But the monsoon current, extraordinary though it may appear, reaches Lhassa across two hundred miles of arid steppe lying as high above sea-level as the summit of Mont Blanc, and, dropping no rain upon this wilderness, descends upon the heart of Tibet in showers which are sufficient for the growth of rice crops. The Tibet Expeditionary Force was amazed to find Lhassa not only damp and rainy during the Indian rainy season, but, though ten thousand feet above sea-level, pervaded by the mugginess of the Indian monsoon. It is then not impossible that the monsoon current may at one time have forced its way across the glaciers of Kashmir. It has now withdrawn; and some ruined walls in a sandy desert whisper a tragedy of famine, despair, and abandonment.

The accounts given by Greek historians of Alexander's invasion (which are in great measure extracted from the writings of men who took part in it) refer to the north-western Panjáb in terms which appear to indicate that twenty-two centuries ago it received a more copious rainfall than at present. Forests of timber trees appear to have stood where now there is only camel-thorn: indeed we learn from remains of (geologically) quite recent date that, further back, there were marshes haunted by elephants and rhinoceros. The country along the rivers Jhelum and Chenáb is referred to as flourishing and densely populated. It is now so indeed, but owing to the gigantic canals with which British engineers have irrigated land that formerly was an arid thorn-growing wilderness. On its return from India the Greek army marched along the arid Mekrán coast west of Karachi. It suffered terribly ; but at the present day such an enterprise would be altogether impossible.

There is, however, no reason for believing that, within the last few centuries, there has been any permanent change in the weather. European travellers of the time of the Moghal Empire give very shocking accounts of famine mortality ; and if, during the last thirty years, famines have become a prominent feature in Indian economic history, it is because famine-relief has established itself as an organised department of State energy, and failures of rain and their consequences are carefully inquired into and recorded. We shall have more to say regarding famine-relief later on. But it may be remarked here that although the Bombay branch of the monsoon is much stronger than that which enters Bengal, it is less certain to force its way inland: consequently, fluctuations of rainfall are more violent in western than in eastern India, and famines would be more numerous than they are had not the population accustomed itself to them, in its density and in its habits. On the great cultivated plateau of the Deccan, which overlooks the Bombay coast, the people hardly expect more than two good harvests in five. This difference in penetrating strength is due to difference in coast-line. On the Bengal side the land slopes gradually to the sea, and the sea wind sweeps inland without obstruction. But on the Bombay side there is, a few miles from the coast, a mountain wall, two thousand feet high, against which the sea wind dashes itself. It drenches the mountain-side with rain and gradually creeps over

Deficient rainfall: famines.

the summit; but it has suffered a grievous loss of moisture. On the seaward edge of the plateau there fall annually about one hundred and fifty inches of rain; Poona, only twenty miles inland, receives only a seventh of this quantity. Curiously enough, as the current spreads further inland, the rain which it yields gradually increases. A couple of hundred miles further from the coast the fall is half as much again as it is at Poona. So we have seen Lhassa watered by a current which had seemingly spent its humidity upon the southern face of the Himalayas.

Cyclones.

India would, however, fare badly were she dependent upon the gradual diffusion of sea-air across the continent. With the moistening of the ground the indraught weakens, and would not of itself suffice to bring heavy rain during August and September. But from time to time the Bengal current is caught up by cyclones, generated in the Bay of Bengal, which whirl across India, following the range of forest-clad hills that divide the peninsula from the Ganges valley, and spreading their skirts to the foot of the Himalayas on the one hand and far down the peninsula on the other. As they approach the Bombay coast the western current circles and rises to meet and reinforce them. The country lives in hope of two such cyclones—in the first half of August and towards the end of September. In some seasons cyclones appear to become habitual, one following the other with much regularity. It is, indeed, often remarked in India that the weather forms habits which influence it for months at a time. A season that commences normally will proceed with satisfactory regularity, and it seldom happens that after an irregular opening it settles down to the course which the country expects of it.

Excessive rainfall: its disastrous consequences.

We think of India as suffering from deficiencies of rainfall, and it is when the rain fails, or is short, that telegraphic messages arouse our sympathy for impending losses. But excessive, or over-continuous, rain also causes widespread hardship. The crops may stand high in the fields. But, affected by blight, or preyed upon by insects, they may yield no produce and may, for all good to the cultivator, be as if they had withered from the start. Man's existence depends upon the repression of the insect kingdom, and any excessive moisture which disturbs the adjustment of Nature affords occasion for the infinite possibilities of insect multiplication. A cotton crop which to all appearances is flourishing is often ruined by a little worm that makes its home in the bolls : armies of caterpillars suddenly appear, marching across the fields in solid battalions several yards deep, stripping leaves and flowers with the completeness and regularity of a machine. If the cold-weather rains be unduly prolonged, or are attended by fog, the wheat on heavy land will surely be blighted. I have seen wheat, extending over half a million acres, which two months before harvest promised a bumper crop, yield at harvest time two or three pounds of shrivelled grain to the acre. In crop diseases, as with diseases of mankind, India does things on a large scale. And if the cold-weather rain has come and gone as it should, there is still a dreadful risk of hail-storms. They are due in the days of the wheat harvest, when the country is a sheet of gold and the cultivators are preparing with

Hail-storms.

thankful rites to welcome the harvest home. A cloud streams out across the sky, black, lightning-shot, with lurid yellow lining : there is a rush of cold wind, some violent peals of thunder, and the hail sweeps across the fields, cutting down the brittle crops as if by the scythes of a line of war-chariots, stamping them into fragments which are swept away by the wind, leaving nothing but muddy stubble, whitened and pitted with the hailstones, where just now stood the promise of a year's subsistence. No one who has witnessed such a catastrophe will forget the wailing and lamentation which follow the storm through the village. In the Maratha country the fear of hail has driven men to invoke the powers of magic, and every good-sized village has a hedge priest, or medicine-man, whose business it is to meet approaching storms and by incantations to divert them. He is perhaps as fortunate in his prognostications as the Meteorological Reporter to Government, and is at all events a more picturesque personality, with more power for allaying the apprehensions of mankind.

In India of all countries it is evident that the rain-clouds bear threats as well as blessings. Happy in its rainlessness is Egypt, where the crops are rooted in moisture, but expand their leaves and flowers in unbroken dryness and sunlight.

Rainfall and insects.

The insect troubles of the rainy season are a well-worn theme of Indian experience. In some parts of the country one realises that it needs but a little to give insects the victory and to expel humanity from the land. This is particularly the case in the moist climate of Assam. No sooner does evening fall than myriads of flies, beetles, and moths swarm out into the twilight and drive mankind within fortifications. Not only does one dine and sleep within mosquito-nets: nets are required for the horses in the stable. In the villages the cattle are housed in lofts, standing on piles, so that fires can be kindled below them, and the insects may be repelled by a veil of smoke. It is curious to see the cattle at evening time walking unconcernedly up step-ladders to their stalls. Small flying beetles are prodigiously numerous: even in the Assam hills, five thousand feet above sea-level, they will suddenly descend upon the garden and strip every leaf from the rose bushes in a single night. And here we must mention that most loathsome beast the flying bug; in appearance something like a black ladybird, but exhaling an effluvium which English people have well-nigh forgotten. The smallest opening in curtain or window gauze suffices for them: they alight on the dinner-table, find their way into one's soup, and, more dreadful still, sometimes creep into one's hair. It is sufficient to mention that a touch excites them to increased secretion. But it is on the river steamers that one realises that insects crowd the air as bacteria the water. Below each deck-light is a thick whirling column of life which one has fairly to push one's way through; and occasionally the vessel passes through clouds of flying bugs which invade it by thousands. One gathers them off the dinner-table with spoons and segregates them in finger-bowls.

Malarial fever is independent of rainfall if, as was formerly the case at Ismailia, there are breeding-places for the anopheles mosquito. But in India it is nearly always associated with the drying-up of the rains. It costs many

Fever.

more lives than cholera, plague, or famine, and, where endemic, weakens and indeed emasculates the population. Outbreaks sometimes occur of extraordinary virulence. Such a calamity afflicted the districts round Agra in 1878. The courts were closed for a month because neither clerks, nor suitors, nor witnesses could attend them: the cotton fell to the ground as there were no hands to pick it: the mortality was such that villages lost more than half their inhabitants, and long stretches of wheat land reverted to coarse grass. Funerals were neglected: bodies were carried in carts to the burning grounds: I witnessed an incident of unusual pathos—a man walking sadly thitherwards with his two little dead children slung on poles across his shoulders.

Rainfall in deluges.

The Bengal branch of the Indian monsoon establishes a world's record in rainfall. Some hundred and fifty miles from the shore of the Bay of Bengal the Assam range of hills runs out into the plain, crossing the path of the monsoon current with an abrupt scarp rising to 4000 feet above sea-level. Against this barrier the rain-clouds hurl themselves, climb upwards, and condense as they ascend in sheets of falling water. Cherrapunji, on the edge of the plateau, ordinarily receives 450 inches of rain: it is reported to have once received 50 feet. One conceives of such a place as an uninhabitable cataract. Not so: it is a flourishing village, and was for many years an army sanatorium. For six months of the year the weather is clear and bright, and during the monsoon the rain falls chiefly at night, and sunny days are quite frequent. The plains below are deeply flooded, and large steamers can make their course across country if they please. One evening in August, leaving the steamer some fifteen miles from the hills, we embarked in light coracles, half-roofed with canopies of bamboo, so low that it was impossible even to sit up under cover. Throughout the night in pouring rain we were paddled towards the hills, avoiding the current of the stream and pushing our way through half-submerged thickets of dense grass which swished along the boat-cover—a night impression not easily to be forgotten. At break of dawn we were landed on a sandy bank. Before us the stream, now become a torrent, rushed with clear, cool water down a rocky bed. Beyond the stream our view was closed by a wall of long grass. Behind us rose the cliffs, dark blue, scarred in places by bare precipices down which tumbled a lace-work of waterfalls, in places dense with vegetation. The rain ceased: we climbed the scarp by a steep, winding path, discovering that what seemed thickets of jungle were really hillside gardens of oranges, betel-palm, pepper and bread-fruit trees. As we mounted the cliff-side the stifling heat of the plain fell away below us, and when at last we stood on the summit, refreshed by a cool breeze that surged with the noise of a hundred water-falls, we understood the imagery of the Delectable Mountains. Below us, looking back, stretched an immense, apparently limitless, sheet of water, dotted, as with débris, by half-submerged trees, patches of tall grass, and by villages which seemed to float like wasps' nests adrift on the surface of the water. They are built upon artificial mounds upon which the cottages are clustered, rising in close tiers one above the other. Each family has its boat, and spends its day in fishing and in fetching grass for the cattle which are cooped up within the houses. If the flood rises extraordinarily the houses are deserted, and the population with its cattle sets itself afloat till the waters fall. In these curious conditions a species of rice has been developed which lengthens its stalk with the gradual rise of the water and can even prolong it to eight or ten feet.

Three months later there will be a transformation. Below us will stretch a brilliant green carpet of rice in which the brown of the villages will hardly be apparent. There are silver lines marking the course of slow-streamed, tortuous rivers. The lake has become a garden, and we can see from our Ararat that the Deluge is ended.

ii.—The Land of India.

WE are frequently told that India should be regarded not as a country but as a continent; and to support this idea there is the striking fact that the peninsula of India is in its geological history absolutely distinct from the northern plain of Hindustan proper—the plain in which Calcutta, Benares, Delhi, and Lahore are situated. The peninsula formed part of a huge island, cut off from the mainland of archaic Asia by a sea which washed its northern shores. The open plains that now connect the peninsula with the Himalayas are composed of silt brought down by rivers into this sea. Borings near the sea at Calcutta, and six hundred miles up the Ganges valley at Lucknow, have revealed that the silt extends downwards to at least five hundred feet below sea-level and probably much farther. Northern India is then the creation of the rivers that flow through it just as Egypt is the creation of the Nile. It is a mass of river silt which fills up a chasm in the earth's surface. The sea which originally occupied this chasm extended, in (geologically speaking) recent times, northwards over a large portion of the area now occupied by the Himalayas. The upheaval of the Himalayan mountain range is of comparatively recent date. Long before it existed the peninsula of India stood high above the ocean. It stretched westwards far beyond its present limits, and not

Geological history of the country.

improbably was continuous with Africa. Only on this hypothesis can we explain the many close connections between the faunas of the two countries. Since those far-off days the balance of sea and land has been reversed: land then extended far into the southern, and sea into the northern hemisphere.

The northern barrier of the Himalayas.

India is secluded by the Himalayas, just as Italy is secluded by the Alps, from the country north of it. In both countries a mountain wall overlooks to the southward an alluvial valley, south again of which rises an elevated peninsula. But behind the Alps fertile valleys lead down into a still more fertile plain, while the Himalayas are the southern buttresses of an enormous plateau—the plateau of Tibet—which lies ten thousand feet and more above the sea-level, and is, outside the Arctic or Antarctic circles, the most inhospitable region of the world. This barrier has protected India from military or political aggression on the part of her greater and stronger rival, China.

Himalayan scenery.

Himalayan has often been compared with Alpine scenery. Both exhibit the dark green of pine forests, the light green of grassy slopes and meadows, and the dazzling white of snow-peaks; but in the Himalayas these elements are not in the close combination which gives Alpine scenery its brilliant effects of contrast—forest and grassy slope leading right up to the glaciers and forming one picture with the snows that overhang them. The Himalayan snow-peaks stand far back from the limits of vegetation, and rise from a barren wilderness of scarred hillsides and stony valleys. To those who approach them they appear as tremendous monuments of desolation: there is nothing to recall the softer aspects of nature. In Kashmir snows and forests are set closer together, and are mirrored in a lake which may fairly be compared with the most picturesque waters of Switzerland. In the eastern Himalayas, owing to the prevalence of clouds and moisture, big forests flourish at higher elevations than elsewhere. But, generally, snows and glaciers are remote from the furthest limit of oak or pine trees, and, viewed from the forest, occupy but a small space on the horizon. Some of the peaks rise to double the altitude of Mont Blanc. But to feel them overhanging him the mountaineer has to climb to so high a level that much of this difference in height is discounted. We must, however, except from these somewhat disparaging comments the view of Kinchinjunga from Darjeeling. This giant of the hills stands well to the south of the snowy ridge that forms the boundary of Tibet, and, viewed from the outer hills, is a magnificent spectacle. It rises 22,000 feet above the point of view: it towers above the intervening ranges, and, though sixty miles distant, it dominates the landscape. Another wonderful view astonishes those who voyage up the river Brahmaputra. The outer hills of the Himalayas run close alongside: suddenly a valley opens out a prospect right into the interior, framing a snowy peak which rears itself more than 23,000 feet above the river.

The western Himalayas.

The rainfall attracted by the Himalayas decreases very rapidly from east to west. The western Himalayas offer but few suggestions of tropical scenery, even in the hot valleys which carry their drainage into the plain. The prevailing trees are firs, oaks, and cedars, and grassy slopes abound. The hillsides and valleys are, for their resources, densely populated: indeed, the area actually cultivated supports, acre for acre, more persons than in many of the most crowded districts of the plains. Every practicable slope is terraced with little fields, rising in tiers one above the other, and the numerous springs which emerge from the rock are skilfully led to irrigate them. In the early summer the terraces are yellow with barley: later, they stand high with maize, or thick with brilliant green rice. An amaranth yielding a small grain is commonly cultivated: it is of the same family as the cockscomb of our gardens, and one variety, like the cockscomb, flowers in bright red, another variety in orange. In September you may see hillsides ablaze with these colours, in fiery contrast with the pervading shades of green. The villages generally lie above the fields that belong to them, so that their drainage may filter to the crops: the houses are of rough stone, flat-roofed, crowded together. The people class themselves as Hindus, and speak, with a patois of their own, the language of the plains. They are smaller and fairer than the people of the plains, and their women are often exceedingly pretty.

Eastwards the rainfall increases, and there are great changes in the character of the trees and of the people. A Mongolian type appears in the Gurkha inhabitants of Nepal, a race not unlike the Japanese in features—short, thick-set, and courageous—which provides the Indian army with its most dashing infantry, with regiments that are the 'Green Jackets' of the East. The Gurkhas, however, class themselves by religion as Hindus. Still further East the last traces of Hinduism vanish,

The eastern Himalayas.

and the mountains which lie round Kinchinjunga—behind the British hill-station of Darjeeling—are inhabited by people akin to the Tibetans, who are Buddhists in name and observe the outward forms of that religion. Their monasteries are high-peaked buildings perched for the most part on the ends of mountain spurs. The main edifice includes a temple, a library and a sacristy, and exhibits many resemblances to the monasteries of Europe. The temple is three-aisled, on the general lines of a basilica. Round the side aisles are chapels, each with a picture of a saint. The main aisle ends in an altar furnished with vessels, decked with flowers and overhung with large pictures—often three in number. The library is well supplied with books—long rectangular packets of bark-strips, which are kept in pigeon-holes, tier upon tier. Amongst the treasures of the sacristy are handsome silver vessels and a wardrobe of vestments in embroidered Chinese silk. Round the outside of the main building is a stone parapet overlooking the valley that slopes steeply below it: at the back are the houses of the monks, grouped as in a village. I well remember an evening visit. As I walked up the hillside the air throbbed with a deep buzzing sound like the pedal note of an organ: this was from a trumpet ten feet long, made in three sliding compartments like a telescope. These trumpets are characteristic: smaller ones are often made of human thigh bones, and it is said that one monastery uses for this purpose the bone of an unusually tall British bombardier, whose grave, at Darjeeling, the natives could not be restrained from rifling. On the parapet I found the head Lama, dressed in a woollen cassock of dull red, over which he wore a cape of a darker shade. Round his waist was a rope: on his head a biretta, and as he paced the terrace he slowly turned a hand prayer-wheel. The sun went down: a pallor crept over the snows of Kinchinjunga above me, and as I gazed at the crimson glow on its highest pinnacles the faint tinkling of bells came to me across the valley—the angelus of other monasteries that crowned the mountain spurs around and below me. This was 8000 feet above sea-level. Yet just below the monastery was a dense tropical forest of magnolias. The hills here face the Bay of Bengal, and the air is warmed by currents of moist wind. For some months of the year the forests are wrapped in mist, and the trees are festooned with lichens which hang down in tresses three or four feet long. It would seem that the forest was in mourning weepers.

The enclosing walls of India.

At each extremity of the Himalayan range—beyond the Panjáb at one end and Assam at the other—by a gigantic contortion of the upheaving thrust, mountain chains have been forced up which run north and south, at right angles to the line of the Himalayas, so that the plains of northern India terminate in two enormous angles. Within each of these angles there are hills which have, it may be surmised, been squeezed up by lateral pressure—the Salt range at the western, and the Assam hills at the eastern extremity. In each of these angles earthquakes are of frequent occurrence, due very possibly to subsidence of the earth's crust as the angular pressure is relaxed. The Assam hills rise to a considerable height: long stretches range over 5000 feet, and the highest of their peaks attain 10,000 feet above sea-level. The scenery of these hills is varied and very beautiful. Their feet are set in tropical jungles: pine forests clothe their higher slopes: they support a plateau of open grassy moorland. From their western summits there opens out perhaps the most extensive view in the world—right across the Brahmaputra valley and over the opposing Himalayas to the snow-peaks round Kinchinjunga, distant as far as London is from Dartmoor.

The northern India plains.

Along the foot of the Himalayas, between these two angles, stretch the plains of northern India. These plains were formed by river action, and broad rivers intersect them. The word 'Panjáb' means five waters, and refers to five rivers which flow westwards and southwards through this province, and, uniting in the lower reaches of the Indus, fall into the Arabian Sea to the north of Bombay. In the contrary direction seven large rivers flow eastwards towards Calcutta: they are spread at wider intervals apart than the Panjáb rivers, but, like them, unite—in the Ganges—before they gain the Bay of Bengal. The Ganges shares its delta with another mighty river that descends from Assam to the east—the Brahmaputra—the upper course of which is still in the unknown, a geographical mystery—which it remains for exploration to unveil. It is agreed that the Brahmaputra is the Sanpo of Tibet, which, rising at the back of the Himalayas, near the midway point of the range, flows eastwards through Tibet, passes close to Lhassa, and then forces its way, curving southwards, through stupendous mountain gorges till it reaches the head of the Assam valley and flows, as the Brahmaputra, in a direction almost precisely contrary to that in which it started. We know the Sanpo as it courses through the open valley of Lhassa: at this point it is 10,000 feet above sea-level. A short way further down-stream the river plunges downwards beneath the shadow of high snow mountains, and falls 9000 feet in a distance of 250 miles. Imagination depicts gigantic cataracts; but this section of the river's course is absolutely unexplored. Its investigation from the Assam side would be confronted with no special difficulty: troublesome hill tribes infest the path, but the hope of money would probably conciliate them. Four years ago some explorers were organising an expedition. But the scruples which now oppose themselves to any British undertaking in Tibet were fatal to their prospects, and this interesting portion of the earth's surface is sketched upon our maps by conjecture only.

Indian rivers.

The rivers of India undergo each year two complete transformations. During the cold weather a stream of comparatively clear water meanders through a waste of sand, approaching sometimes one, sometimes the other, of the scarped banks that limit this expanse on either hand. Before the river has accomplished half its course its sandy bed may attain a breadth of a mile or more, and further down a breadth of four or five miles. It is a desert in miniature over which the sand blows in clouds, lifeless save for sleeping alligators or flocks of sandpipers which haunt the edge of the water. As the hot weather advances the stream is swelled by the melting of snow on the mountains: with the coming of the rains it rises into a sea of turbid water, which fills the bed from bank to bank, its surface crisped by waves and smoothed in places by circling eddies.

In October the torrent falls, and in a month the sand-banks re-emerge, and the stream shrinks into insignificance amongst them. The rivers seldom overtop their banks, and flood the land, until they have reached the lower half of their course, where the slope of the country—and of their beds—is flattened, and the current loses velocity. There, in periods of heavy rainfall, they sometimes spread for miles over the fields, damaging the rice crops but improving the land so long as the main current is not diverted across it, and the spread of flood water is nearly stagnant. In full current the river lets fall only the heavier particles of the silt with which it is charged—that is to say, the sand—and a field over which the current has been deflected is ruined by a sandy deposit. Losing velocity, the water drops fine mud, and this is generally as fertilising as manure. River floods reach their greatest extension in eastern India, where the seaward slope of the country is remarkably small. The floods of the Brahmaputra sometimes extend to a breadth of eight miles, and, as we have already seen, the country south of the Assam hills is deeply submerged every year. Such little slope as there is towards the Brahmaputra is neutralised by the height of the Brahmaputra flood, which holds up the rivers that meet it and converts them into practically stagnant lakes.

The reclamation of the plains from the sea.

It is difficult to realise that the great plains of northern India have been reclaimed from the sea by the gradual accumulation of river sand and mud. Yet so it is. The muddy discoloration of the sea which one remarks at the mouths of great rivers—sometimes extending a hundred miles or more from land—

indicates the growth beneath the waves of countries that are still to be. The valley of the Nile as far south as Keneh was once a sea gulf, running parallel to the Gulf of Suez, but in a contrary direction. The sea once touched the feet of the Himalayas. Below the shadow of the mountains the accumulating river silt gradually rose to sea-level and formed mud-flats which, raised and pushed out seawards, have grown into a valley—or rather a plain—that now stretches 900 miles away from the mountains. The sea water has left its traces in the efflorescence of poisonous salts—a mixture of sulphate of soda, carbonate of soda, and common salt—which in places sterilise large plains several square miles in extent, and in the midst of luxuriant cropping produce cancerous patches of irregular shape upon which cultivation impinges but which it may not invade. The salts are concentrated upon the surface in places where the subsoil is of very close texture and is constantly passing moisture upwards by capillary action. During the hot weather these blots on fertility glisten with a dazzling white crust of salt. As the mud-flats at the river's mouth were raised by flood deposit the river currents gradually cut channels through them, and thenceforward it was these channels and their banks that grew upwards most rapidly, since they received river silt all the year round, while to the flat expanses between them silt was carried only in high flood time. The river bed and its banks gradually rose above the general level of the country, bearing the stream as if upon a raised aqueduct. Breaches occurred when floods were high, and the current then deserted its channel, left it high and dry, and selected a new course in lower ground on one or other side of it. The new channel, like the old, was gradually raised, then breached and deserted. In this fashion, by forming for itself successive new channels, the river raised the land's surface in a series of parallel ridges, working its way sideways across its valley and back again by deserting its channel as soon as it had raised it. We can see this process actually continuing to this day in the lower reaches of the Ganges, where rivers are continually shifting their channels.

Effect of surface slope.

It is obvious, however, that the land surface can be raised by river action in this fashion only when the river current is sufficiently slow to part with its silt. This is the case in the lower reaches of the Ganges, where the slope of the country is not more than 6 inches in the mile (the fall of the Nile valley), and the slope of the river bed, owing to its curve, is considerably less than this. But as we ascend the river and pass the middle point of its course the slope of the country increases very rapidly. It is 9 inches to the mile above Allahabad; 18 inches to the mile above Agra, and 2 feet to the mile above Delhi. It is this rapid increase in slope that raises the Ganges valley to an elevation over 800 feet above sea-level at its head beneath the Himalayas. It is difficult to understand how river silt could have been deposited on so steep a slope, and the conclusion can hardly be resisted that since the process of silting began, the upper portion of the valley has gradually been forced upwards by subterranean action, so that the river beds have been gaining in fall and their currents in velocity. In their upper reaches the rivers of the northern India plain are now wasting, not accumulating forces: they cut away more than they deposit, and their channels lie deep below the level of the country.

Scenery of the plains.

During the cold-weather months the plains of northern India—from Patna upwards to Lahore—are carpeted with green. Fully half their area is under wheat, barley, varieties of peas and linseed, which stretch in an expanse of verdure, broken by clumps of dark-foliaged trees, but by no field hedges. In some tracts, through the wheat and barley fields mustard is sown in straight parallel bands, some twenty feet apart, and, when the mustard is in flower, as far as the eye can reach, the green is regularly striped with yellow—a formal arrangement of colour which, bizarre though it may appear from description, is really beautiful, especially under the rays of the setting sun. In March and April the green is replaced by the golden yellow of harvest. The crops are reaped, and the country relapses into desert. Five months later it will again be dressed out, but in crops of a tropical character, tall millet and maize, hemp, sugar-cane, and cotton. The country is no longer open : a horseman could not push his way through the fields. Eastward of Patna rice is the dominating—indeed almost the sole—crop grown Through Bengal, from west to east, there is a strip of wheat that marks the track along which for six centuries passed and repassed armies of wheat-eating Moghals. For the rest, rice is supreme, and it remains so, broken by thickets of tall jute, till, travelling eastwards, we come upon the tea-gardens of Assam.

South of these plains the edge of the peninsula —the northern shore of the island of old time—

is marked by a rock escarpment which runs east and west, roughly speaking, along the line between Calcutta and Karachi. Ascending it, we come upon a plateau which, broken by cross-ranges of hills and by deep river valleys, extends throughout the length of the peninsula, and, with fringes of low country along the coast-line, to the sea which washes either side of it. The ancient rock bed of this plateau has, over much of its area, been covered with a sheet of black 'trap' rock or basalt—in some places several hundreds of feet thick—which lies horizontally over the older rocks, exactly as if it had overflowed. It is indeed supposed to have welled up from below as a flood of molten lava which submerged the island as it then existed. This was before the beginnings of life, for the rocks that underlie the basalt are entirely devoid of fossil remains. But the basalt is intersected by horizontal beds of gravel, containing fresh-water shells, which are apparently the remains of lakes which formed on the surface after one eruption of lava and were overwhelmed by another.

The peninsula.

The north-western end of the plateau is of no great elevation and merges into the desert of Rajputána and the southern Panjáb. Crossing it in a southerly direction we are gradually led upwards over broad plains and low ranges of sparsely wooded hills till we emerge on the edge of a precipice overlooking a deep valley. The river Nerbudda flows below, through an expanse of cultivation, and across it, twenty-five miles away, the horizon is closed by the dark-blue outlines of a range of mountains. These

The scenery of the peninsula—to the north.

are the Satpuras, which cross the peninsula from Calcutta to Surat. They rise to 4000 feet above sea-level, cover a breadth of about 150 miles, and have acted as a rampart between southern India and the northern plain. Till the British Government pierced them with roads and railways they offered an impenetrable barrier to military expeditions, and an attack upon southern India from the north could only be delivered from the western extremity of the range, where a dip in the hills affords an easy pass. The pass is guarded by the fortress of Asirgarh, perched on the summit of an isolated, flat-topped hill, with steeply scarped sides, which rises a thousand feet above the roadway.

Rivers of the peninsula—to the north.

The Nerbudda flows westward into the Arabian Sea. North of Bombay the mountains which overlook the western coast-line descend to the level and offer a passage to the river through a plain which is so fertile as to be called the Garden of India. Southwards the coast hills are high enough to throw the drainage of the peninsula eastwards, and the Nerbudda and its neighbour, the Tapti, are the only rivers which can penetrate to the Arabian Sea. The Nerbudda is one of the sacred rivers of India. Its source in a high valley of the Satpuras, deep-set in jungle, is a place of pilgrimage; and to perform a circuit of the river on foot is an efficacious means of obtaining grace. One not unfrequently meets bands of ascetics who devote three years of their life to this task. Starting from the river mouth they march along it to its source, and return to the sea by the opposite bank.

The black soil of the peninsula.

The soil of the Nerbudda valley is characteristic of central and southern India. It is of a black colour: when wet so sticky as to be unworkable, and when dry of a stone-like hardness, with a surface much broken by cracks and fissures. It is derived from the basalt that is the rock-cap of a large area of the peninsula. Much of the basalt decomposes easily, being composed of rounded lumps, which disintegrate in layers like an onion, set in softer material. The detritus of the basalt is of a dull red colour when washed out by surface drainage, and gives this colour to the rivers when swollen by rain. The silt when deposited turns black under atmospheric action, or with the growth of vegetable matter, and the blackness of the soil when the fields are bare gives a peculiarly sombre appearance to the landscape. This black soil, or 'cotton soil' as it is commonly called, covers quite a third of the open area of the peninsula. On the uplands it is shallow, and will only bear crops during the monsoon: in the valleys, where it is deep, it cannot be touched till the rains are over. It is then sown with wheat or linseed and yields fairly without manure, since it is rich in phosphates and very retentive of its moisture. In the Nerbudda valley its depth is exceptional. During the rains the valley is an impracticable morass, but in the cold weather it is a sea of green wheat lying between two dark-blue ranges of mountains. It is an interesting fact that the soil of Egypt is of similar origin and character. It also is derived from nodular basalt which occurs in the highlands of Abyssinia: the silt gives the name of 'red water' to the Nile floods that are charged with it, and forms when deposited a blackish coloured soil, which hardens and cracks in the heat of summer, but which, if the surface is kept open, is extraordinarily retentive of moisture.

Hill ranges—the Satpuras.

Parts of the Satpuras are exceedingly wild; but they contain valleys and plateaux which are open and well cultivated, and even their highest slopes are used as summer pasturage for cattle that provide food for an undiminishing number of tigers. At Pachmarhi is the most picturesque scenery of the range. Here a group of sandstone mountains escaped the overwhelming flood of basalt, and overlook in precipitous outlines a grassy plateau, dotted with fine trees, that lies 3500 feet above sea-level. The sandstone takes a red colour from iron with which it is infiltered, and the contrast between the red of the overhanging cliffs and the green of the trees and herbage is very similar to that which we admire in the Dolomites. The rock is easily worn by water, and the edge of the plateau has been cut into deep precipitous cañons, 700 or 800 feet deep, within which flow clear streams, fringed with tree ferns. Some of these deep cañons are little more than a stone's-throw broad: park-like glades lead up to them, and looking into the chasm one is charmed by the bell-like whistle of an ouzel—known as 'the idle schoolboy'—which haunts its recesses. In the face of a rock which stands out into the plateau are some sculptured caves which tell of the days of Buddhist anchorites. In a valley hard by, human sacrifices were celebrated only two generations ago. From a steep rock which overhangs the valley the victim leapt on to a platform below: close to the platform stood the Raja's throne

—so near that he might be sprinkled with the blood of the sacrifice.

South-wards from the Satpuras.

Crossing the Satpuras we descend upon another broad cultivated valley, in which Nagpur is situated and the productive cotton-fields of Berar. The valley is, in fact, a continuation of the open black soil plain that stretches far and wide over the western portion of the peninsula. Beyond it, dense jungle reaches southwards to the river Godavari. Eastwards the valley ends in the hills which here form the cross watershed between the Arabian Sea and the Bay of Bengal. Beyond this watershed a large oval-shaped oasis of cultivation, 7000 square miles in extent, opens out amidst the hills and jungles which sweep down towards the sea. It is known as Chattisgarh, and was apparently colonised from northern India, retaining peculiarities of northern India in its crops and its language. As the coast is approached, cultivation again appears, expanding into the broad, rice-growing plains of Orissa which lie about the mouth of the river Mahanadi, and here form the littoral of the Bay of Bengal.

The Deccan.

Beyond the Nagpur and Chattisgarh plains we enter upon southern India properly so called, or the 'Deccan.' Save at high levels we are too far south, for cold weather, and rice, millet and cotton can be cultivated all the year round. The surface of the peninsula becomes curiously tilted. The highest ground in the country lies close above the western coast-line. In fact the backbone of the country is situated along its western border,—because, it is surmised, land that lay still further west has been washed away. The mountain wall that has withstood the sea, and now runs north and south alongside of it, supports to landward a high plateau 2000 to 3000 feet above sea-level, which slopes away towards the eastern coast. The great rivers of southern India, the Godavari, the Kistna, and the Tungabhadra, flow into the sea east of the peninsula, but rise on its western margin.

The mountains of the western coast-line.

This mountain chain is the most striking geographical feature of the peninsula. Rising in scattered hills, a hundred and fifty miles north of Bombay, its peaks attain, over Bombay, a height of 4000 feet. Farther south it rises to double this height and spreads out into the grassy plateau of the Nilgiris. Its southward course is then broken by a remarkable gap which admits the breezes of the Arabian Sea to blow across the peninsula. It again rises to over 7000 feet above sea-level and descends in a confused mass of hills and valleys till it meets the sea west of Cape Comorin. For the northern half of its course the mountain chain is extraordinarily barren and desolate. The heavy rain which its seaward face attracts finds no resting-place upon its precipices: its landward face receives comparatively little, and during six months of the year is scorched by winds of extreme dryness. The peaks which rise above the plateau are steep-sided and flat-topped: they are often narrow, isolated pinnacles which seem to stand sentinel over the passes, and have in fact been commonly used as fortresses. Farther south the air gains moisture and the basalt covering gives way to crystalline rock. The hill outline grows softer, and vegetation becomes more abundant, till in the Nilgiris we ascend to grassy downs, with copses nestling in their hollows, that in scenery and in climate recall memories of England. Between the mountain chain and the sea is a strip of low land which, towards the north, is an open chess-board of rice-fields, but further south is covered, with dense, tropical vegetation, and produces the spices that first introduced India to European commerce. The edge of the Nilgiri downs commands a striking prospect of forest that falls seaward over descending hills and valleys. Clearings in this forest are opened out by the coffee plantations of Coorg and Travancore.

Scenery of the Deccan.

Surveyed from the mountains that rise behind Bombay, the Deccan plateau offers a desolate prospect. Indeed, of all the countries that are cultivated, it is probably the most cheerless. There are no trees save the few that with some cactus hedges mark the situation of straggling villages. The land undulates eastward in low folds of ash-coloured soil which, except in the dips, lies thin upon the rock, and on rising ground is covered with loose stones. These do not, however, prevent it from being cropped in favourable seasons, though to the cultivator and his bullocks its tillage must be as the ploughing of shingle. The rainfall is precarious. In hollows, wells are dug and patches of land are irrigated, but the main crops—tall millet, cotton, and the sesame oil seed—are unirrigated, and with a scanty rainfall cannot be depended upon to yield satisfactorily more often than two years in five. In such a country one comes across the ruins of a large city of Bijapur and wonders whence came its former prosperity. The people have become inured to hardship, and are sturdy and self-reliant. From them were recruited the Maratha horsemen who broke down the empire of the Moghals, and for half a century terrorised the whole of India by their depredations. As one passes eastward the rainfall increases, and the country on either side of the Godavari becomes dense with jungle. Still further east the basalt gives place to crystalline rock, and, with a still heavier rainfall, rice takes the place of millet, irrigated from multitudes of tanks that are cleverly constructed across the valley-heads. There succeeds a forest-clad wilderness bounded by a line of hills that overlook the open rice country which fringes the Bay of Bengal.

If we cross the peninsula on a more southerly line, we shall find that the basalt has disappeared; the rocks are crystalline and the soil yellow. The western range has risen from 4000 to 8000 feet, and the plateau (of Mysore), which it supports, from 2000 to 3000 feet. The characteristic crop of the plateau is a small millet with ears that grow in fours, like a bird's claw. The descent from the plateau to the eastern sea is broken by two isolated masses of lofty hills, outliers of the main range. As the ground falls, rice-fields take possession of the landscape. Poor inland, they are of great fertility near the seacoast, more especially in the river deltas. There are five of these deltas along the coast; the rice crops stand in them so thick as to give the appearance of a solid mass of vegetation. The cultivators are exceedingly prosperous: sleek in appearance and not uncommonly wearing heavy gold bracelets, they offer a striking contrast to the hard-bitten Marathas, on the other side of the peninsula, whose virtues have been

The southern end of the peninsula.

fostered by a precarious rainfall and an ungenerous soil. At the extreme end of the peninsula a level stretch of red soil, closely cultivated with cotton, runs out into the sea which separates India from Ceylon.

iii.—The People.

Persistence of nationality.

In western Europe nations that have been overwhelmed by conquering immigrants have retreated into corners of the continent, or have, by intermarriage, merged themselves with their invaders and lost their racial identity. There may be Basque blood in central France; there is certainly Celtic blood in England; but it is diffused through the general population, and neither Basques nor Celts subsist in these areas as separate tribes. In India circumstances are entirely different. For at least twelve centuries, by a rigid prohibition of intermarriage, each race has preserved its individuality. Such of its members as took refuge in the hills and jungles live in communities of their own: those who preferred their homes to freedom, and were content to live in subjection to their conquerors, have none the less maintained their racial distinctiveness and even in some cases their tribal language. Intermingled with the invaders, they remain a peculiar people. With them, as with the Jews, the doors of home life are not unlocked by the interests of a common citizenship.

Consequences of racial distinctiveness.

A conquered race that does not intermarry with its conquerors remains in isolated subjection: it is at the bottom of the social scale and remains there, since it forms no alliances that can raise it in the world. Accordingly, amidst the humblest castes of Indian society, we may find races that once ruled provinces of their own. Within the last century and a half an aboriginal tribe known as the Gonds has fallen from dominion into the lowest servitude. They are the original inhabitants of the tract now known as the Central Provinces, which embraces the western Satpura hills and the fertile valleys to the north and south of them. Gond dynasties held sway here, and the country was known—is still known in village talk—as *Gondwána*. The race is hardy and courageous, and, if generally somewhat unintelligent, could build fortresses which can be compared with those of mediæval Europe. One of them, that now overlooks a forest clearing, with the forest pressing close behind and on either side, was encompassed with high walls of red sandstone, well built and elaborately crenellated, pierced by imposing arched gateways that are surmounted by the Gond crest — an elephant trampling a tiger, a lively testimony to victorious struggles of the past. The walls are over five miles in circuit. But the town they once enclosed is vanished: there only remain a few huts in a wilderness of tall grass and thorn brake. In the middle of the eighteenth century the Gonds were overwhelmed by the tide of Maratha conquest. The Marathas had for some years past been filtering into the country and had secured a footing in the services of the State. Consequently a single victory sufficed, not merely for conquest, but for dominion. Yet with such traditional respect was the Gond dynasty invested that the Maratha rulers found it expedient to preserve to its representative the title of Raja and to issue their orders under his seal. A century later, on taking over the country, we found and continued the Raja in the dignified ease of a State pensioner. But his people had lost everything. There were some who in the recesses of the hills maintained villages of their own, cultivating the hill slopes in poverty-stricken independence. In the plains they had become the Gibeonites of the community; and their strength and endurance only qualified them for field labour or domestic drudgery.

Distinctions of caste.

From a people the Gonds have sunk into a caste, and the largest of the Indian castes are probably tribal in origin. But the vast majority of them represent differences not so much of race as of environment. Every walk of life is occupied by a caste or castes of its own, which may not marry with nor even eat with other castes. No one can, for instance, be a weaver, a carpenter, a barber, or even a scavenger, unless he is born one—unless his parents belong to a caste that has appropriated this or the other means of livelihood. Nor is each caste of occupation general throughout the country. Each province has a separate gradation of its own: to the carpenters of Calcutta, for instance, the carpenters of Madras are strangers, between whom intermarriage would be an unthinkable impossibility. The one caste that pervades the whole of India is the Brahmin, and this is subdivided into numberless sections between whom there can be no alliance of bride and bridegroom. The Muhammadans form a community of their own, shut off from the Hindus by differences of creed as well as of race; and there are Hindu castes, such as the Sikh, which have come into being as the disciples of religious reformers. Indeed, castes of this description, the product of local religious revivals, are coming into existence at the present day.

Prohibition of intermarriages between castes.

There are certain castes which claim to be hybrids, and to have sprung from intermarriages between men of a higher and women of a lower caste. The Eurasian community, which is an element of some importance in the society of the larger cities, has sprung in modern time from alliances between Europeans and Indians. It is certain that in ancient days, before the caste system had become firmly crystallised, mixed alliances were not prohibited. The marriage of women with men of inferior caste has probably always seemed as abominable as it is regarded at present. But men took to themselves wives or concubines from lower grades of society until the occupants of these grades, resenting the position, made it an ordinance of their caste that women should not marry outside it. Eurasian girls may, of course, mate with Europeans, though their marriage with Indians offends popular sentiment. But within the Indian community intermarriage between castes has for at least twelve centuries been absolutely prohibited.

Heterogeneity of the population.

The effect of this permanent maintenance of human types is that the population is heterogeneous to an extent that it needs actual experience to appreciate. It is no question of rich and poor, of town and country, of employer and employed: the differences lie far deeper. The population of a district or a town is a collection of different nationalities—almost different species—of mankind that will not eat or drink or intermarry with one another, and that are governed in the more important affairs of life by committees of their own. It is hardly too much to say that by the caste system the inhabitants of India are differentiated into over two thousand species of mankind, which in the physical relations of life have as little in common as the inmates of a Zoological Garden.

Unifying sentiments—their weakness.

There are, however, certain general similarities which have the effect of binding this complicated society into loose confederacies. There is the tie of religion, which, respectively, unites all Hindus and all Muhammadans: there are the ties of a common language and a similar method of dress which draw together the people of a province and engender the nearest approach in India to a national feeling. But the sentiments which community of religion or language may arouse cut across one another and are mutually destructive. Hindus and Muhammadans are intermingled in all provinces. Those who are alike in language may differ in religion, and those who agree in religion may be quite unable to understand one another's speech.

Misclassification of the lowest castes as Hindus.

From the religious point of view the people of India are generally ranged under two heads—as Hindus or Muhammadans. But this classification is very misleading since a large proportion of the lower castes are not really Hindu in either religion, customs, or sympathies. In the hills of the eastern frontier there are tribes which are of a distinct racial type, and are absolutely untouched by Hindu influences. They stand as far outside Indian society as Tibetans or Chinese. The tribes which inhabit the hills and forests of the peninsula, or drift in casual labour about the plains, are also distinct in race and language from the villagers who employ them. But living in close contact with Hindus they have adopted some Hindu customs, and in particular the observance of the Hindu caste system. Similar is the condition of a mass of degraded humanity which has lost all traces of any tribal origin, and lives in practical serfdom to the people of the plains. Such are the Chamárs of northern India, the Mahárs of Bombay, and the Pariahs of Madras—very large communities which are regarded by the respectable Hindus with the deepest contempt. They do not observe the Hindu taboos: they do not reverence the cow: they will eat animal food, will skin dead cattle, and will perform the necessary but degrading offices of scavengers. The Brahmin priesthood will have nothing to do with them, and those of them who desire a priesthood maintain separate 'black' Brahmins of their own, whom the genuine Brahmins regard with derision. The term which best describes these people is that of Helots: it indicates precisely the contempt in which they are held, and the origin of this contempt in pride of conquest. But the most convenient title for them is that which they have earned by working as 'coolies.' They are far more numerous than is generally supposed. It is impossible to draw a strict line between them and the Hindus, since the two communities merge one into the other and are connected by a chain of caste gradation. But it may safely be estimated that the classes which are regarded and treated as Helots, which do not observe the Hindu food taboos and do not acknowledge the Brahmin priesthood, include at least a quarter of the population.

The contempt which this large community endures is of the most surprising character. Coolie families must live in a separate quarter of the village: they are not permitted to draw water from the village well: in some parts of the country they are not permitted to walk along streets that are inhabited by the higher caste. A case came to official notice in Madras where the village postmaster, being a Hindu, would not allow Pariahs to come to his post-office: they had to throw their letters down at the end of the street and leave them to be collected there. On the west coast a coolie meeting a Brahmin on the road has to step aside some distance into the field, lest the air passing him should offend the other's nobility. Addressing a superior, a low-caste man will hold his hand across his mouth to prevent any contamination by his breath. Even indirect contact is polluting, and I have known a Brahmin clerk charged with the distribution of leases to low-caste tenants throw the papers on to the ground for the latter to pick up as best they could.

Condition of the lowest castes.

The Hindus are distinguished by the most rigid scruples as to food. The most degraded of the coolie class draw the line nowhere. Not only will they devour the carcases of dead cattle: they will eat food that has been cooked and left by others. Some of them eke out their subsistence by an occasional diet of rats, snakes, or lizards. I was sympathising with some Gonds over a poor rice harvest. 'Yes,' they replied, 'but we have done very well this year in field-mice.' Riding through a village I came across a gypsy encampment. The village headman expressed very

Disregard of the Hindu food taboos.

bitterly his disgust that these people should have camped on his land, 'for,' he said, 'they live on alligators and make the most loathsome smell in cooking them.' This was the case. There was a river hard by in which alligators abounded: these the gypsies caught with trimmers and roasted whole in long underground ovens. It may be observed here that gypsies are very numerous in India and differ very little from their fellows in Europe, whose Indian descent is proved beyond doubt by close similarity of language. These illustrations of gross feeding are extreme cases. The vast majority of coolies are more discriminating in their appetite, and manifest increasing prosperity by greater particularity in their diet. Indeed, coolie castes are forming which sometimes outdo the Hindu in the scruples of their food taboo. One of them will not touch lentils because, being of a pink colour, they are suggestive of blood. But most of the coolie class drink spirituous liquor, and from their income is mainly derived the large excise revenue of the Indian Government.

Still lower depths of society.

Below the coolie class are people whom it would be libellous to group with them—men known as Aghoris—who eat human flesh. I came across one of them who lived on a sand-bank in the Ganges, and arrested the corpses which floated down-stream. Carrying a human skull, they blackmail shopkeepers by threatening to throw it upon their stalls, and to pollute irretrievably their stock-in-trade. If the police are not by at hand the shopkeepers submit: to touch such a man in personal violence would be to incur a still more dreadful pollution. There are actually ten thousand persons who at Census time classed themselves as Aghoris. All of them do not practise cannibalism, and some of them attempt to rise in the world. One of them secured service as cook with a British officer of my acquaintance. My friend was in camp in the jungle with his wife and children, when his other servants came to him in a body and refused to remain in service unless the cook was dismissed, since they had discovered, they declared, that during the night time he visited cemeteries and dug up the bodies of freshly buried children. The cook was absent, but they pointed to a box of his that emitted a sickening smell. The man was incontinently expelled: but for long afterwards the family was haunted by reminiscences of the curries they had eaten.

Usefulness of the coolie castes.

Without its coolies India would do badly. They provide labour for a community which considers labour degrading. At harvest-time they move about the country in thousands, gathering in spring-time wheat, and in autumn millet and cotton, which cover too large an area to be harvested by the regular farm labour. Their hands have made the canals which have increased so enormously the produce of the country, and the railways which have enhanced its value. They supply a very large proportion of the mill-hands who work the hundreds of factories that are making Bombay and Calcutta great industrial centres. As emigrants to Natal, Mauritius, the West Indies, and even to Fiji, they produce most of the cane-sugar that is consumed in Europe; and, though subjected to depressing regulations in those places which are exclusively white in sentiment, but make use of dark labour, they rise in the West Indies to considerable affluence, and have even become the owners of race-horses. Over a million of them are employed in the tea-gardens of Assam and Ceylon, which without their assistance would relapse into jungle. Without their labour on roads and railways the effective annexation of Burma would have been impossible. In the past they have been too much amazed at the undiscriminating tolerance of the British Government to take full advantage of it. But they are gaining in intelligence as well as in prosperity. Missionary endeavour has borne good fruit amongst them, and they are aspiring to educate their children and to advance in the world. Their ambitions excite in the higher castes irritation and disgust; and a new chapter of Indian history will begin when these Helots of India gain the self-respect which inspires enthusiasm and the knowledge which can turn it to effect.

The Hindus—their origin.

Hindus that may properly be so called constitute about half of the total population. The term includes the descendants of conquering races that entered India from the north-west, and such of the aboriginal inhabitants as have linked themselves with their conquerors, anciently by intermarriage and now by respect, accepting the authority of the Brahmin priesthood, the sanctity of the cow, and a multiplicity of caste taboos. Hinduism, by associating itself with those it had despoiled, spread its influence over the continent: but it has sacrificed its purity to its ambition, and has become vitiated by the superstitions of its adopted children. The conquering race is commonly known as the Aryan: it was allied in stock to the nations of Europe, and spoke a language that is closely akin to Greek and Latin. Ethnologists hold that the Aryan invasion of India was a long-continued process, that there were several distinct floods of conquest which came to rest in Rajputána and the north-western portion of the Indo-Gangetic plain, but from which streams of emigrants pressed their way further east into Bengal, and southwards some distance into the peninsula. It is obvious that bands of adventurers entering India over the mountain passes of Afghanistan or the Pamirs can have brought very few women with them. They must have intermarried very largely with the daughters of the soil, and have generally lost their purity of race. Indeed, in southern India, now nominally Hindu, there is practically no admixture of Aryan blood : the people are of aboriginal descent, and are Hindu by adoption only. The purest Aryan blood is probably to be found in Rajputána.

Aryan traditions—their effect.

By the Hindu writings and traditions the Aryan colonisation of India is represented to have been much more extensive and complete. According to an ancient hymnal that was composed many centuries before Christ, Aryan society grouped itself in three classes—the Brahmin (or priests), the Kshatriyas (or warriors), and the Vaishyas (or traders). The two latter are now commonly known as the Rajputs and the Banias. These classes still nominally exist as separate castes. Their members rank far above men of all other castes, and pride themselves on the title of 'twice-born.' They include about a tenth of the total population. Judging from this social distinction—rooted in such great antiquity—one would conclude that the Aryan invaders contented themselves with monopolising the control of religion, the management of the army, and the conduct of trade, leaving the aboriginal inhabitants to pursue their cultivation. The 'twice-born' have since learnt the advantages of controlling agriculture also: Brahmins, Rajputs, and Banias now hold much land, not merely in large estates, but in small holdings of four or five acres—just sufficient for the support of a family. But however small may be their farms, however poor they may be themselves, they cultivate by hired labour only, and with very few exceptions will not touch a plough or engage in manual labour. To them the plough and mattock are taboo. According to their own accounts, the Aryans have settled upon the land, but will not touch it.

Home-abiding instincts.

At one time the Hindus must have possessed the spirit of enterprise. They pushed their way into the recesses of the country, founding kingdoms, even in the remote valley of Assam. They sent forth expeditions which effected a footing in Siam, and even in Java, leaving unmistakable vestiges in temple architecture. But at present they have a horror of crossing the sea: it is taboo, and a high-caste man on returning from a voyage is obliged to undergo a formal ceremony of purification. There are, however, certain classes which have no such scruples. Sikhs will enlist as policemen in China. The coolie castes will, as we have seen, venture across the sea for higher wages than India can offer them. But the trading caste—the Banias—display the completest contrast to the conservative quietism of the ordinary Hindu. Their headquarters are in Rajputana, but they pervade the whole of northern India, monopolising the money-lending business as well as certain branches of trade. Banias may be found on the extreme eastern frontier of Assam selling opium to tribesmen who are the terror of the countryside. Once established in a locality they grip its business as with tentacles, and villagers have been known to defend themselves by laying Bania advance agents under a rigid interdict of fire and water. Banias have opened shops throughout the length of Egypt, and in South Africa their enterprise is very largely responsible for the dislike that bars the country against all Indians who do not belong to the labouring class.

The Muhammadans.

Muhammadans number about a quarter of the population. They also represent waves of conquering invasion. But their immigration in force is comparatively modern, commencing about the date of the Norman conquest of England. At intervals during the succeeding seven centuries, Tartars, Afghans, Persians, and Turks poured across the frontier, sometimes retiring with their plunder, but more frequently settling upon the land. The Muhammadan aristocracy of India are those who can trace their descent from these settlers. But the Muhammadans, like the Hindus, added immensely to their numbers by proselytising, with the difference that the Muhammadan convert was admitted within the inner pale of Islám, and was not, like a convert to Hinduism, relegated to the outer enclosure. Muhammadan missionaries penetrated to the rice-swamps of eastern Bengal and converted the population with a rapidity which calls to mind the successes of early Christian missionaries amongst the barbarians of Europe. Nor were the methods employed solely persuasive. In the neighbourhood of

Dehli there are many villages that are shared in equal portions by two communities, one Hindu, the other Muhammadan. So far as personal appearance goes they might belong to different races. But both communities are of the same Hindu ancestry. The Muhammadans were converted in the time of a Moghal emperor who wished to increase the proportion of Muhammadans round his capital, and who thought that the fairest method of doing so was to oblige half the inhabitants of a certain number of villages to change their faith. The converts are still known as 'new Muslims.'

Muhammadans form half the population of the Panjáb, and two-thirds of the population of eastern Bengal. Elsewhere they are much less numerous, though they are found throughout the country, numbering three millions in so distant a province as Madras. They will be treated of in detail later on, and it suffices to mention here that, like most Hindus, they have generally lost all spirit of other than military enterprise. A rule of their religion prohibits the taking of interest: this has seriously prejudiced them in making money. The memory of their domination still clings to them, and landlords find Muhammadan bailiffs more effective than Hindus in collecting rents. Curiously enough the most enterprising Muhammadans are those of seaport towns on opposite sides of the continent—Bombay in the west and Chittagong in the east. These are astute and adventurous traders.

Their condition.

Crossing the differences between one caste and another, between Hindu, Muhammadan, and Coolie, are the peculiarities of language and dress that are most commonly associated with nationality.

Separative differences: dress and language

On the Afghan frontier the language is Pushtu, akin to Persian. The men wear loose, baggy trousers, a long coat, and a large turban wound round a pointed skull-cap. Leaving the frontier districts we meet with a language akin, not to Persian, but to Sanskrit, which is spoken by seven million persons in the west Panjáb, and, with dialectic variations, in Sindh. Thence eastward down the Indo-Gangetic plain, to a line some distance within the frontier of Bengal, the people speak varying dialects which may be conveniently classed together as Hindi, since, although of somewhat different origin, they are drawn together by the Hindustani (or Urdu) which became the *lingua franca* of Upper India in the days of Moghal rule. Speaking Hindustani one is understood more or less throughout this large area. The dialects which differ most largely from the general are those spoken at the extreme west and at the extreme east of this area—in the Panjáb and in the Bihar division of Bengal. The Hindus generally use, in writing, characters which are those of Sanskrit or closely resemble them. Muhammadans use the Arabic characters. This difference in script in a mixed population complicates the provision of village schooling. Hindi extends southwards to the Satpura range, and crosses the Satpuras to reach the plain of Chattisgarh. It is spoken, with differences of dialect, by 135 millions. The dress of these people is generally white. The Hindus wear a loin-cloth which is substantially a long kilt, the back lower edge of which is drawn between the legs and tucked in above in front, thus being converted into the semblance

—in northern India.

of a pair of breeches. The Muhammadans wear trousers. Both have long coats fastened across the breast, those of the Hindus overlapping towards the right, and those of the Muhammadans towards the left. This curious distinction is universal. Generally it may be said that, throughout India, the loin cloth marks the Hindu and trousers the Muhammadan. The former differs from province to province in length and voluminousness: the latter are worn narrow in some places, broad in others. The coats may be longer or shorter. But these two types of dress pervade the country, and the most striking differences of costume between one part of India and another are in the shape and colour of the turban. In the Hindi country turbans are white, much smaller than those of the Afghan type. In undress small white skull-caps are much affected.

Bengal.

East of the Hindi area Bengali is spoken by 44 millions. It has a written character of its own, which is used by the generality of Bengali Muhammadans as well as by the Hindus. The Bengali Hindus wear a longer and fuller loin cloth than that of up-country people. They generally go bareheaded. To the east and south of Bengal Assamese and Uriya are spoken respectively. They are closely akin to Bengali, but Uriya has a script peculiar to it. Assamese and Uriyas dress similarly to the Bengalis, but the former gain in distinction by using a cream-coloured silk which is derived from species of silkworms that are locally cultivated. Sheets of this material are draped round the shoulders. The Assamese are a good-looking race, and an Assamese gentleman in his flowing drapery might have stepped from the pedestal of a classical statue.

All these languages, Hindi, Bengali, Assamese, and Uriya, are akin to Sanskrit. South of the Uriyas, going down the eastern side of the peninsula, we meet with languages which are of indigenous origin. Telugu, to the north of Madras, is spoken by 21 millions; Tamil, to the south of Madras, by 16 millions. The people of the south generally affect bright colours in their dress, and a crowd of Madrassis is a very gay spectacle. Crossing the peninsula and going up its western side, Malayalim is spoken along the south-western littoral; north of it comes Kanarese. Each of these four indigenous languages has a script peculiar to it. Further northward we meet again in Marathi (spoken by 18 millions) with a language related to Sanskrit. Its use extends half-way across the peninsula and right up to the western Satpuras. Further north again dialects of Gujaráti and Rajasthání (spoken by 20 millions) take us from the seacoast, north of Bombay, across Rajputána to the Panjáb. They, and also Marathi, possess written characters of their own. The Marathas dress in white, but wear smaller coats than up-country Hindus: they are easily distinguished by their large red or yellow 'cart-wheel' turbans. In Gujarát and Rajputána the turbans are also bright-coloured. But they are smaller, and in winding are given a peculiar twist.

The peninsula.

In this brief survey we have not taken into account languages that are spoken by the hill tribes of the interior. But it indicates sufficiently the extreme diversity of the Indian people. Omitting hill tribes from consideration, there are thirteen languages distinct in vocabulary, construction, and written character. On their frontiers, in village speech, they merge one into the other. But a man knowing only one of them would be able to make himself intelligible in no other.

Differences in physique.

In appearance the people of India display far more diversity than we find amongst the nations of Europe. There is the type we associate with the Afghan race, marked by olive complexion, aquiline features, grey eyes, and a very long nose. Men of this type are generally bearded, and recall very closely the characteristics of the Jews.[1] They are most numerous amongst the Muhammadans of the north-west frontier. Further east, Muhammadans who are descended from invading immigrants not unusually exhibit some Tartar features: they are of shorter stature than the Afghans, with brown eyes, sometimes set a little obliquely, shorter noses, and less abundant beards. Another (Hindu) type is quite European in essentials: the men are tall, no darker of complexion than Italians, with hair that is often tinged with brown, possessing very regular features. Their noses have been determined by measurement to be as fine as those of the average Parisian. This is the type of the Aryan invaders: it is most prevalent in Rajputána, whose Aryan settlers seem to have brought their own women with them. A fourth type reminds us, although distantly, of the negro: short statured, black complexioned, with black, often curly hair: the nose as broad as that of the negro, but the face lacking the coarseness of the negro in lips and jaw. This represents the Dravidian race, which is supposed to be aboriginal in India, and at one time to have entirely occupied the country. It is at its

[1] It is a curious fact that one Afghan tribe calls itself by the name of the 'Children of Israel' (Beni-Israel).

purest amongst the hill tribes of the peninsula, but is general throughout the whole of southern India. A fifth type is the Mongolian, an eastern variety of the Tartar. The stature is short and broad: the face flattened: eyes set obliquely, and the lower jaw coarse and heavy. This type is universal amongst the hill tribes of eastern India. These five varieties of mankind have contributed to form the people of India.

Ancient intermixture of races.

Throughout the country the lowest castes, whether of the hills or of the plains, display the characteristics which have been described as Dravidian, and are very nearly or quite pure in aboriginal descent. The upper classes are the result of intermarriages, which, now absolutely prohibited, were common before the epoch, perhaps twelve centuries ago, in which the Hindu caste system crystallised into its present rigidity. The Aryans maintained the purity of their race in Rajputána. To the north and west, in the Indo-Gangetic plain, they intermarried very generally with the Dravidians whom they found in possession, and produced the hybrid type which is commonly known as the Hindustani. Comparatively few penetrated into Bengal and married there, and fewer still into peninsular India. It is generally accepted by ethnologists that the Bengalis have a considerable admixture of Mongolian blood which reached them from the north-east. Their features very commonly exhibit Mongolian characteristics, in particular the heavy development of the lower jaw. They represent a mixture of Dravidian and Mongolian elements, slightly touched with a strain of Aryan.

Diversities due to migration.

Since tribal intermarriage has ceased, migration has added to the variety of the inhabitants, though it has not disturbed their blood. Families who migrate take their women with them, and in their family life preserve for generations their native speech. Brahmins, in particular, have found their way throughout the country, often summoned and settled in small colonies by rulers of Dravidian race. These settlers carefully preserve the purity of their caste. Far up in the valley of Assam—amidst a race strongly permeated with Mongolian blood—one may meet with Brahmins who exhibit the most refined and classical type of European features.

Tendency to separate, not to combine.

Had intermarriages continued, the inhabitants of a locality speaking the same language might have lost their fundamental differences of origin, might have grown together and have formed a nation. But development has proceeded on quite different lines: sympathies have centred in the tribe and have deserted the locality. No national type has been evolved, and there cannot be said to be an Indian nation—or even a nation in India. It is true that some localities display a definite and general type of disposition. The Bengalis decidedly have a character of their own: so also have the Marathas. But similarities of human nature, which can overflow the barriers of caste, and can maintain themselves independently of interbreeding, must appertain rather to the locality than to the race. So we observe that English families settled in Ireland become as Irish as the Irish-born, and in South Africa assimilate the features of the Boers.

Fully half of the two hundred and ninety-two[1] millions of India are massed in the Indo-Gangetic plain. Outside China there can be in the world no rural area so densely inhabited. Each square mile contains from five hundred to six hundred persons, and in some districts there are nearly eight hundred to the square mile. Two cultivated acres provide on an average for three people: in some localities two persons live upon each acre in cultivation. It is only a very small proportion of the population that lives in towns. There are seven towns with more than a hundred thousand inhabitants: Calcutta, with its suburbs, contains nearly two millions. But their contribution is lost in the immensity of the total.

Distribution of the population

—in northern India

In the peninsula humanity is much less crowded. Cultivated tracts of black soil seldom contain more than two hundred persons to the square mile, and usually not more than one hundred and sixty. The fertile coast-line is more closely inhabited, approaching the standard of the Indo-Gangetic plain. Density reaches its maximum in the river deltas, which can support a person to each acre. On the other hand there are vast tracts of hill and forest, each square mile of which does not provide subsistence for twenty roving aborigines.

—in the peninsula.

It would appear that unless fresh avenues of livelihood are opened by the extension of manufacturing industries, India is inhabited by nearly as many persons as it can support. So great is the tension of population upon the land that it snaps when affected by any shortness of crop, or by epidemic disease, and there

Fluctuations in the population.

[1] Including the population of the Native States.

result, not so much oscillations of growth as catastrophes of decline. Outbreaks of cholera claim thousands of victims: but they are dreaded because the death they bring is sudden, not because it is widespread, and they are much less destructive than the insidious attacks of fever. Twenty-five years ago malarial fever literally decimated the districts round Agra. Still more dreadful were the losses suffered ten years ago by some districts of Assam, which were gripped by a malignant disease, the course of which was something like that of the sleeping-sickness of East Africa. Malarial fever has reduced to stagnation the population of large areas in Bengal. In famine times, when crops have failed, death gathers an abundant harvest. The ten years, 1892-1901, were darkened by a succession of disastrous seasons: the crops were dried up because rain failed, or blighted because it was over-abundant, and there were famines in northern, central and western India. They were most intense in central and western India, which at the end of the decade were left with seven millions less people than they had supported at its commencement. Five of the seven millions inhabited Native States. It must not be understood that these losses were all due to starvation. It is feared that numbers died of hunger. Native States have not the means nor the organisation for the relief of famine on the scale adopted in British India. But multitudes perished from diseases that followed unusual privations, or from fever that seemed to be caused by the abnormal course of the rains. Taking the whole of India together, the population during the thirty years, 1872-1901, increased by 1½ per cent. during the first, by 10 per cent. during the second, and by $1\frac{1}{2}$ per cent. during the third decade. Since the last census was taken in 1901 there have been terrible losses from plague.

Infanticide.

The practice of infanticide seems to indicate that population is reaching its limit. This crime used to be prevalent amongst certain castes of northern India. In families which were threatened with many daughters female infants were killed immediately after birth by being drenched with cold water, poisoned with opium, or smothered. It is a disgrace to a man if his daughter is unmarried when she attains a marriageable age. Women can, of course, not marry outside their caste. Within their caste they can marry into a caste group above them, but not into a caste group below them. Accordingly, women tend to become over-numerous in the higher classes of their society—a development with which we ourselves are acquainted—and a large family of daughters is a serious calamity. The Government decided to check infanticide. It had but indirect measures to its hand. The children of each village were inspected, and, if below a certain age girls were in default, the parents were obliged to contribute to special police charges. Rough as was this procedure it sufficed as a corrective. In India a firm declaration by the State may of itself be able to turn the course of popular morality. But the inspecting officer could not afford to be careless. In some cases he found that a stock of young girls followed him about the country, to be drafted amongst the children he was about to inspect.

Losses from malaria are recovered but slowly, since the disease weakens the constitution of those whom it does not destroy. But Nature restores famine losses with extraordinary energy. With the return of favourable harvests the birth-rate rises at a phenomenal rate: every young woman one meets has a baby in her arms. An observant native official gave me a lively description of the situation: 'Nowadays,' he said, 'if one looks at a woman she has a child.'

Recovery of famine losses.

iv.—History—Up to 1000 A.D.

The Vedas: 1500-600 B.C.

OUR first glimpses of Hindu life in India are afforded us by a collection of Sanskrit hymns, formulas, and incantations known as the Vedas. Their composition extended over a long period of time: it is estimated that nine centuries intervened between the production of the earliest and of the latest passages. The language of the earliest hymns differs no more from classical Sanskrit than the Greek of Homer differs from that of Herodotus. Sanskrit had settled into its classical form in the fifth century B.C., when Herodotus was writing his history. But from internal evidence the most ancient Vedic hymns are conjectured to have been composed so far back as 1500 B.C., at the time the Israelites came out of Egypt. In this case they are the earliest literary attempts of the European families of mankind that possess artistic merit. These are the opening lines of the first hymn of the *Rigveda*, addressed to the Fire flame:—

> 'I sing the Fire flame: Priest of the Household:
> Divine himself and Minister of the Sacrifice:
> God's Messenger that shows us gold:
> Worthy to be praised by us as by our fathers:
> He shall lead down to us the gods.'

The hymns indicate by incidental references that at the time of their composition the Aryans had entered India, but were still confined to its north-western corner. The memory of snow mountains was still with them. Wealth consisted *par excellence* in cattle : horses were prized, but, as in the days of Homer, were driven in chariots, not ridden ; gold and copper were known, but not silver, nor, perhaps, iron. Grain was cultivated, but the food most frequently mentioned was milk and clarified butter. Society had evidently not long emerged from the pastoral stage. The people delighted in beer-drinking, and found nothing shameful in intoxication. The family lived under the direction of the father, holding in reverence the family hearth. At marriage the bridegroom went in procession with his friends and relations to the bride's house, where they were entertained with a repast which (horrible to modern Hindu ideas) included beef. Taking the bride's hand, the bridegroom led her round the nuptial fire. They then returned together to the bridegroom's house in a carriage drawn by white bullocks garlanded with crimson flowers. Above the family came the tribe : to each tribe a separate tract was apportioned. Kingship was sometimes hereditary, sometimes determined by election. A priesthood had developed, but had not become hereditary. The gods were imagined as elemental forces, and were worshipped under names which recall with curious similarity the titles of Greek and Roman deities. Associated with this belief was that in the spirits of ancestors, which has come down to modern Hinduism, almost unchanged, through twenty-five centuries. There were frequent wars, and society was organised on a warlike basis. This description might almost serve for early Greek or Roman days. It was the close similarity of the Sanskrit language to

Latin and Greek which first brought us to realise that the Aryans were a member of the European family that had strayed away to the East.

Changes during the Vedic period.

By the time the later hymns of the Vedas were composed—in the sixth or seventh century B.C.—great changes had occurred. The Aryans had pushed their way up to the Ganges. The Brahmin priesthood had separated itself off from the rest of the people and become hereditary. There were also hereditary warrior and business castes, immeasurably below which were placed the aboriginal Helots.

Lack of Hindu histories.

From this time onwards for fifteen centuries we have an uninterrupted stream of Sanskrit literature. The text has come down to us in far better preservation than that of the Greek and Latin classics. These writings were evidently of Brahmin composition. They include religious and magic rituals, fantastic cosmogonies, highly speculative works on philosophy; treatises on grammar, mathematics, astronomy, medicine, and law; poetry—epic, lyric, and dramatic; —but no historical work whatever. There are mythological romances such as that in which Geoffrey of Monmouth told of the landing of Brutus in the island called after him Britain; but they have no pretence to be historical. They resemble the more fantastic of the monkish chronicles of mediæval Europe, and like them, were composed to exalt the status of the priesthood. This is the more surprising, as in other branches of literature Brahmin authors attained a high degree of merit. Their epics are inordinately long (the chief of them, the *Mahábhárata*, is eight times as long as the *Iliad* and *Odyssey* combined) they are overladen with descriptive and swollen with much didactic matter. But the action is picturesque and proceeds with dignity. Their dramas possess real merit, and anticipated the Elizabethan school in combining prose and verse, and in the use of dialect for the meaner characters. To their mathematicians we owe the system of decimal notation that we use to-day, and the discovery of algebra. But mere worldly affairs, such as history or natural science, had no attraction for them. The Brahmins were a class apart, and their interests were centred in their class and in the fruits of their own meditations. They were not kept in touch with the world by having to recruit from it in order to maintain a celibate priesthood. Hence it comes that for Hindu history we are dependent upon the testimony of foreign observers—of Greek soldiers and diplomatists, of Chinese pilgrims, of Muhammadan travellers, of European adventurers and traders, whose acquaintance with the country was superficial, and who were liable to error. For instance, the two Chinese pilgrims, to whom we owe our realisation of India during the fifth and seventh centuries of our era, both lead us to understand that money was unknown, whereas numerous coins of these and earlier periods are extant. By the careful study of inscriptions and coins, we have been able to piece together a skeleton history—lists of dynasties and kings with an approximate chronology. But it is only by the assistance of foreigners that we can attempt to clothe the skeleton with flesh and blood.

The first datable fact in Indian history is the life of Gautama (or Sakya Muni), the founder of Buddhism. He died in 486 B.C., about the time of the battle of

Salamis. The theory of the transmigration of souls, upon which his teaching rested, had been propounded in India very much earlier—certainly by the epoch when it was being taught by Pythagoras in southern Italy. But he gave the theory a moral interpretation. Through transmigration the soul was exposed to punishment for offences committed in a previous existence, and this idea accounted for the apparent injustice of this world. We suffer what we have deserved, though we may not now be deserving it. Gautama was of princely, not Brahmin, descent. Struck to the heart by the failure of man's life, its pain, its unhappiness, and the sordid futility of its end, he abandoned his young wife, his riches and his power, to become first a student and then a teacher. The Way which he taught was a lofty morality, regardful of others as well as of self, though only for self's advantage. But seeing that existence is an endless chain of successive lives, turned as it were by the Wheel of Destiny, and that life itself is a penalty, the chiefest object of man was to escape from his treadmill by the annihilation of his identity—by attenuating the vitality of his soul, so that it should not have strength to transmigrate, but should flicker out, like a dying flame. This end he could attain by a rigid self-absorption, and the new religion proclaimed itself by the endorsement of the celibate life, of the hermitage, and of the monastery.

The rise of Buddhism, 450 B.C.

On the Master's death fragments of his bones were distributed as reliques to monasteries about the country, and were enshrined in huge mounds of masonry known as *stupas*. Three of these stupas have yielded their reliques to the exploration of archæologists. Amongst the show-cases of the Calcutta Museum one can reflect upon a small crystal vase containing a morsel of charred bone, half smothered in little gold-leaf flowers—the remains of a teacher whose name as Buddha —or 'The Illumined'—commands in Asia to this day a wider reverence than that of any other before or after him. In India his doctrine for upwards of a thousand years struggled with Brahminism, was defeated by it, and is now practically extinct, though a belief of similar character and of about the same antiquity—Jainism—is still widely held amongst the trading classes. Buddhism retreated to Ceylon, Burma, and Tibet, but has found in the Far East a broader dominion than India refused to it. Corrupted by idolatry, by magic, and by superstition, it affords to mankind a definite, if erroneous, solution of the problem of life. Why should the just suffer with the unjust? The question is put to us in that ancient morality-play, the Book of Job. But we are so stirred by the splendour of its language and the power and vividness of its imagery that we forget to press for a satisfying reply.

Architectural remains of Buddhism.

But though Buddhism is, in India, only a memory, its influence is still alive in the religious architecture of the country. The stupa was a development in masonry of the earthen barrow: it was as solid as an Egyptian pyramid; and a sacred edifice is still conceived as a mass of material to which the enclosure of space is subsidiary. The Buddhist pagodas of Burma are solid from foundations to apex; and solidity is the characteristic of the Hindu pagodas of Madras and of the temple spires which dominate the village landscape of northern India.

India next comes into history through her contact with the Greeks. Alexander the Great invaded the country in 326 B.C., and spent a year and a half in the Panjáb. But his victories carried him no farther than half-way to the Ganges, and left no mark whatever upon the country. His campaign was described by some of his companions, but their accounts are for the most part only known to us through the pages of authors of much later date. It is clear that the Hindus had reached a high level of civilisation. Their leaders were regarded as brave and chivalrous. The attention of the Greeks was attracted by numbers of naked ascetics whom they described as 'gymnosophists': so is the attention of the modern traveller. Alexander's conquest was a passing experience; but his successors influenced northern India very greatly. Amidst the struggles of the generals who divided his empire, a Greek kingdom came into being in north Afghanistan, and held its own for a century and a quarter. It is known to us by a coinage of great artistic merit which first taught the Indians to use double dies in minting. And it inspired Indian artists with the spirit of sculpture. The north-western corner of the Panjáb was thickly strewn with Buddhist monasteries, which have left behind them a very large number of deeply cut bas-reliefs illustrative of the idolatrous tenets which corrupted the religion three centuries after the death of its founder. Buddha was figured and worshipped as a god, and incidents of his life-history furnished an abundant theme for artistic representation. The bas-reliefs exhibit a remarkable blend of Greece and India, and are superior in design and execution to

Greek influences, 326-130 A.D.

any sculpture which the Hindus have produced during the succeeding two thousand years.

The four empires of India.

During historical times four Empires have held the whole of the Indian continent under their sway or influence, inspired respectively by Buddhism, Hinduism, Muhammadanism, and Christianity. The first of the four came into being, in the Maurya dynasty, two years after Alexander's retreat from the country. Its seat was in western Bengal, and its capital at Patna. Its founder, Chandragupta, is known to us by the writings of a Greek envoy, Megasthenes, who was accredited to his court by the Seleucid king of Syria, and amused his leisure by describing the people and country. His original writings have been lost and are known to us only through the quotations of later authors. These give us a glowing idea of State efficiency. The various duties of government were distributed amongst departments, which were administered by committees of officials. Special attention was given to the army, which was controlled by a council of thirty members. But there was a particular department charged with the concern of irrigation. The people were contented and prosperous. The capital was of large size—nine miles long by a mile and a half broad. It was defended by an elaborate wooden palisade. Traces of this palisade have recently been discovered.

The Buddhist Empire, 321-184 B.C.

Asoka.

The Buddhist Emperor of India was Chandragupta's grandson, Asoka. By negotiation and by conquest he extended his dominion to the south of the peninsula; but under feelings of remorse for the misery caused by his campaigns he attached himself devotedly to the religion of

Buddha, and for some time wore the habit of a monk in a Buddhist monastery. He forbade the taking of life for food or sacrifice, and abolished the royal hunt which had delighted Megasthenes in the time of his grandfather. He made the promulgation of the faith a duty of his officials, and he despatched missionaries to carry it to southern India and to Ceylon. He conceived a remarkable idea of promoting morality by advertisement. Moral maxims and exhortations to their observance were exposed to the people—set up on stone pillar tablets or engraved upon rocks. Twenty-one of these inscriptions are extant to this day. Some of the rock inscriptions were on hillside paths to catch the eyes of passing pilgrims; and in the depths of the forest you may come across a cliff-side from which, under festoons of creepers, you are addressed with advice by the first Emperor of India. History repeats itself; and in the present day good Christians admonish us by hanging texts of Scripture in railway station waiting-rooms.

The Maurya Empire lasted under a century, and perished before the Romans had done with Carthage.

Early Tartar invasions.

We next learn from Chinese sources of the beginning of an invading torrent from central Asia, which during seventeen centuries, in successive waves of conquest, overwhelmed India with floods of misery. It commenced with an irruption of Scythians shortly before the beginning of the Christian era, and ended with the massacres of Nadir Shah in 1738. The Scythians appear to have wandered southwards and westwards, and an interesting speculation connects them with the origin of the Maratha race. Certainly the Marathas in the days of their activity scoured and plundered the country as wild troops of horsemen after a fashion which is associated with the Scythian type. A Tartar tribe which followed penetrated as far east as Benares, and appears by its coinage to have surpassed in civilisation the conquered Hindus. The dynasty adopted Buddhism in its later or idolatrous form ; and it was in its day that the Buddhist monasteries of the Peshawar Valley were decorated with their best specimens of Græco-Buddhist art. But its dominion did not outlast a couple of centuries.

In the fourth century after Christ there uprose the second Empire of India. It represented the culminating triumph of Brahminical Hinduism. About 320 A.D., at the time when Constantine the Great was founding the Greek Empire, a dynasty known as the Gupta overshadowed its rivals. Like the Maurya dynasty, it arose in western Bengal and held Patna as its capital. The second monarch of the line, Samudragupta, extended his victorious campaign to the south of the peninsula, and though his dominion over these distant regions was but vague, he could claim to have imposed his authority upon the whole of India. In the early years of the fifth century a Chinese pilgrim named Fa Hian reached India on foot to gather information about the Buddhist religion in the country of its birth. He left a diary behind him which, mainly a record of his religious experiences, gives us some account of the state of northern India during the middle period of Gupta rule. Patna was a large and flourishing city, with two Buddhist monasteries, one belonging to the original iconoclastic and the other to the later idolatrous faith. The festivals of the Church were cele-

The Hindu Empire, 320-480 A.D.

brated with great magnificence. But Hinduism was the cult of fashion: the king was an enthusiastic patron of Sanskrit literature, and Brahmin poets showed their gratitude by courtly eulogies. These were the palmy days of Sanskrit authorship. The better classes of the people abstained from meat and from spirituous liquor. The government was mild and the people contented. Punishment was not inflicted with cruelty. It speaks wonders for the public tranquillity that during six years Fa Hian should have been able to travel about the country on foot as he pleased. But this dynasty had no longer life than its predecessors. It endured but little more than a century and a half. Northern India was submerged by an irruption of the Huns. This was the time when they first pressed upon the boundaries of the Greek Empire.

About a hundred and sixty years later—towards the middle of the seventh century—India was again visited by a Chinese pilgrim named Hiouen Tsang, who held by the later or idolatrous form of Buddhism. He travelled to seek for manuscripts and to visit the holy places of the Master's life and death. It seems extraordinary that in days which appear to us as days of violence and confusion, when western Europe had relapsed into barbarism, a defenceless Chinaman should have walled from China to India across the desolate Pamirs—the roof of the world—and through the wild passes of Afghanistan. The journey to India took him four years. On the completion of his mission he returned by the Khotan route, and spent the rest of his days in translating the manuscripts he had collected. He has left a diary which is more informing than his

Harsha, 606 A.D.

predecessor's, and affords us a comprehensive picture of northern India at the time of the Saxon Heptarchy. The country was strongly governed by a king named Harsha, who held his court at Kananj (near Cawnpore), but showed Tartar descent in his restless touring and the cruelty of his punishments. Mutilations were common and torture was practised. But the Chinaman found everything to admire. The religious tenets of the king were at first unsettled; but he finally elected for the later form of Buddhism, commanded Hiouen Tsang to his court, and welcomed him with distinguished honours. The conversion of the king was met by a conspiracy of Brahmins, and it is a fact significant of the times that some of them were executed and large numbers were banished. At the present day a Hindu jury can hardly be brought to convict a Brahmin of a capital offence. The bathing festival, which now annually attracts hundreds of thousands of pilgrims to the confluence of the Ganges and Jumna rivers at Allahabad, was foreshadowed in quinquennial assemblies which Harsha used to summon at this spot: the month of gathering remains the same. Property was secure and men could till their fields in peace, paying land revenue, which was calculated at one-sixth of the produce. There was no corvée for public works, and the State paid for its labour. Harsha's rule extended over the whole of northern India: he attacked the peninsula, but obtained no footing in it. On his death the country fell into anarchy. A Chinese embassy which had been despatched to his court found on its arrival that a stranger was in possession. The embassy was attacked and plundered. It retreated to Tibet, and returning with a force of

Tibetans and Nepalese, defeated the usurper and carried him in bonds to China. India relapsed into her darkest ages.

The dark ages—650-950 A.D.

These lasted for some three hundred years—from the middle of the seventh to the middle of the tenth century. For this period coins are almost wholly lacking: civilisation declined, and society was torn and dismembered by the struggles of rival chieftains or of competing adventurers. At this time, in fact, an observer who compared India and Europe would find little of essential difference between them. It is noteworthy that these troubles and anarchy were not caused by any invasion from outside. For once central Asia left India to work out her own salvation: and, unchecked by the prestige of a foreign ruler, mutual jealousies seem to have dissolved all vestiges of a central government. From these struggles emerged India as we know it, with its rigid gradation of exclusive castes. In Europe the pretensions of the feudal barons were checked by the coalescence of those who dwelt in towns, by the formation of defensive urban societies. In India man withdrew himself into a caste as a refuge from oppression, and prided himself, in fact, on being not a citizen but an outsider.

Rajput baronies.

These troublous centuries were marked by the ascendency of Rajput clans, which from the Indus to the borders of Bengal seized tracts of country and settled upon them as feudal lords. The Rajputs claimed descent from the warrior caste of the Vedas: but it is clear that except perhaps in parts of Rajputána they have a large admixture of indigenous blood. It is probable that the marauding clans strengthened themselves by the admission of outside adventurers. In times of urgency recruits are welcome, and tradition informs us of definite cases in which men of other castes received adoption as Rajputs.

Brahmin influence.

As in mediæval Europe, priestly influence was consolidated by civil dissension, and the Brahmin hierarchy strengthened its position. It attached itself to the Rajput barons and lent them the assistance of religious authority and of literary compliment. In return Brahmins were permitted to enlarge and fortify their privileges. We have an instance of the process in the history of Manipur—an oasis in the jungle which divides India from Burma, inhabited by a people akin to the Burmese. Two centuries ago Brahmin missionaries converted the people to Hinduism. The notion of caste is quite foreign to the race, but they are now stricter in its observance than the most strait-laced Hindu. Not only are the Hindu food taboos scrupulously respected: a Manipuri considers his house polluted, and will dismantle it, if a European so much as takes shelter in its verandah. The Brahmins invented a chronicle which traced Manipuri descent from the warrior caste of the Vedas; and they were privileged to occupy large tracts of land free of revenue to the State. During the dark ages of India Brahmin colonists were summoned to all parts of the country to organise caste and develop a ritual, and were granted revenue-free lands in which their rights were secured by the direst imprecations. A curse inscribed upon a copper-plate grant which came to my notice declared that a trespasser would become 'as one who cohabited with his own mother before the idol of the god.'

By the end of this period some notable Hindu kingdoms had emerged from the confusion. Chiefest was one which occupied the country round Cawnpore. The praises of Bhoj, its Raja, are sung in popular legend, and he is as familiar a character to the people of Hindustan as King Bladud is to the inhabitants of Bath.

Rajah Bhoj—885 A.D.

So far we have dealt in the main with northern India. Of the history of peninsular India we possess but an outline. Inscriptions and coins give us lists of dynasties, which rose and fell with the fluctuating tide of conquest, names of kings, with their triumphal notes of victory, and an approximate chronology. There is little testimony from the outside. The travels of Hiouen Tsang led him to the extremity of the peninsula, and we learn that Buddhism in his days had its votaries throughout the country, and that cities in which he sojourned were large and flourishing. But we know little of the constitution of society or of forms of government.

Southern India.

The people of southern India are for the most part of Dravidian stock, and of Aryan blood there is very little. Brahmins have immigrated from the north, have established a ritual, and have organised society on a caste basis. They have probably recruited their numbers by the admission of local families of influence or ability. Of the Aryan warrior or trading classes there are no authentic traces, and in southern India Hindu institutions are simply imitative.

At the commencement of the Christian era the Andhra dynasty had for nearly two centuries held sway over the northern part of the peninsula. It adopted Buddhism, and left its memory enshrined in a stupa[1] of extraordinary magnificence and elaboration. The dynasty held its own for nearly five centuries, and during this period the Pallava dynasty, which ruled over the south of the peninsula, appears to have enjoyed a similar stability. It is clear that the country was prosperous. It conducted a considerable trade with the Roman empire, and Pliny remarks upon the large size of its sailing-ships and upon the magnitude of the sums it received for its produce. Roman coins are still forthcoming in abundance for collectors. And it is noteworthy that the design of a sailing-ship appears on the coins of the Andhra line.

The Andhra dynasty, 180 B.C.-400 A.D.

On the western, or Malabar, coast there survive ancient colonies of Jews and Christians which link Indian with Mediterranean history during the early centuries of our era. The Jews fled here for refuge from the troubles that followed the destruction of the Temple. Their descendants hold their own to this day. Four centuries later Nestorian Christianity, expelled from Europe and Africa under the ban of heresy, stretched itself eastward, sent its missionaries through Persia to India, and established a Church which took pride, later on, in ascribing its foundation to St. Thomas the apostle. For a thousand years its members retained a peculiar (Syrian) rite, and acknowledged a patriarch who lived at Babylon or at Antioch. Its repose was disturbed by the arrival of the Portuguese, who pressed it very determinedly to accept the authority of the Roman Pontiff. After many vicissi-

Jewish and Christian settlements.

[1] At Amraoti, on the river Kistna. It has been used as a quarry by the villagers around, and is now a ruin. Specimens of its sculptures are on the staircase of the British Museum.

tudes of allegiance, part of the Church has been affiliated to Rome, retaining, however, some peculiarities of rite and dogma.

From the fall of the Andhra line till the Muhammadan invasion of the peninsula—ten centuries later—we have little information but of a conflict of dynasties, and the record hardly extends beyond a list of names and dates. No dynasty succeeded in subjugating the whole peninsula; but it is an interesting fact that the Pallavas, in the south of the peninsula, maintained their authority, with varying phases of fortune, for more than eight centuries. We have found no such continuity in the north.

v.—History—After 1000 A.D.

Muhammadan invasion.

We now approach the Muhammadan period of Indian history. Invasion across the north-west border recommenced. The peculiarity of the invaders consisted in their religion. In race they did not differ essentially from many of the tribes that had poured across the frontier during six earlier centuries. We speak of the great empire which the Muhammadans ultimately established as the 'Moghal' empire. This is the name by which it is known to the people. The word is the same as our 'Mongolian,' and indicates correctly that the invaders were very largely of Tartar descent. We may also think of them as Turkish. A dialect of the language now spoken in Constantinople was the tongue of the founder of the Moghal empire.

In the eighth century of our era—within a century of the death of the Prophet—a band of his Arab disciples invaded Sindh and annexed it. But their dominion was of short duration and had no effect on Indian history. It was not till the period of the Norman conquest of England that the Muhammadan invasion really commenced. For more than a century and a half it was limited to frequent plundering incursions organised by two dynasties that successively established their headquarters in Afghanistan. The marauding armies were exceedingly numerous and treated the inhabitants with unconsidering brutality. They came for plunder and nothing else. There was much to plunder, and they came often,—over a considerable period every other year. From one of these dynasties sprang Mahmud of Ghazni, the most powerful Muhammadan sovereign of his time. He led seventeen raids into India, and is still throughout the Muhammadan world regarded as the type of insatiable avarice. The Persian poet, Sádi, in his admirable collection of tales and verses known as the *Rose Garden*, relates of an apparition of Mahmud that nothing but his burning, restless eyes remained of him—vitalised, where all else had perished, by the rage with which he saw his treasures in the hands of others. For a century and a half northern India endured a martyrdom of robbery, torture, and massacre.

Commencement of Muhammadan rule—1192 A.D.

At the end of the twelfth century there was a change of policy. The Hindus confronted the force of plunderers with a large army. It was defeated, and the Muhammadans decided to annex. Northern India was apportioned between five governors. One of them, Kutb-ud-din, whose headquarters were at Dehli, is celebrated for the construction of a tall fluted campanile which is one of the most peculiar and most beautiful of Indian monuments. These governors soon asserted their independence of the Afghan dynasty, and established royal houses. But the kingship of Dehli took precedence over the rest, and ultimately assumed an imperial authority.

Military kingdoms, 1192-1526 A.D.

The Muhammadan kingdoms of this period were of the military type, and their most successful rulers were generals who commanded the influence of the army. Some of them began life as slaves. Dynasties were often changed, and reigns were of short duration. Within a period of three centuries and a quarter Dehli witnessed the passing of five dynasties and of thirty-four kings. In military activity the most conspicuous of its rulers was Ala-ud-din, who in 1291 A.D.—a century after the establishment of the kingdom—carried his victorious arms throughout India, even to the extremity of the peninsula, where he built a mosque to commemorate his adventure. But the king who has most claims to recollection is Firoz Shah, who, by constructing the Western Jumna Canal, initiated the great irrigation system of northern India. Ala-ud-din's conquests had no permanence, and their effect was merely to clear the way for the establishment of seven other Muhammadan kingdoms, which divided between them the central Ganges valley, Bengal, and the northern portion of the peninsula.

Fresh Tartar invasions.

The country was ruled by these military governments for three centuries and a quarter—down to the arrival of a new Turkish invader in 1526 A.D. During most of this period Tartar hordes pressed across the north-western frontier. They were repelled, often with great difficulty, often after they had gained successes; and the people of the Panjáb must have endured hardships beside which those of the Thirty Years' War were merely passing troubles. The greatest of these Tartar raids was led by Timour the Lame—at the end of the fourteenth century. It poured over northern India like a dreadful pestilence.

Hindu passivity.

It is significant that no rebellion was attempted by the Hindus. The sentiments of the conquerors towards the conquered are illustrated by the amazing fact that one of the Dehli kings decided to transfer the population of this city to a site in the Deccan which seemed to him to be preferable. Thousands of men, women, and children were driven forth to attempt to walk, with their household chattels, a distance of over seven hundred miles. This, we may hope, was an instance of peculiar cruelty. The aspirations of the soldier-kings were by no means limited to the parade-ground. They introduced central Asian architecture into India and improved upon it; and the mosques with which they embellished their head-quarters are amongst the most interesting and the most impressive monuments of Islám which the world contains.

The Hindu kingdom of Vijayanagar, 1336-1565 A.D.

In the face of imminent destruction the Hinduism of southern India roused itself for a supreme effort and founded a kingdom whose capital, Vijayanagar, repelled for two centuries the advancing forces of Islám, and became, perhaps, the largest and most magnificent city which the Hindus have ever founded. The leaders of this movement were two brothers, the Dioscuri of India. They were assisted by the counsels of an eminent Brahmin scholar. But Hinduism kept no record of its achievements, and the history of Vijayanagar would be represented by a deserted wilderness of ruins on the bank of the river Tungabhadra, did we not possess Muhammadan accounts of attacks upon it, and the impressions that have been recorded by some European travellers. They were amazed at the size of the city and the splendour of its festivals. They computed the army at a million men. They mention that irrigation works were inaugurated with human sacrifices. This superstition still lingers in southern India. Quite recently, some villagers who had constructed a tank were proved to have seized a passer-by and to have immolated him on the embankment.

By the defeat of the king of Dehli, in 1526 A.D., Bábar secured a footing in India. This extraordinary man was the fifth in descent from Timour the Lame. He spoke and wrote a dialect of Turkish, and his character illustrates some of the most salient traits of the Turks as we know them to-day. He was of adventurous disposition and of intrepid courage: but he was emphatically *bon garçon*, and in a diary which he left behind him he records, with the complacency of Pepys, scenery he has admired, sport that has favoured him, bathes he has enjoyed, and dishes that have pleased him. He was fond of wine and saw no reason to abstain from it. He was, in fact, blessed with the sporting temperament. Sometimes a fugitive, sometimes a king in central Asia and Afghanistan, he ended a career of singular vicissitude by establishing his family on the throne of Dehli.

Bábar, 1526 A.D.

His grandson, Akbar, was the Solomon of India. His conquests subdued northern India and led him some distance into the peninsula. But he is better known for his civil administration than for his victories. To his singular tolerance the evidences of religion seemed inconclusive, and he delighted in religious discussions which brought together in debate the professors of different faiths, Christianity being represented, we are told, by some Portuguese priests. He finally attempted to establish a religion of his own. He governed Muhammadans and Hindus with equal justice and with equal firmness; and,

Bábar's successors—Akbar.

with the assistance of a Hindu financier, he initiated a land revenue valuation survey, some traces of which exist to this day. The court of his son, Jehangir, received an English ambassador from whose despatches we may gather ideas of magnificence which are in accord with the splendid architecture that is the glory of this dynasty. To Akbar's piety we owe the great tomb which commemorates the name of his father, Humayun: he built one of the Agra palaces, and that other palace—still more splendid—which in lonely magnificence at Fatehpur Sikri displays the uncalculating grandeur of his ambitions. Under Jehangir, Akbar's tomb at Sikandra was constructed, and the enamelled mosque at Lahore. Moghal architecture reached its zenith in the reign of Jehangir's son, Shah Jehán. He built the great mosque of Dehli, the Táj Mahál mausoleum, and completed at Agra a palace in which he died as the prisoner of his son. He spent his last days in a balcony overlooking the Jumna, which commanded a prospect of the graceful white outlines of the building that commemorated his wife.

The Moghal Empire—Aurangzeb, 1687 A.D.

His son, Aurangzeb, is known to us as the 'Great Moghal.' He was of sterner mettle than his predecessors, strict in his religion, severe towards the Hindus, and spent most of his long reign in military enterprises. For twenty-five years he lived under canvas. He gradually subdued the rival Muhammadan states of the Deccan, and the Hindu kingdom of Vijayanagar having fallen, no obstacle remained between him and Cape Comorin. The third, or Muhammadan Empire of India, was established.

But its foundations were on sand. Already the Maratha power had arisen which was to bleed the empire to death.

History was as attractive to the Muhammadans as it was contemptible to the Hindus, and from the tenth century onwards we have chronicles, some of which are of high merit. Naturally, Muhammadan historians are impressed with the achievements of their victorious rulers. But we have the independent testimony of European travellers to the power and magnificence of the Great Moghal. Their pages abound with curious anecdotes of capricious extravagance. On one occasion Jehangir weighed himself in gold and jewels and distributed his weight in charity. But the condition of the cultivator was miserable in the extreme. The theory of the day, in the Hindu kingdom of Vijayanagar as well as in territories ruled by Muhammadans, was that all the land of the country was the property of the Crown, and that the people cultivated it merely on such terms as the Crown conceded to them. They were left with bare subsistence only. Upon a similar theory have been based the exactions of King Leopold in the Congo.

Aurangzeb died at the commencement of the eighteenth century. Fifty years more and the Moghal sovereignty of Dehli had fallen, torn by dissension and shaken by Maratha attack. The vigour of Bábar's successors barely outlasted two centuries. The decline of the empire was hastened by the last of the raids from central Asia. Nadir Shah, a Persian adventurer, descended upon India, defeated the Dehli army, and brutally massacred the inhabitants of the city. Extorting a huge ransom, the Persians withdrew, leaving behind them a trail of ruin and misery.

We have now to take account of a new power—that of the Marathas—which, Hindu in its origin, followed methods of conquest that were out of all accord with Hindu tradition. Its home was in the arid plains which undulate over the Deccan plateau east of Bombay. The Marathas may possibly have within them some Scythian blood: such a connection might explain the rapid transformation of a community of peasants into bands of guerilla horsemen, as active in movement and in plunder as the Huns of Attila. But the climate and the soil which reared them will suffice to account for a hardiness of disposition which, manifested a century ago in warlike enterprises, has always enabled them to support in patient courage the losses of recurring famines. The founder of the Maratha power, Sivaji, was of the peasant class, and so were the generals who succeeded him in command and established ruling dynasties. But shortly after the death of Sivaji, the general control of Maratha activity came into the hands of a Brahmin family, whose representative, with the title of Peshwa, maintained a hundred years' rivalry with the English in directing the civil and military affairs of the Indian continent.

The Marathas, 1650-1817 A.D.

The enterprises of Sivaji had commenced before the death of Aurangzeb. Fifty years later the Marathas had gained practical possession of northern and central India, and by raids into the Panjáb, Bengal, and southern India, had secured the payment of annual subsidies which were nominally calculated at a fourth of the revenue. 'The Maratha ditch' outside the city of Calcutta testifies to the terror which their name inspired. Their earlier policy stopped short of annexation. For many years they spared the nominal authority of the Moghal emperor, though the emperor was in fact a prisoner in their hands. But later on they administered as well as subdued; and four large principalities—those of Gwalior, Indore, Baroda, and Nagpur—provided established centres for the Maratha power. The ruler of Gwalior—Sindhia—trained his soldiers in European tactics by the employment in high command of French officers. The Maratha confederacy was broken in 1803 by the victories of Sir Arthur Wellesley—better known as the Duke of Wellington—and of Lord Lake. But it was not finally dissolved till fourteen years later; and there still remained the dispersal of large bands of professional marauders (known as Pindaris), which, organised under Maratha auspices, surpassed the Marathas in greed and cruelty. A favourite method of torture that was employed by them to compel villagers to give up their jewellery was to enclose the head of the householder in a bag of cayenne pepper.

The Pindaris.

Before the establishment of British rule one more effort was made by an Indian people to found a sovereignty of their own. The Sikhs, who for seventy years maintained a military government in the Panjáb, were united by a religion, not by the ties of race or caste. They were members of a sect which rejected Brahmin formalism and admitted into fellowship men of all castes by a process of initiation. The doctrines which they followed had been enunciated by a teacher

The Sikhs, 1780-1849 A.D.

in the fifteenth century, and were the outcome of a more general religious movement that is believed to have had its origin in Nestorian Christianity. It was fundamental in this reform of faith that God was a Spirit, and that He could communicate His ordinances through the mouths of teachers. A copious literature gave expression to ideas that were in lively revolt against the idolatry of Hinduism and the pretensions of its priesthood. The Sikhs held in special reverence the book of their doctrine: it is still carried at the head of every Sikh regiment. Under Muhammadan persecution a religion of Methodist quietism was inflamed by an ardent spirit of resentfulness. It took upon itself a military organisation, and its soldiers fought with the burning but steady courage of Bible Christians. In the year 1800 a man of great capacity — Ranjit Singh — obtained control of the movement, consolidated its military energies, and directed them with extraordinary energy and prudence. He reigned for thirty-nine years, and by the time of his death the Sikh army had become a powerful fighting force, disciplined by the influence of some European officers. Its control then passed into the hands of a military democracy which maintained with the English two of the fiercest wars that delayed the advance of British supremacy. The conflict ended in 1849, on the field of Gujrat. Eight years later, the loyalty and valour of the Sikhs illuminated the dark days of the Indian Mutiny.

Bábar had commenced his raids upon the Panjáb when India was invaded across a new frontier. The Portuguese fell upon her by sea. Five years after Columbus had sailed for America, Vasco da

Gama doubled the Cape and landed upon the west coast of the peninsula—a country well known to Europe for the spices, gems, and cotton fabrics it exported by the route of the Red Sea and Egypt. The Portuguese desired to possess themselves of this valuable trade; but they did not come merely as traders. They aimed at establishing such a dominion as Spanish adventurers were carving out in Mèxico and Peru, and their representatives were entitled 'Viceroys,' and claimed authority for the Portuguese Crown in virtue of a grant from the Papal chancellery. For two and a half centuries, almost coincident with the period of the Moghal Empire of Dehli, they struggled to maintain an authority which never penetrated beyond the coast-line. They were at times as greatly pressed by Muhammadan coalitions as was the crusading kingdom of Jerusalem, but they repelled the assaults of Islám with all the courage and more than the success of the Crusaders. They withstood with much glory attacks by the navies of Egypt and Turkey. For a century—till 1600 A.D.—they monopolised the Indian trade. But their authority was undermined by the enterprises of other European nations, and was finally subverted by the Marathas. The Indian dominion of Portugal is now represented by Goa and two other little towns on the western coast-line. If some Portuguese leaders showed the callous cruelty of Cortes or Pizarro, others, and eminently the great Albuquerque, were wise and benevolent administrators: in St. Francis Xavier, Portugal introduced to India the first Christian missionary; and the breadth of her ambitions, the variety of her exploits and her

The coming of the Portuguese, 1498 A.D.

courage in adversity, were a worthy theme for the epic of Camoens.

By the end of the sixteenth century a strange competition was on foot for the exploitation of the trade of India. Merchants from England and Holland, joined later on by French, Danes, and Germans, settled on her coasts, in trading concessions, each determined to do, not only the best for itself, but the worst for its rivals. Their jealousies were increased by proximity: all five nations had concessions in the neighbourhood of the present city of Calcutta. The merchants of each nationality were banded in an association which aspired to a monopoly, not only against foreigners, but against unassociated merchants of its own country. Each association endeavoured to secure its position by forming intimate connections with Native rulers: in the time of Akbar several English merchants travelled as far Dehli. But the fortunes of these associations were involved in the dissensions which divided in Europe the nations to which they belonged. The merchants from Holland and from Denmark yielded to the English, who succeeded in ejecting them from every foothold in the country. The Germans also gave place; but they have since recovered their position, and German merchants are numerous and influential in the mercantile communities of Bombay, Calcutta, and Rangoon. With the French the struggle was more severe: they, like the English, had gained possession of territory, had developed a military force, and had made political alliances with Indian princes. Each side had thus equipped itself with partisans for a conflict, which, urged on both sides

European struggles for the Indian trade, 1590-1760 A.D.

by leaders of address and courage, lasted over a period of sixteen years. If Clive was victorious, it may justly be said that Dupleix, Bussy, and Lally deserved victory. But they were left unsupported by their country; and four dots, on or near the coast-line, are all that the map now shows of French military endeavours.

The British Empire.

The development of the British Empire in India falls within the domain of well-known history. Compared with the progress of European conquest in Africa, its growth was by no means rapid, and nearly a century intervened between the victories of Clive and the settlement of the map of India substantially as we know it. With each advance of the boundary, grave difficulties arose in providing for the administration of territory that was not sparsely inhabited by semi-barbarous tribes, but was crowded with an intelligent population. By the battles of Wandiwash, Plassy, and Buxar, fought between 1757 and 1764, French rivalry was extinguished, and British influence made dominant in Madras and paramount in Bengal. More than a generation elapsed before the brothers Wellesley—one as Viceroy and the other in military command—subdued the Muhammadan ruler of Mysore and broke the power of the Marathas. By the former of these conquests British territory in Madras was extended to nearly its present limits. Fourteen years later the main portion of the Bombay presidency was annexed, and the Bengal presidency was extended up the valley of the Ganges. Thirty-seven years passed before the annexations of Lord Dalhousie added the Panjáb, Oudh, and the Nagpur districts to the territories administered by British officers, and constituted British India nearly as it stands at present. Twenty years after the empire had been established its dignity was formally recognised by the addition of the Imperial title to the British Crown.

The causes of British success.

Amongst the causes that contributed to the success of the British three deserve special mention. Firstly, constant warfare and frequent changes of dynasty had eradicated all racial and religious sentiment from military service, and had rendered the soldier's calling a matter of livelihood. In Europe, at one time, military service also became a cosmopolitan profession. In consequence, the British found no difficulty in enlisting Native troops, and needed only European officers and a leavening of European soldiers to create a strong military power. To British victories Native regiments contributed largely. The day of reckoning came in the Mutiny: but in that day were also manifested great loyalty and kind feeling, and at the present time Native troops constitute two-thirds of the rank and file of the Indian army. In the second place, the officers who represented England in India were, on the whole, well supported by the English Government. England might disapprove of their policy, and of the personal gains that attended it: Clive and Warren Hastings were both impeached before Parliament. But, while sometimes condemning the methods of her sons, England was always willing to profit by their successes, and never denied them assistance when they were in straits, or declined responsibility on the score that the East India Company stood between her and the Indian people. Thirdly, the circumstances of Indian service were such as to attract men of adventurous disposition and determined character. The pay that was offered was small; but the chances of distinction were great, and, by private trading, men of energy and capacity could expect to add enormously to their emoluments and even to acquire fortunes. These were the days when the retired 'Nabob' attracted the ridicule and the envy of English society.

The foreign and military policy of the growing empire was determined by the Viceroys and the Home Government. These authorities also from time to time imposed upon the civil administration principles that could not have grown out of Indian experience. Such were the freedom of the press, the substitution of English for oriental systems of education, and the association with the Government of elected popular representatives in the management of local affairs and in the framing of laws. But the development of the civil government of the country, in its various branches, was the achievement of the English permanent officials, who, in original status but clerks in the East India Company's mercantile offices, now constitute the various Indian services. To Warren Hastings, himself of the permanent Indian staff, belongs the credit of first effectually organising an honest and painstaking administration. For the last half-century the Indian Civil Service, open to all who could win admission by study, has been mainly recruited from the English middle classes—a society, which, tinged with Puritanism, holds strongly by the Bible and teaches it to its children. Its sons generally carried to India with them the moral notions which this

The direction of British policy and of administration.

teaching imparts; and, braced by high responsibility, and removed from the temptations of personal or family interests, they succeeded in elaborating an administration which, autocratic though it may have been, and jealous of its authority, was probably the most benevolent that the world has ever seen.

vi.—Religions—Indigenous and Hindu.

To the student of comparative religion India is a museum of illustrative specimens. It furnishes types of every idea which has occurred to man under the promptings of his religious sentiment: it presents a tableau of the existing beliefs of the world with signs to indicate the course of their development.

Animistic beliefs.

The earliest form of religious idea is that termed 'animism'—a vague feeling that the objects with which a man comes in contact, animate or inanimate, possess wills of their own, and have the power and the desire to oppose him. This notion accounts for the bad luck which often occurs to us: chance is, we feel, an unsatisfactory explanation: it is simpler and easier to believe that we are unfortunate because we have been deliberately thwarted. The idea is present to most men when missing a train or when wrestling with a collar stud. It is obvious in small children, who will beat a table or chair against which they have stumbled. Xerxes affords us a classic illustration in the chains with which he punished the unruliness of the sea. The more peculiar is an object, the greater is the risk from it. Riding about India, one frequently notices daubs of vermilion applied to trees of unusual size, to rocks, or other prominent objects. Red paint is supposed to conciliate them. It was necessary to entertain a special watchman to prevent country-people from disfiguring with red paint the skeleton of an elephant in the Lucknow Museum. I have seen a great crowd of people prostrate themselves before the first locomotive engine that entered their district; and unless precautions are taken vermilion will surreptitiously find its way into locomotive running sheds. The inclination to propitiate a strange object is common amongst the lower classes of India, and has earned them amongst Muhammadans the scornful title of 'wonder worshippers.' In places where tigers abound they are propitiated with magical rites. It is an interesting fact that these rites will succeed only when they are performed by a man indigenous to the locality: local forces will only recognise local men. Hindu villages in the jungle often maintain an aboriginal medicine-man to propitiate the forest powers that surround them. Inquiring why Hindus would not take up land in a fertile but waste district of Assam, I was told that they had no means of finding out the local influences and of conciliating them. The existence of such influences was indisputable. A further stage is reached when the power of inanimate things is supposed to reside in spirits that pervade them. The belief in dryads is universal in India. They appertain especially to the large fig-trees (*banians* and *pipals*) which are commonly planted in the little market squares of Indian villages or just outside the houses. You may see sometimes numbers of little earthenware saucers, suspended by strings from the branches, in which the dryads are fed by offerings of curds.

But the extraordinary reverence in which the Ganges is held affords undoubtedly the best illustration of the attachment of religious imaginings to a physical object. Although frequently apostrophised as 'Mother Ganges,' it is clearly the river that is worshipped and not any deified abstraction of its qualities. It is difficult to convey to English readers the enthusiastic affection with which the river is regarded. Russian pilgrims undergo the extremity of hardship to bathe in the Jordan. But they are influenced by an association of ideas. The Ganges is adored in itself, and itself sheds the grace that is attained by baptism. Its sanctity is pre-eminent at certain places on its course, as at Hardwár (where it issues from the mountains) and at Benares. To bathe in the river is a potent means of securing salvation, and on festivals, generally at the periods of new or full moon, hundreds of thousands of persons—men and women—congregate at the river's side and immerse themselves in the water. When the full moon occurs at night the spectacle is not one to be forgotten. The sands along the river's edge are densely crowded with people, dressing or undressing, haggling with the priests (to whom fees are payable); and the shallow water is alive with bathers immersed to the middle, plunging below the surface for a counted number of times, and sending ripples of black and gold across the reflected moonlight. You will see strong forces of police guarding the approaches, for if uncontrolled the eagerness of the crowd would crush the weak under foot; and a young Englishman passes on horseback, seeing that order is preserved and that the bathers do not get into deep water beyond the limits staked off for them. The bathers walk into the river along little plunge-boards, a row of which projects into the stream. Each belongs to a family

The river Ganges.

of Brahmins who are called 'sons of the Ganges': they distribute between them the area of the province and send out touts twenty miles and more along the roads to direct the clients that they consider belong to them. A fee is payable for each person that steps on the board; the profits are very large, and their distribution not unfrequently leads to rioting. It is meritorious to carry Ganges water to distant shrines and pour it over the idol, and one meets long lines of pilgrims each carrying two glass phials of water, slung on a rod over his shoulder. It is near to the heart of every Hindu that his bones after cremation should be thrown into the stream, and pious sons frequently carry reliques long distances for this purpose. When wood is scarce, bodies are thrown into the river half burned, an ever-present danger in time of cholera. Benares, the sacred city of the Hindu, with its long river frontage of steps and temples, is the refuge of the aged who wish to die by the edge of the river of peace.

Fetishes.

The mischievous influences by which we are surrounded can be neutralised by the use of charms or *fetishes*. In English nurseries children will often face with more courage the terrors of darkness if they are permitted to take some favourite toy to bed with them. But it is not only amongst our children that we find the germs of this superstition. How many of us carry charms on our watch-chains, and use mascots for the bridge table and even on the motor car! In India fetishes are in common employ. A curious one I came across was a little bag of highly polished wheat-grains that was the guiding and directing genius of a band of professional housebreakers. The grains could foretell good luck or bad, and in this respect were more serviceable than an ordinary fetish; but they were formally worshipped by the tribe, and their possession gave authority to the leader. There are few Indian children who do not wear a neck amulet—a little silver case containing a written incantation. This again is more elaborate than the primitive fetish. Caste life affords an illustration truer to type. In a large number of castes the representative implement of the caste is held in reverence, and once a year is formally worshipped. Horses in India are led, not by the bridle, but by a thick cotton leading-rope which is passed over the headstall, and such a rope is carried by every Indian groom. I asked my groom one day to tie up with his leading-rope a dog that would not follow. He absolutely refused, and I discovered that the rope was the fetish of his caste and was formally adored and propitiated in the course of an annual caste festival. To touch a dog with it would have been sacrilege. The clerk every year keeps a festival known as the worship of the ink-bottle, the weaver propitiates his loom, the professional wrestler the clubs with which he exercises his muscles, the scavenger his brush, and even so ambiguous a caste as that of tent-pitcher has a fetish of its own—the mallet of its trade—and the man who is so disrespectful to his mallet as to sit upon it is judged by his caste committee and fined one and eightpence. This amount seems to be not an uncommon penalty for minor breaches of caste rule. Still more remarkable is the fact that high-caste men very frequently carry about with them a fossil ammonite and adore it under the assumption that it represents divinity. A Brahmin subordinate holding responsible office under Government, intelligent, well educated,—a graduate of the university,—was charged with having assaulted a coolie. He explained that an ill-conditioned village headman, when asked to give the customary assistance in pitching his tent, had sent some particularly low-caste coolies. 'So long,' he went on, 'as they concerned themselves with my tent and furniture, I bore it in silence, but when I saw one of them lay hands on the basket in which I carry my god, I could not contain myself, and I struck him.' The god he referred to was one of these ammonites.

Another conception of primitive religion—the *taboo*—exercises a very powerful influence on Indian society. The taboo is a prohibition, the essence of which is that it should be unreasonable. Some tribes in the Assam hills consider that certain occurrences lay them under an interdict. Such are a birth in the household, or a visitation of sickness, or the spectacle of a burning village. During the period of interdict, which may extend to a week, it is *taboo* to do anything whatever but eat and drink. The people are confined to their houses: they may not attend to their crops: no official of Government may enter their villages. The magistrate of the district, visiting a friendly tribesman, found the door closed against him. He asked what was the matter, and was told through the keyhole that a bitch had just had a litter of puppies, and that he could not come in. But we need not go to hill tribes for illustrations of the taboo. The Hindu caste system is permeated by it, and, indeed, depends upon it. The prohibition of caste intermarriage may possibly be explained by an insistent feeling of trade

Taboos.

unionism. But no rational explanation can be given of a food taboo that is in force irrespective of cleanliness or wholesomeness. We can, however, find in our own society traces of the feeling. Schoolboy life is complicated by taboos, generally affecting dress, of the most irrational description. And some of our adult notions of 'good form' rest upon nothing more solid than unreasoning prescription.

Of all the vagaries into which religious imaginings have strayed, none is more curious than the notion that certain animals are useful as interpreters of the supernatural, or as intermediaries between man and the forces that oppress him. Birds by their flight could tell Romans, Greeks, and Arabs of good or bad fortune: victims could reveal the future by the condition of their intestines. As totems, animals have been adopted as the genii of tribes and societies. The animals that were held sacred in Egypt would in their diversity have formed a menagerie: they included crocodiles, fish, ibis, and hawks, as well as all the domesticated beasts. It was death to kill one: during the Roman occupation of the country the officials were hard put to it on one occasion to repress rioting that had been excited by the killing of a cat. Later on, the people of each district seemed to have concentrated their reverence upon one kind of animal, and would kill without scruple the animal that was worshipped by their neighbours. In India, monkeys are respected by all but the hill tribes. But there is an explanation of this in the assistance they gave to the hero of the great national epic. Peafowl are taboo in up-country plains' districts. Snakes, even poisonous, are held in respect: I have known villagers refuse to kill a

Animal-worship

cobra, and families will offer milk to a cobra which has invaded their houses. There are temples that are dedicated to the snake: one of them stands on the Simla golf-links. But in India all animals sink into insignificance by the side of the cow: she may almost be called the presiding genius of the country. Kine-killing is, in Hindu eyes, the worst of sacrileges, and provokes the bitterest quarrels between Hindus and Muhammadans. It is a stumbling-block between us and the Brahmin priesthood, and provides a stirring war-cry for the disaffected. The cow, like the Ganges, is apostrophised as 'mother': white, with soft eyes set in dark eyelids, she stands as a type of the patience of India. It is meritorious to set a bull-calf loose upon the country: sacred bulls wander unchecked through the narrow streets of Benares, poking their heads into the vegetable and grain stalls that line the thoroughfare. A Maratha Brahmin, when death approaches, is lifted from his bed to the earth: a cow is brought in, and, as life fades, her tail is placed between his dying fingers. The origin of these feelings has baffled all inquiries. In the earlier Vedic hymns cattle are held in great esteem, but not more so than horses, and the slaughter of cattle for sacrifice and for food is expressly recognised. The laws of Manu, written after the commencement of the Christian era, permit of the killing of kine to feast an honoured guest, or for sacrifice; and, though plainly deprecating the practice, seem averse from it, rather from a desire to spare animal life generally, than from any special regard for horned cattle. In Egypt the cow represented Hathor, at one time the most popular goddess of the country: there was a special cult of the Apis bull which was perhaps reflected in the worship of the golden calf of the wilderness. At the time of Herodotus the cow was sacred in Egypt: but so were many other animals, and male kine could, as in ancient India, be sacrificed and eaten provided that a scrupulous ceremonial was observed. But it is difficult to believe that a cult of Egypt penetrated Asia to reach Indian soil, leaving no traces of its passage across the intervening countries. Possibly the sentiment was borrowed from the Mongolian tribes of the north-eastern frontier. They are peculiar in abhorring milk and butter: bulls are slaughtered for food, but only on great occasions: they are highly prized, and fines that are levied for tribal misconduct are made payable in them as a severe penalty. Cow-killing is under its strictest interdict amongst the Mongolian people of Nepal, though they do not hesitate to sacrifice the buffalo. It may seem that to reject as unclean the products of a cow is the reverse of respecting the animal. But ethnologists are agreed that ceremonial uncleanness is often a sign of an ancient taboo. To Muhammadans, dogs are unclean. Yet the reformed Government of Turkey, with all its wishes, has not ventured to proscribe the troops of dogs that infest and pollute the streets of Constantinople.

Cult of the spirits of the departed.

The more ancient is the civilisation, the more backward the condition of man, the more substantial is his belief in the separate existence of his soul. A tribe of the Assam hills, when burying a kinsman, fences the grave with thorns, which may prick his wandering spirit and prevent it from returning to trouble his home. Circumstances once deputed me to superintend the execution of a man and a woman of the lowest caste, who in conspiracy had poisoned the latter's husband. They were brought out from the condemned cell, and I asked the man whether I could do anything for him before the end. He wished to say a few words to his accomplice: he briefly reminded her of an old *pipal* tree which stood by the road to their village. They believed that the soul of one who came to a violent death haunted the place that was last in his thoughts, and they died contentedly together in the assurance that they would meet again amidst the foliage of the tree. This calls to mind the theme of the Willow Pattern plate. Whatever be its formal religious belief, each Hindu family keeps every year the festival of its ancestors, when cakes are offered to the last seven in the line of them, decreasing in size with the remoteness of the relationship. The doctrine of transmigration is accepted more or less vaguely: it is cited to justify the protection of animal life. Ancestor-worship is in direct conflict with this belief; but the incongruity is no greater than others which puzzle attempts to understand the religious ideas of the country. The individuality of the soul was, of course, a cardinal principle of the religion of Egypt: it was the custom annually to visit the cemeteries, and to place offerings of food on the graves. This custom may still be traced in Muhammadan Egypt, and we are reminded of it, especially in Paris, by the modern observance of All-Souls' Day.

Hero-worship.

Indian beliefs are further affected by the glamour of hero-worship. One of the two great epics of the country celebrates the trials and the victories of Rama, a traditional prince of Oudh. By the deceit of a stepmother, Rama was excluded from succession and exiled, accompanied by Sita, his faithful wife. In exile he undertook labours such as those of Hercules: his wife was torn from him in revenge and carried away by a giant that ruled Ceylon, but was finally recovered, after infinite labour and peril, by the assistance of an army of monkeys. The tale illustrates resignation, brotherly love, wifely fidelity, and manly courage. It was undoubtedly composed several centuries before our era, and in the sixteenth century it was rendered into the vulgar tongue by Tulsi Dás, a poet of extraordinary fire and skill. The poem is familiar in all ranks of Hindu society: the unlettered know passages by heart, and enjoy very greatly evening entertainments at which a Brahmin is engaged to read it aloud. He reads for hours at a time. Tulsi Dás moralises by the way to very high purpose, and his precepts have profoundly affected the Hindu character. The incidents of the tale are annually brought to mind by open-air pageants, the parts of which are taken by private citizens. They are on a very large scale, with very brilliant costumes, giving entertainment to many thousands of spectators, and ending up in a burst of fireworks, consuming the huge basket-work figure of the giant of Ceylon. The people of Assam delight themselves with such entertainments all the year round, but on a smaller scale, and on the stage of a rough bamboo theatre.

In Brahmin theology Rama is an incarnation of the god Vishnu. But in popular ideas he is a god in his own identity: by repeating his name and that of his queen one may earn grace, and the pious will utter the formula 'Ram Ram Sita Ram' many thousand times over.

Such are the vague beliefs and sentiments that thread their way through the consciousness of the Indian people—that form the mosaic foundation upon which has been reared a superstructure of idolatrous Brahminical theology. It is this theology which, presented to the eyes by temples and images, is generally taken by Europeans as the Hindu religion.

Grotesqueness of Hindu idols.

The first impression that strikes the observer is the extraordinary grotesqueness of these images. The gods they represent are in substance the forces of Nature, not accepted as they stand, as in the simple Nature-worship of the Vedic hymns, but conceived as the attributes of deities which a later imagination has endowed with substantial forms and more or less human qualities. The forms that have been given to these deities represent the profound pessimism of the Hindu mind.

Like the Greeks, the Hindus, unguided by revealed religion, sought the Divine not outside the world, but within it, and looked to the workings of Nature for clues to the disposition and will of the gods. To the Greek the smiling brilliance of the sea, valleys dense with olive gardens, hills running up through vineyard terraces to slopes of pine trees or banks of flowers, suggested forces which were, above all things, beautiful, and which, if occasionally hostile to man, opposed him rather in caprice than with malignancy. In very different guise does Nature appear to the Hindu. Beauties there are: but they lack the gaiety of Mediterranean scenery. The forest depths are dark: the river, swollen with rain, is a resistless torrent, threatening the fields and dwellings of mankind : the hills are guarded for wild beasts by thorny jungle, dense grass, or rocky precipices. Nor is Nature depressing in sentiment only : she often appears to overhang humanity as a tormenting spirit. She sends forth hordes of birds and beasts to prey upon the crops and to dispute with the cultivator the fruits of his care and labour. Perched aloft above his fields on a rough platform, the cultivator and his sons, with slings, rattles and shrill cries, all day and all night, watch and repel marauding tribes of parrots and starlings, deer, wild pig, and sometimes elephants. By a strange fatality the ripening of the spring crops is the season for hail-storms. At times descending clouds of locusts strip the land of all its herbage, and even the forest of its leaves. And above all these disasters impends the supreme calamity of famine : the anxious watching of the merciless skies, the withering of the crops, ruin, and the hungry cries of children. Death steps alongside of life. From the edge of the forest the tiger besets the grazing cattle, and sometimes, depraved by the taste of human blood, spreads a panic through the countryside : villages are deserted and crops allowed to fall ungathered. There is fear of death in the routine of domestic life : the cobra lives in the shelter of the cottage, and the women of the house must be cautious when shifting furniture, fetching fuel from the yard, or bringing vegetables from the garden. Before vaccination was introduced almost every child bore the marks of smallpox. At times cholera, fever, and plague overshadow the country, scourging the people with death and anguish : then unceasingly the funeral pyres are burning. These are the baleful aspects of Nature in India. At times she smiles upon mankind.

There are seasons of bountiful crops, of healthiness and prosperity. Village life has its idyllic side: the promise of harvest is gilded by brilliant sunlight: in their cottages the poor have joys which are unknown in the slums and alleys of Europe. But Nature, which gives the increase, also appears to destroy it, and the deities that inspire her forces present themselves to the popular imagination in shapes that are cruel and repulsive. The most popular of the divine hierarchy of the Hindus—the goddess known as the 'Great Mother'—is depicted as an ogress. She is black in face: her eyes are fierce: blood drops from her crimson mouth and protruding tongue: she is garlanded with human skulls.

The trinity of Brahmin theology.

Brahmin theology has deified Nature in a trinity of aspects. Brahma represents creation: having created, the god is passive, and very few temples exist in his honour. Vishnu represents the continuity of existence; and Siva the breaches in this continuity which result from birth and death. Vishnu appeals to the philosophic view of life; but he is popularised by numerous incarnations in which his actions attract a wider sympathy. His most popular incarnation is that of the god Krishna, whose exploits illustrate and excite the perilous association of religion with the erotic. Siva appeals to the emotional view of life. He is known *par excellence* as the 'great god'—the Lord of Birth and Death. *Salvâ reverentiâ*, this dual conception is exactly expressed by the lines of Tennyson:—

> 'Thou mad'st these orbs of light and shade,
> Thou gavest Life to man and brute,
> Thou gavest Death; and lo! Thy foot
> Is on the skull that Thou hast made.'

But reflections upon birth and death bring us close to the margin of the obscene and the terrible; and the cult of Siva has degenerated into phallic-worship in one direction and into demon-worship on the other. The divorce of religion from morality reaches, however, its utmost limit in the cult of the female deities who have been imagined as companions of the gods, and most of all in the worship of the consort of Siva known as Durga, or Kali, which reaches the acme of its popularity amongst the people of Bengal. She is propitiated by bloody sacrifices of buffaloes and goats. To the extremists among her followers sexual restraint is a denial of her authority. In her name prostitution has become a temple service, and her attributes have corrupted deplorably the instincts of youth. Strict Hindus generally class themselves as votaries of Vishnu, Siva, or of Siva's consort, and signify their devotion to one or other by marks of red or white paint, borne on the forehead drawn upright if for Vishnu, horizontally if for Siva, and curved, with a dot, if for the goddess. Besides these gods there are countless others. The Hindu Pantheon has been complicated by the desire to subdivide, which has multiplied so extraordinarily the Hindu castes. Brahminism recognises the influence of many hundreds of thousands of gods.

Many of the most learned Brahmins will smile at these beliefs. To them religion expresses the transcendental conception of their philosophy—that life is an illusion, a procession of misleading shadows, behind which there lies, veiled, the reality of the eternal. To an Englishman these ideas appear very unpractical, except, perhaps, when he stands alone under the stars, or, withdrawing

Esoteric Brahminism.

for a moment from his pursuits, he thinks of the feelings he may experience one day, when he lies a-dying.

There have been revolts against polytheism and against the authority of the Brahmin priesthood.

Movements of religious reform.

We have already considered in outline the reforming movement which was led by the Buddha in the fifth century B.C. Buddhism has forsaken India for other countries of Asia: but a parallel movement—Jainism—still animates one section of Indian society. This creed came into existence about the same time as Buddhism: but it rejected less strictly the tenets and authority of the Brahmins, and has degenerated into a form of polytheism. According to its belief the highest object of asceticism is to secure, not the annihilation of self, but transcendent individual sanctity, and saints of great eminence are objects of worship. Its votaries are possessed by a most scrupulous regard for life of all kinds: with few exceptions they will not plough for fear of cutting a worm: they will not sit down before carefully brushing their seats that they may run no risk of crushing an insect: extremists prove in their bodies the strength of their convictions, and pride themselves upon the lice for which they provide a home. But Jains show a keen appreciation of natural beauties: they construct their temples upon hills that overlook charming scenery, and Mount Abu, the headquarters of their faith, 'rises with its gems of architecture like a jewelled island from the Rajputána plain.' The Jain community devotes itself to trade and money-lending—pursuits that are not harmful to animal life. Amongst them men can earn titles of

The Jains.

honour by the profuse celebration of a religious ceremony. On a platform under a large awning are set up numbers of little brass images and vases decked with flowers and prettily arranged, as for the decoration of an altar. The giver of the entertainment invites his caste-fellows; they attend in thousands from the country-side, and are feasted generously. On the great day of the festival the host with his relations mounts a large wooden chariot, and is drawn by an elephant several times round the altar. His triumph is commemorated by the grant of a title, which is coupled to his name by people generally as well as by his caste-fellows. There are three of these titles, each to be acquired by a definite amount of expenditure. The cost of the lowest exceeds £3000.

The teachings of Kabir.

It is a remarkable coincidence that at about the time of Luther a wave of spiritual revolt should have been passing over India as well as Europe. In the first half of the fifteenth century it produced a teacher named Kabir, whose sayings are still current throughout a great part of northern India. He insisted upon the Unity of God, the fellowship of man, and the direct responsibility of man to God, and he condemned all caste rules, sacrifices, and the intervention of the Brahmin priesthood. From his doctrines sprung the aspirations which, a century later, animated the prophets of the Sikhs and were formulated in their scriptures. His teaching moved the hearts of both Muhammadans and Hindus; and it is said that at his death both parties claimed his body. His spirit appeared and bade them uncover the bier. On raising the cloth they found only a heap of flowers, which they divided, half being burned by the Hindûs and half buried by the Muhammadans. He is supposed by some to have derived his inspiration from the Nestorian Christianity of southern India, but in this case he simplified very greatly the doctrines he received. The enlightenment of his views has won him most adherents amongst the poor and illiterate. But his writings, mainly of the proverbial order, are the source from which conversation, in all classes of society, draws its favourite texts. Their popularity is, however, as nothing compared with those of a successor, Tulsi Dás, the translator of the Ramáyana. In his imaginative hands the epic conducts us to thoughts which approach those of Christian doctrine,—the sinfulness of man, the infinite mercy of God, His incarnation for the purpose of redeeming man; and he extols, as the highest of our emotions, an ecstatic, self-abandoning love for the God that cares for us.

Of Tulsi Dás.

The influence of these reforms has been greatest in the Hindi-speaking districts of Upper India. But about their time there also arose a reforming teacher in the plains of Bengal. Chaitanya taught very similar doctrines, and initiated, in the Sankirtan, or procession of song, what is perhaps the only form of congregational worship that is known to the Hindu. From his influence have sprung the Hindu monasteries of Assam, which recall in many particulars the monasteries of Burma. They do not represent exclusively Brahmin foundations: some of them are the resort of a lower caste of which Chaitanya was a member. In each an abbot presides over a company of celibate monks who live in cottages clustered round a large prayer-

Chaitanya.

hall. Beyond the cottages are fields belonging to the monastery which are cultivated by the monks. Each monastery has its lay-disciples, by hundreds or by thousands, scattered about the country: they render each year a small subscription to the abbey funds. The abbots command immense respect, especially such of them as are high-caste Brahmins. From time to time they make progresses about the country, receiving honours which are almost divine, being carried aloft in high palanquins, from which they are lifted into their seats so that their feet may not touch unhallowed ground. They inculcate in their disciples a pure morality; their influence is altogether for good, and they have not shrunk from exerting it on occasions in furthering benevolent objects of the Government. Assam adjoins Burma, and the wild hill passes that separate the two valleys have for long time past been crossed by parties of adventurous Burmese. Some of them have settled in Assam, and it is an interesting fact that in this province alone institutions should flourish which reproduce under a different creed so many of the features of Burmese monasticism.

Hindu forms of worship.

With respect to religious ceremonies, Hindu worship is, as already mentioned, essentially individual and not congregational. In the northern India plains, temples are very numerous. From each little village, a mile or so distant from its neighbours, a white temple spire springs upwards, in contrast with the dark-foliaged trees amidst which the houses are half-concealed. At morning- and evening-time one hears the temple bells, or the strident note of the shell-trumpet that calls the god to service. Women flock to the building carrying oblations of flowers: one sees much fewer men. Flowers are offered: formulas are repeated. There are at least three practical methods of obtaining grace,—by baptism in sacred waters, by adoration of the image of the god, and by circumambulation of his sanctuary. In the northern part of the peninsula temples are less numerous: indeed, in some places, with a thriving population, there are none at all. Generally, men do not take their religious duties very seriously, and they are more concerned with the little rituals of magic that usher in the seasons, and with the propitiation of the influences that haunt their village lands than with the more formal ceremonies of doctrinal religion. But all will admit the obligation to undertake a pilgrimage. There are shrines throughout the country. One is situated hard by the glaciers of the Himalayas, another on the seacoast at the extremity of Cape Comorin. On the east coast is the famous temple of Jagannáth, beneath whose processional car devotees would in past years fling themselves. In the plains of northern India there are Muttra and Benares; and numerous bathing fairs are annually held at places on the great rivers. To visit holy places is as desirable as it was in England in Chaucer's days. But one may make the pilgrimage by railway, and on festival occasions vast crowds are assembled by special trains. The pilgrim traffic is a most important asset of the Indian railways. There are still, however, thousands who prefer journeying on foot: passing through the hills of central India one may come across a footpath along which there streams for hours together a line of men and women on their way to Jagannáth. The men

Pilgrimages.

are usually carrying phials of Ganges water, and cheerily salute the stranger with an invocation to Mahadeo, the Great God. In the Himalayas one may meet with ascetics measuring their way to the snow shrine by their body's length, with a full-length prostration at each step taken.

Sacrifices.

On special occasions sacrifices may consist in the beheading of buffaloes or goats: wooden stocks are sometimes used to keep the victim's head in position. But they are generally limited to oblations of grain or flowers. When performed by Brahmins they occasionally have a very curious significance. Missing my train at a road-side station, I had an aged Brahmin as companion in misfortune, and we waited together in the shade of a tree. Time passed, and at last he undid a bag which he carried, and clearing a space on the ground, prepared for a sacrifice. He set out a number of little brass vessels, cups and platters, placing water in some and flowers in others. Uttering formulas, he proceeded to take first one and then another, shifting the water and moving the flowers. At times he took a spoonful of water from one of the vessels and emptied it on the ground. When the ceremony was ended I inquired whether I was right in supposing that he was offering a meal to the god. He assented. I asked what was the meaning of his manipulations with the spoon. 'That,' he replied, 'was the expectoration of the god.' A Brahmin in preparing his meal will, if he has time, set out portions of it in little brass pots for the gods whose fellow he is, summoning them to take their share by a blast on a little shell-trumpet. He sits down to eat in ghostly company.

The ascetic life is the natural fruit of the pessimism of India. In no other country is such transcendent merit attached to mortification of the flesh. Ascetics press their martyrdom to almost incredible limits: they will spend their days outstretched upon a bed of spikes; they will hold up an arm till it withers in the socket: literally they treat the body as though it were a slave. The devotee is saluted everywhere as 'Maharaja': men of wealth and position constantly in their declining years resign their possessions to their heirs and wait for death in nakedness and poverty by the Ganges at Benares: nay, it is no uncommon thing that young men of education, the products of our universities, should relinquish their interests and their ambitions, and join the wandering army of devotees who, literally in sackcloth and ashes, seek grace in an unending round of pilgrimages. Two illustrations may be given. We were photographing the little temples which surround the holy source of the river Nerbudda, in a valley deep set in the wild hills of central India. On the steps there was a group of ascetics, their nakedness hid by little but ashes, and masses of dishevelled hair. One of them came up, and courteously remarked in excellent English, that he feared one of his companions had moved and spoilt the picture. It turned out that for several years he had been assistant to a fashionable Calcutta photographer.

Asceticism.

Travelling by rail between Calcutta and Madras, I noticed at a station a tall, striking figure, yellow-turbaned, dressed in a long red gown, across which there hung a chain of silver amulets. He was attended by two nearly naked servants who, entering my compartment, spread on the opposite bench a black antelope's skin. On this their master sat himself cross-legged. After some minutes of expectant silence, I offered him the salutation due to a Brahmin of position. He cheerfully returned it, and we entered into conversation, which I found he could conduct in fluent English. With Indian frankness he related to me his history. He was a graduate with honours, of the Madras University: he had served the Government in the police department, in which he had attained responsible rank, and which (as he was careful to show me by the production of certificates) he left with the highest character. He had 'found religion,' and for several years had wandered as an ascetic over the continent, visiting every shrine of importance, even to one on the ice-bound confines of Tibet. He confessed to disappointment, and, at the time of our meeting, had taken service, as family priest, with a Hindu lady of rank. When we parted he pressed into my hand a number of tracts, written by himself in excellent English, on such theosophical subjects as the identity of man's soul with the Spirit of God.

The hill tribes have simpler methods of attaining self-absorption. In the jungles you may chance upon a swing suspended in front of a little thatched shrine. In it the Gond priest swings himself into a form of ecstasy.

vii.—The Muhammadans.

THE foundations of the Hindu religion are lost in the maze of speculations with which men endeavour to account for the unreasonableness of life's circumstances. The origin of Muhammadanism—of the faith of Islám—is altogether clear. From the historical point of view this religion is, like Christianity, derived from Judaism. Founded in Arabia during the seventh century, at a time when Greek Christianity had spread over all the countries of the Levant, its doctrines protest against the teachings of Greek Christianity, but are nevertheless coloured by them. The name of Our Lord, pronounced *Ísa*, and that of the Virgin (*Maryam*), are well known to all Muhammadans, and are never used by them without the prefix of a title of reverence. But the influence of Judaism is still more apparent. The teachings of Muhammad, which form the Korán, and the authoritative commentaries on the Korán, make frequent references to the history of the Old Testament. Muhammadans are quite familiar with its leading incidents. Their children are frequently named after the Hebrew patriarchs. Abraham, Isaac, Jacob, Esau, Ishmael, and Joseph are specially common, although, correctly pronounced, they may not strike the English ear immediately.[1] Crossing on one

Origin of the Muhammadan belief.

[1] It should be added that names are also taken from the New Testament.

occasion from Karachi to Bombay, I listened to a discussion amongst the Muhammadan deck-passengers as to whether a whale we came across was of the same kind as the fish which swallowed Jonah. Their respect for the Old Testament and for the Gospels has led Muhammadans to group Jews, Christians, and themselves together as 'People of the Book,' and as fundamentally distinguished from the people of all other creeds. The distinction is indeed immense: it is the distinction between revealed and unrevealed religion—between a God that is searched for in Nature and a God that is found outside it, whom we realise as existing apart from Nature, and to whom we can appeal against her injustices. To those who sought the Divine in the workings of Nature, ideas were material and worship was idolatrous. Nature would only give hints in omens and auguries and through the oracles that were associated with the beauty or wondrousness of certain localities. But God, revealed as a Spirit, could communicate with the spirit of mankind, and could declare His ordinances to His chosen prophets.

Locality and religion.

The religions of Chaldea and Egypt grew up in cultivated plains and appealed to the anxieties of mankind for the course of the seasons. Hinduism is also a religion of the plain; but it is deeply tinged with the mysteriousness of hills and forests. Islám had its birth in the desert, where Nature is at her simplest and does not prompt the imagination by the diversity of her forces. It was in the desert that the Children of Israel were given the Law and the Commandments. The cardinal principle of Islám is the Unity of God: this is an absolute dogma which admits of no complication—not even for illustrative purposes. He can be represented by no material form: idolatry is abhorrent, and Islám permits of no graven images even for artistic purposes. The Sultan of Turkey may not put his head upon coins, and Muhammadan architectural decoration is purely formal. The Jews were sharply distinguished from most other nations of their time in the congregational character of their worship: believers united in the services of the synagogue. Congregational worship is a prominent feature of Muhammadanism, and it has exerted a powerful influence in keeping men together, and in counteracting the disintegrating tendencies which have divided so minutely the Hindus. The religious services of the Muhammadans are impressive in their discipline and their simplicity. Ranged in straight lines, one behind the other, the worshippers follow the words of the ministrant with genuflexions and prostrations that fall exactly together. The effect may be formal — may even suggest drill — but no one has witnessed the service but has been moved by its congregational effect, by its suggestion of unity in word and action. The worshippers disperse, but they take home with them the idea that they belong to a firmly welded community. This conviction is strengthened by a democratic sentiment that possesses real vitality. Before the majesty of God all men are equal. Whatever be the difference in rank or fortune, one Muhammadan can appeal to another as his brother, and society is bound together as by a kind of freemasonry.

One may notice many points of resemblance with

Puritan Christianity. There is the same disdain of embellishments in worship and the same relish for lengthy pulpit discourses. No separate priesthood is recognised, and the ministrant (Imám) is but a leading member of the congregation. The Mullahs of whom one hears are not priests but preachers: they rouse the feelings of the people, but do not act for them in prayer or sacrifice. A similar fatalism enmeshes the judgment: a similar militant fierceness hardens its attitude towards unbelievers. Nay more, the Muhammadans, like the Puritans, are fond of manifesting their piety in naming their children, and men are commonly called by such names as 'The Servant of God' (*Abdullah*), 'The Unity of God' (*Wahidullah*), 'The Mercy of God' (*Rahmatullah*), and 'The Slave of the Almighty' (*Abdul kádir*).

Coincidences with Puritan Christianity.

But saints are held in a reverence which can hardly be distinguished from adoration: the uneducated undoubtedly worship them. The saint's shrine is in most cases his tomb. Such shrines are scattered all over the country,—sometimes a little masonry grave with a niche in which a lamp is kept burning, sometimes a large domed building with an hereditary staff of ministrants (called 'servants') who are supposed to be the descendants of the saint and live by the offerings of the faithful. Such institutions have their special annual days of festival, when Muhammadans collect in thousands. Hindus attend also, and the occasion becomes a fair which is welcomed by all classes for business and amusement.

The adoration of Saints.

Islám surprises us by the sensuality of the joys which the faithful are offered in its Paradise—by material conceptions of the hereafter, that, demoralising to men, must have lowered men's ideals of womanhood. But we must remember that the message of Muhammad was addressed, not to the weary and heavy laden, but to the vigorous and full-blooded sons of the desert.

Conceptions of the hereafter.

There are over 62 millions of Muhammadans in India: in British provinces they form nearly a quarter of the population. Islám invaded India from its north-western corner, and we should expect to find its adherents decrease in number as we travel eastward and southward. With one very remarkable exception this is the case. In the Panjáb and Sindh it is the creed of more than half the population: in the United Provinces of only a seventh: in Bombay of a tenth, and in Madras of only a fourteenth. The exception is in the eastern districts of Bengal, where Islám formed, by conversions, a fresh centre of growth, and has been embraced by two-thirds of the population. It appears that the Muhammadan population is increasing more rapidly than the Hindu. During the last decade of the census its rate of increase was four times that of the rest of the population. This great disparity is due in great measure to the fact that there are few Muhammadans in the areas which suffered so terribly from the famines of 1896-1900. But, this consideration apart, Muhammadans are multiplying more vigorously than the Hindus, owing probably to their meat diet, to their dislike of child-marriage, and to the remarriage of their widows. In race there is a strong admixture of Afghan blood in the Panjáb: elsewhere those descended from immi-

The Muhammadan population.

grants are chiefly of the central Asian stock which may be loosely described as Tartar, and which they themselves style Moghal. But a large proportion are converts from Hinduism or from aboriginal superstitions. Two millions of the Muhammadans of the Panjáb retain a caste title which indicates that they were originally Hindus. The 'new Muslims' of the districts round Dehli have been already mentioned. There are converts among men of rank, who record their descent by uniting the Hindu title of Raja to a Muhammadan name. In eastern Bengal there are families of Afghan, Moghal, and even Arab descent. But the mass of the Muhammadan population is aboriginal, and owes its creed to conversion. Islám is still gaining steadily, if slowly, by conversion. The equality on which it places its adherents is, of course, a powerful attraction to the lower castes.

Distinctiveness of the Muhammadans.

But although a large proportion of the Muhammadans are of Hindu or aboriginal blood, their separation from the rest of the population is absolute. Muhammadans are distinguished by their dress, by the fashion of wearing beards (which amongst Hindus is not nearly so general), and above all, by their names, which are generally scriptural or significant of doctrine, and are entirely different from those used by Hindus. The various titles of honour with which the Government acknowledges eminent services or merit are in two distinct classes, one for Hindus, the other for Muhammadans. The latter are further distinguished by the prayers which no sense of false shame prevents a devout Muhammadan from offering at certain hours of the day wherever he may chance to be. A European is surprised, and perhaps a little shamed, to see a Muhammadan fellow-traveller in a railway carriage stop his conversation, spread his prayer carpet and perform his devotions when the hour for prayer has arrived. In hopes of a personal resurrection, the bodies of the dead are, as with us, buried in cemeteries, not cremated, according to the Hindu practice. So it comes that the Muhammadan, though living *in partibus infidelium*, never forgets that he is separate in communion from unbelievers, that he belongs to a freemasonry, the signs of which are public, not secret—which proclaims itself to the world and does not merely reveal itself to members of the brotherhood. For the rest Hindus and Muhammadans generally live together amicably enough. They do not occupy separate quarters in towns or villages. But when Muhammadans are touched in their pride of religion they are prepared instantly to rise in asserting it. And causes of disagreement are by no means infrequent. A Hindu religious procession may disturb Muhammadan worship as it passes a mosque—nay, if feelings are embittered, may offer open insult. The Muhammadans retaliate by polluting a Hindu temple, and a riot ensues which taxes to the utmost the firmness and the discretion of the officers of Government. A Muhammadan procession carrying a mimic shrine may find that its emblem will not pass below the branches of a *pipal* (fig) tree. The Hindus will not permit the branches to be cut: the Muhammadans will not abate one inch from the dignity of their shrine. But the most fertile cause of strife is the sacrifice by Muhammadans of cows at the festival which commemorates the sacrifice of Abraham. By a misapprehension (for which there is no authority in the Korán) they consider themselves bound to keep the occasion by the sacrifice, not of a ram, but of a cow. This ceremony offends the very tenderest of Hindu scruples, and leads to bitterness of animosity, to rioting, and to bloodshed. All that the Government can do to obviate quarrels is to take its stand upon the Custom which both sides respect, and to permit of these sacrifices only in houses where it has been usual to offer them.

Sects.

The unifying force of Islám has checked schism, and religious divisions are few in number. The principal one is that between the Sunnis and the Shias. These sects differ in the respect they pay to certain commentaries on the Korán: but they are mainly divided by a radical difference of opinion as to the proper method of appointing sucessors to the Prophet. His first three successors were selected democratically by the faithful in disregard of the claim of his son-in-law, Ali. Ali succeeded to the fourth vacancy: his sons, Hassan and Hussain, were attacked by a rival and were killed, heroically fighting, at the battle of Kerbela.[1] The Sunnis accept the succession as it stands: to the Shias the first three successors were interlopers. In fact they hold that the Caliphate should have descended by inheritance, and they reckon the sons of Ali as the chiefest of martyrs. They commemorate their martyrdom during the festival of the Muharram, and carry in procession mimic shrines artistically constructed of bamboo, coloured paper, and tinsel, which they escort with shouts of lamentation. The Shias have their headquarters in Persia: in India they are much

[1] Tradition is incorrect in respect to Hassan, who took no part in this battle, and ended his life under different circumstances.

less numerous than the Sunnis, but are an important element in the population of the two large cities of Lucknow and Hyderabad. The Muharram celebrations afford, however, entertainment to the whole of the population, and Hindus may often be seen taking part in the processions. A Muhammadan sect known as the Wahábis became very prominent in India some forty years ago. It represented the strictest views of Muhammadan Puritanism, and held views that were politically of importance, since they asserted that India was an alien country in which Muhammadans should always be at war with unbelievers of all classes. For many years past one has heard but little of it. At the other extreme are the Súfi doctrines. They introduce into Muhammadanism the idea of ecstatic communion with God—an idea which (as we have seen) was popularised amongst the Hindus by the poet Tulsi Dás. The Súfis illustrate their ecstasies by similes drawn from the wine cup, which it is difficult always to recognise as allegorical. The poems of Omar Khayyám illustrate the philosophical cynicism into which these ecstasies not uncommonly faded.

The Moplahs.

There is on the Malabar spice coast—far away from the general Muhammadan life of India—a colony of Arabs which settled there some nine centuries ago. Their descendants—known as Moplahs—have sunk to the position of small cultivators. But they possess a courage which has made them the terror of their landlords, and has within recent times opposed itself without thought of death to the controlling operations of regular troops. The Moplahs afford a curious instance of the long transmission by inheritance of the quality of courage in such a climate of moist, enervating heat as ordinarily dissipates it.

The domestic arrangements of the Muhammadans rest upon the belief that a woman who is not in love with her husband is liable to go astray in mixed society. Marriages are arranged, and love may or may not follow; moreover, a wife's love must be suspected of inconstancy when, under a system of polygamy, she shares her husband with others. Accordingly, from the time they become marriageable, women are strictly secluded in their homes. Little girls can attend school, where they commit to heart chapters of the Arabic Korán—as unintelligible to them as to our children would be the Scriptures in Latin. But on emerging from childhood they enter the zenána, or harem, and henceforth the outside world reaches them by hearsay only. Their existence even is ignored: it is bad manners to refer to the wife of a visitor, except in the vague phrase 'your veiled ones.' The narrowness of an outlook which is limited to the home must lessen the educative effect of the mother's influence: ignorant as she is of the world and its manners, she cannot give her sons those early impressions which assist us so greatly in the conduct of life. But the Muhammadan lady does not repine at her seclusion: rather does she esteem it as a mark of dignity. The poorer classes cannot afford much domestic privacy. But when one of them rises in the world his wife will eagerly retire behind the purdah (curtain). After all, the social circle of the Muhammadan lady is probably not more restricted than that of many English bourgeois families. For her husband, society consists of men only. But his manners have not

The Muhammadan woman.

suffered: his courtesy suffers nothing in comparison with that of the most polished European men of the world. It is permitted to marry four wives: but in most cases a husband finds one quite sufficiently expensive. He can divorce a wife by uttering a formula three times in the presence of witnesses. But to assert this right is expensive. For it is a marriage obligation of the husband's to settle upon his wife a substantial dowry which must be paid over to her if she is divorced. So practically safeguarded, the married state is much less unfavourable to the Muhammadan woman than it is often supposed to be. But polygamy is exceedingly injurious in the domestic quarrels it engenders. Brothers by different mothers are hardly of the same family, and in these circumstances no respect can be claimed by the eldest son. Muhammadan inheritance is not unfrequently disturbed by the bitterest jealousy: the Emperor Aurangzeb conquered in pitched battles two of his brothers before securing his throne.

General condition.

There are everywhere men of high rank, wealth, and intelligence at the head of the community. But the general condition of the Muhammadans is one of poverty and depression—all the more bitter as they have the memory with them of Imperial fortunes. In the Panjáb and Sindh and in eastern Bengal they are cultivators. Elsewhere they prefer town to country life, and particularly affect the industries of weaving and dyeing. They rarely acquire riches. They have against them two important provisions of their customary law. In the first place, the method in which property is divided amongst heirs tends to its *morcellement*: the widow and each of the children are entitled to fractional shares: land is subdivided into minute fragments, and the sharers in a holding are often so numerous that their names can hardly be recorded in the Government land registers. The Muhammadans apply to the inheritance of land a rule which the Prophet intended for sheep and camels. In the second place, it is forbidden to take interest for money. The broad-minded may not apply this to debtors who are infidels. But the majority cannot reconcile it with their conscience to take interest from any one. It will even offend the principles of wealthy benefactors that their endowments of land should be converted into Government securities. Taking no interest themselves, the Muhammadans pay it at high rates when they borrow from Hindus, and are thus heavily fettered in commercial competition. In the interior of the country they expect very little from trade or industry. But commercial instincts are developed by the influences of seaport towns, and in Bombay, Calcutta, and Chittagong there are communities of keen and enterprising Muhammadan traders, some members of which are exceedingly wealthy. Muhammadans of Bombay hold in their hands much of the trade with East Africa, and those of Chittagong have played a part of importance in developing the commerce of Rangoon. One section of the former—known as the Khojas—has a curious history. It claims descent by conversion from the disciples of a militant preacher of Syria, who, as the 'Old Man of the Mountains' was the subject of very fantastic legends in crusading days. The Khojas submit themselves to an hereditary chief whose authority extends to spiritual as well as to secular affairs, and renders him an influential personality in Indian society.

Living intermixed with the Hindus, the Muhammadans have not been protected altogether by their religion from the influence of Hindu ideas and customs. They have become infected with scruples about food, and are cut off from Europeans by prejudices that would seem ridiculous in Persia or Turkey. Their religion forbids the eating of pork, the drinking of wine, and (amongst the strictest) the smoking of tobacco. But for the rest it suffices if the faithful abstain 'from things strangled and from blood': they cannot eat the flesh of an animal whose throat was not cut, before life was extinct, in the name of God the Most Merciful. But the Muhammadans of India have added greatly to these restrictions. Thirty years ago there were but very few, even of the most intelligent, who would eat with a European. Like the Hindus (and the ancient Egyptians) they have a prejudice against crockery and glass, and consider that food and drink should only be taken from metal vessels. Nor have their religious beliefs remained uncontaminated. Amongst the poorer Muhammadans there is much gross superstition: they respect Hindu gods, share in the keeping of Hindu festivals, and may even call in Hindu priests. In addition they develop curious mysteries of their own. One of the most remarkable of these is associated with the servants of a well-known saint's shrine in the Panjáb. They go about as ascetics, attended by little withered specimens of humanity, known as the saint's 'mice.' These little creatures are dwarfs with astonishingly small heads,—indeed their skulls do not grow beyond infant size,—and they are idiots. It is said that they are the first-born of those who have prayed at the shrine for

Hindu influences.

children and have vowed to offer their eldest child. But it is also said that their deformity is artificial and is a terrible witness of cruelty to childhood.

Methods of liveli-hood.

A Muhammadan is most contented when he earns his living by service, and Muhammadans abound in the lower grades of Government employ as orderlies, police constables, bailiffs, and petty clerks. Their share of higher office has in great part fallen to the Hindus, because they have stood aloof from the English education which under our system has become a necessary qualification for superior State service. Their attitude has been due in part to jealousy of a foreign tongue which was ousting Persian from official use. Persian was the official language of the Moghal empire and held its own during many years of British rule. It had even been adopted in Hindu States, and was used by the Maratha officials of the kingdom of Nagpur. But the Muhammadans were also alarmed by the divorce of education from religion. The English schools were organised on a rigidly secular basis. Accordingly they maintained an educational course of their own, which began by committing the Korán to memory, and ended by understanding the meaning of its texts—that is to say in a working acquaintance with Arabic. It seems probable that their boys have been prejudiced by learning for repetition chapter upon chapter of Scripture in a language that was entirely unknown to them. There were, of course, some who elected for the Government course of education. But their prospects of obtaining State service were not favourable. The Hindus had anticipated them and were in possession of the ground; they naturally disliked the competition of outsiders, and combined to render the admission of a Muhammadan difficult and his service unpleasant. Thus it has resulted that in eastern Bengal, where two-thirds of the population is Muhammadan, the share held by Muhammadans in the superior grades of State service is quite insignificant.

A new spirit of awakening liberalism.

During the last thirty years a great change has come about: Muhammadans have begun to aspire to English education, to adopt such a European habit of dress as is current in Turkey, to take their meals in European fashion. This reform is almost wholly due to the efforts of one man—Sir Syed Ahmad Khan—who was by far the ablest Muhammadan of his day. In the service of Government he gained much distinction, and earned our gratitude by saving some English lives in the Mutiny. On retiring from service, and taking his pension, he devoted the rest of his life to the welfare of his community. He was a man of dignified presence, indomitable energy, and moving eloquence. He had but little acquaintance with English. But he realised its growing importance, and saw that, if the Muhammadans neglected it, they would forfeit all effective share in the administration of the country. After long endeavour he gained sufficient support to found the Anglo-Muhammadan College at Aligarh, realising two principles: firstly, that religion should be taught as well as literature and science, and secondly, that character should be trained by such a discipline as is enforced at English public schools. Most of the pupils are boarders. It was characteristic of the man that while engaged upon this great scheme he neglected no opportunity, however small, of broadening the views of his countrymen. He lived himself in European fashion; but he had an outside guest-chamber for such of his friends as shrank from changing their customs, and to excite the curiosity of his guests, he brightened its walls with coloured illustrations of eclipses and of the phases of the moon. An envoy sent by the Sultan of Turkey to the Amir of Afghanistan, passing through India on his way, breakfasted at the Aligarh railway station. Sir Syed Ahmad brought on to the platform a number of his Muhammadan friends, and lifting the refreshment-room curtain, showed them the astonishing sight of a Muhammadan of rank sitting at meat with the English officials who had come to receive him at the station. Since those days things have changed indeed, and there are now very few Muhammadan gentlemen of education who would feel awkward in accepting an Englishman's invitation to dinner.

The Aligarh college.

The Aligarh college has grown and flourished. It was exceptionally fortunate in one of its first English principals. Boys come to it from all parts of the Muhammadan world: its cricket teams meet good English elevens with credit: in the service of Government its sons have won special credit for courage and truthfulness. It is much the best Muhammadan college in the world. Like all other institutions it has its dangers. The founder of the college vested its management in a committee: there are some Europeans on the committee, but the administration is practically free from control by the State. The prosperity of the college will be assured when Old Aligarh Boys have secured a leading influence. They will not need persuading that personal jealousies must give way to public spirit, and that discipline must be rigidly maintained however tempting may be its relaxation in individual cases.

viii.—Hindu Institutions—The Caste and the Village.

THE Hindus have preserved two institutions, which are, in general outline, not peculiar to them, but which have in their hands been elaborated and crystallised with remarkable precision. These are the Caste and the Village. The effect of each is to divide society into a number of close compartments, and to discourage communication between them. By the Caste men are grouped according to their race or occupation: the Village groups them according to the locality they inhabit. The two systems overlap: there are many castes in India, and many villages contribute to form the community of a caste. But the two institutions converge towards a single purpose—the development of small, self-contained societies which can resist the shock of outside aggression and of natural calamities. The Caste and the Village may be likened to communities of zoophytes which the tides and currents of the ocean may ruffle but cannot uproot. Streams of conquering Tartars have flooded India again and again; but within the Caste and the Village Hindu society has preserved its organised vitality.

Effect of these institutions.

The peculiarity of the Hindu caste is that a man may not take a wife from outside it, and may not eat with any but a caste-fellow. A carpenter, for instance, may not marry the daughter of a blacksmith, nor can he meet a blacksmith at meals. Caste is an hereditary distinction: a man belongs to a caste because he is born in it. But its effects are further-reaching than those of any other hereditary distinction that the world has known. Where a nation has been formed by a combination of tribes, men belong to their tribes, as to their families, by birth. Trades-guilds or unions have always tended to become hereditary institutions. According to Herodotus the men of Egypt were grouped into different classes according to their occupations, and these classes were hereditary: each man belonged to the class of his father and followed his father's trade. In the later days of the Roman Empire men were classed together by law according to their occupation, and no change of occupation was permitted. But in none of these cases was a man prohibited from marrying outside his class. Intermarriage was permissible, and the children took sometimes their father's, sometimes their mother's places in the social scale. There was a fluidity which is altogether lacking under the Hindu caste system.

'Caste' more rigid than 'class' distinction.

In other countries there have also been prejudices against eating with all comers. We read in the history of Joseph that 'the Egyptians might not eat with the Hebrews, for this was an abomination to the Egyptians.' We learn again from Herodotus that a thousand years later the Egyptians did not like eating with Greeks. But these prejudices affected men of another nation, not their own fellow-countrymen, and although in all societies there has always been some reluctance to sit at meals with men of much lower birth, or inferior status, we can find no parallel to the religious prejudices of the Hindu, which have the effect of declaring that in the physical relations of life persons of all other castes are taboo.

Origin of caste.

The origin of these remarkable restrictions upon human liberty has been the theme of much discussion, but is still undecided. In vague outline it may, however, be imagined. Man has been defined as a 'clubbable' animal: he has a tendency to form societies which will give him the sentiment of fellowship without loss of his individuality. The tribe originated in the family, and was based upon relationship. But men were permitted to join a tribe by adoption, maintaining by a fiction the idea of a common descent. Men of the same occupation naturally come together in a trades-guild: to strengthen their fellowship they are also inclined to adopt the fiction of a common ancestry. These communities, whether of the tribe or a guild, have a tendency to become more and more exclusive, and will in time surround themselves with an impenetrable fence unless the narrowness of their view is checked by the recognition of wider interests. In other countries concentration within their walls has been prevented by feelings of nationality or of religious unity. In India these feelings have never gained strength, and there has been nothing to oppose the exclusiveness of caste. On the contrary, the growth of rigid formality has been fostered by an hereditary priesthood to whom each intricacy of observance was for pride and profit.

It seems clear that caste in its present rigidity is a development of comparatively recent Hindu history.

In the earliest Vedic times Brahmins are mentioned, but as appointed priests, not as hereditary Levites. Some centuries, however, before the commencement of the Christian era, society had become grouped into a number of hereditary communities. But they seemed to have been classes, not castes, and not to have barred intermarriage. In 320 B.C. the Greek envoy, Megasthenes, recorded that no Hindu might marry out of his class, or change his profession: he also mentioned that the men ate their meals alone. But we can hardly theorise upon his observations since, four or five centuries later, the laws of Manu, giving a long enumeration of the classes into which society was divided, expressly recognised intermarriages, and prescribed a very elaborate scale for determining the status of the children of mixed unions. To the Chinese pilgrims who visited India during the fifth and seventh centuries A.D., the most noticeable features of society were Buddhist, and Buddhism was opposed to rigid distinctions of caste. Indeed we may surmise that Buddhism, so long as it held its own, was a force that counteracted the separative tendencies of the Brahmins. It is probable that the caste system acquired its present rigidity during the Hindu dark ages—between the seventh and the tenth centuries—which witnessed the final triumph of Brahminism over the rival faith.

A comparatively late development.

In the present day the process of caste subdivision still continues. Old castes throw off new castes as offshoots. Some members of a caste in which widows may remarry decide that this practice vulgarises their society: others in a caste which holds by adult marriage, desire to win popular

Vitality of caste.

esteem by marrying their children in infancy. They form separate castes and rise in the world. Other new castes may mark a fall in the social scale, such as Brahmins who will touch a plough, or Rajputs who will cultivate vegetables. But different castes never amalgamate unless they are stirred by the ferment of a religious reform. To such a revival the Sikhs owe their separate identity: their society was recruited from many castes. So also is the theistic community, which has of recent years grown up in Bengal under the name of the Brahmo Samáj. But these religious revivals have never gone very far in their work of consolidation. Apart from them, the tendency is still to crystallise in compartments, and new castes are simply subdivisions of larger crystals. The people have, so far, not been affected by the idea of the unity of empire. Educated men are united by a knowledge of English, and they will sometimes —generally in private—treat caste food rules with disrespect. Some have had the courage to marry widows. But to marry outside the caste is still beyond the limits of imaginable daring. In Bengal and Madras school-life has weakened some prejudices, and students of different castes, living together in a boarding-house, will sit down to meals together. But the food must have been cooked by a Brahmin or by a caste-fellow; and in many localities each boarder still insists upon cooking for himself. School influences are also weakening the prejudices of the literary castes against manual labour: in the school carpentry shops you may see boys of all castes practising together. But these relaxations do not affect the observance of caste rites and ceremonies, nor, of course, the prohibition against intermarriage. There is, however, outside the domain of caste, a growing body of importance, composed of Hindus who have visited Europe, America, or Japan, and who object to submit on their return to the ceremony of purification, or to relinquish customs that they have acquired in European society. But these men are, as yet, not sufficiently strong or numerous to stem the current of Hindu exclusiveness: they are as driftwood floating upon its surface. Our sympathies may go out to these reformers. They are attacking the most difficult of strongholds. And their position is weakened by the inconsistencies into which family life betrays them, and which furnish enough material for the ridicule of their opponents. Women never desire a simplification of social and religious observances, and the majority of young Hindus we see in London and at the universities will, on their return to India, not be welcomed by their mothers and sisters till they have purged themselves from the taint of their sea-voyage, and their association with Europeans, by undergoing a ceremony of formal purification.

Never has human society been more complicated or artificial. The people of a caste are isolated from all others by their marriage laws, their social customs, their religious practices, and their precedence. Marriage outside the caste is an impossible abomination. Within the caste it is limited by strict rule. Each caste contains groups, and bridegroom and bride should come from different groups. By a prejudice, some traces of which we can find among ourselves, a man may not marry above him, and a woman may not marry below her. In regard to social customs, the most

Complications of caste life.

prominent restriction is that already referred to, which prevents a man from touching food that has been cooked, or even touched, by any one but a caste-fellow or a Brahmin. There are indeed castes—low down the scale—which are even more particular than the generality, and will have nothing to do with Brahmin cookery. In India one can sit at meat only with a caste-fellow. There may be friendship between men of different castes; but they must separate at meal-times. The expansiveness, the geniality of the dinner-table, which, with us, renders eating and drinking the sacraments of friendship, can in India join no hands across the barriers of caste. This food taboo is constantly in evidence: complicating, as it does, the business of daily life, it is an ever-present reminder that one belongs, not to the brotherhood of man, but to a peculiar people. It grievously hampers the daily life of any one who is not a stay-at-home, and convenient relaxations have gradually been permitted. Water may be taken from the pitcher of a man of low—but not of very low—caste; otherwise, in a land of wells, a traveller might die of thirst. Light refreshments, such as biscuits and sweetmeats, may be purchased and eaten without asking questions for conscience' sake: so also with ice and soda-water at railway stations. But, save for Indians who are anglicised, meals are still ceremonial rites, with, indeed, some such symbolism of sacrifice as attached to the banquets of Homer. In religion again, each caste has its peculiar observances and (as has already been noticed) many castes worship as a kind of totem the chief implement of their trade. Each caste has a governing committee of its own with a jurisdiction which may be compared to that of our courts of Arches, Probate, and Divorce. By its rules and precedence the caste system permanently establishes the most extraordinary inequality between man and man. The Brahmin stands above all in undisputed superiority. His person is sacred: disrespect to him is a serious crime: on his part offences are generally venial: under Hindu rule he enjoyed 'benefit of clergy' of the widest extent. Down the scale caste follows caste in more or less settled gradation. Some castes dispute their position on the precedence list, and some may be bracketed with others. Each takes pride in its position and peculiarities, and jealousy of caste distinctions is absolutely unknown.

The village.

The houses of a typical Indian village are clustered together more after the fashion of a little town than of a village as we know it. Round about there are sometimes broad earthen ramparts which gave the strength of a fortress in time of trouble. Immediately outside the walls there is a strip of common, or waste land, on which each cultivating family has its manure heap, and its threshing-floor, and where the village cattle are collected on their way to and from their daily pasturage. Around lie the fields within an irregular periphery. They are separated by no hedges or fences: they lie open to one another, and, viewed from above, resemble the pattern of some irregular patchwork. In some parts of the village the fields are roughly square-shaped—from one to two acres in area. Elsewhere they form little parallel strips of very small size, as many as twenty sometimes going to the acre. This minute subdivision results from an arrangement under which each holding comprises a slice of each kind of soil in the village. Those who have read Seebohm's *English Village Community*, and remember the field-map it includes, will have a good idea of the distribution of land in a typical Indian village. As in early English days, so now in India, a holding, or 'virgate,' consists of a number of little parcels, that are strewn about the village area, no two parcels lying alongside. It is unnecessary to explain how greatly such an arrangement must prejudice economy and expedition in farm work, and the improvement of land by such processes as draining. On the other hand, with undersized cattle and primitive implements, ploughing is a long operation, and does not cover daily so large an area as to necessitate many transfers from one plot to another. It is not uncommon for land in preparation for wheat to be ploughed and reploughed twenty times over. The tenures upon which the fields were originally held have been a good deal obscured by conquest and by migration. Aliens have found their way into the precincts of the village, and into partnership with the descendants of its ancient patriarchs: manorial rights have been thrust upon the village from above, with over-lordships—sometimes several grades of over-lordship—one above the other. But looking beneath the surface two original types of village appear: one in which the land is held by a heterogeneous collection of persons—of different castes—who represent a mixed band either of reclaiming immigrants or of annexing marauders; the other in which the proprietors are a brotherhood—necessarily of the same caste—who hold the land in a kind of partnership. The latter is probably the more archaic form. The members of the brotherhood in theory hold by shares, not by definite apportionment of land. A man, for instance, whose share is a sixteenth, was entitled to a sixteenth share of the profits, but not, save by incidental arrangement, to hold and cultivate any particular sixteenth of the area. But, as a matter of fact, the fields have generally been allotted, more or less permanently, amongst the members, although part of the area is even now frequently held in commonalty, and is cultivated either by tenants or by members of the brotherhood paying rent to the common purse. Such a distribution would tend gradually to fall out of accord with the ratio of the nominal shares to one another. Some land would gain in value more rapidly than others: the introduction of irrigation would in this way completely alter the relative value of different parts of the village area. Families would die out, and the equitable distribution of their fields would often be evaded by the more powerful members of the community. When, for any reason or other, the allotment of the land became glaringly unfair, there was a recognised remedy in a little agrarian revolution: the fields were pooled, and were redistributed by lot. Such periodic redistributions were of frequent occurrence down to quite recent times in the Chattisgarh tract of the Central Provinces, one of the few localities which escaped annexation by the Moghals, and preserved the traditions of Hindu practice. The members of the village brotherhood were often very numerous, running in large villages into hundreds. But, though owning the land, they did not necessarily cultivate it. Brahmins and Rajputs, holding in some districts a very large proportion of the land, will rarely lay their hands upon the stilt of a plough.

They would be outcasted if they did so. They cultivate either by tenants or by hired labour, the traditional rent paid by the one, or wages paid to the other, being not a cash amount but a share of the produce. Below the proprietary brotherhood, then, there is a body of tenants, and below the tenants a body of labourers, each subsisting directly upon the land, and sharing its produce with the proprietors, in virtue of an arrangement which, till recent years, was defined by custom, and could be modified in no degree by the stress of competition. The village is provided with a staff of rough artisans—such as blacksmiths and carpenters. These also were remunerated by a share of the produce. The blacksmith, for instance, was entitled to so many sheaves of wheat, so many cakes of sugar, for each ploughshare provided by him. Lastly, there are the village servants, the barber, the waterman, and the watchman, all paid by shares of produce, and, more influential than these, the accountant, who registers the receipts and expenditure of the brotherhood and of the village fund. Each village has its fund, maintained by subscription, which provides for the cost of village festivals, of quarrels with adjacent villages, and of conciliating State officials. The village generally lived in a state of rivalry with the villages around it, and had but little communication with them, except through caste guest-friends. Boundary disputes were of common occurrence, and often eventuated in little village wars. In fact the village was essentially a State in miniature, with as complete an individuality of its own as a Greek city.

Narrow, indeed, was the scope for competition in these

complicated little societies. The village stood within a ring fence; and, within it again, each little group was palisaded off from the groups around it. Internal decay there might be. No outlets relieved the pressure of multiplying humanity. But the village, as a self-contained unit, has manifested extraordinary powers of resistance, and has remained a centre of vitality in the darkest days of foreign conquest.

Caste and village limited competition.

The Caste and the Village protected society against the harassing activities of the State. They also limited the disturbance which could be caused it by the enterprise or ambition of individuals —by the aggressiveness, that is to say, of free competition. Each village, each caste, had a sphere of its own, which could not be invaded from the outside: each of them was sufficiently compact and homogeneous to be governed by rules and customs which effectually stifled competition amongst its members. Custom, not enterprise, regulated the apportionment of the land, the profession or trade of the individual, and the rates of remuneration or wages. The forces of Nature, as represented by competition, were regarded not as beneficial, but as injurious; and it appeared that man was happiest and best when shut off from the struggling life of his environment, with his individuality strictly harnessed to the chariot of the commonwealth.

Hinduism and socialism alike in this respect.

This pessimistic idea contrasts very strikingly with the profound trust in the benefits of free competition which, only a generation ago, guided the course of English politics. Alarmed by the misery and degradation of labour that is sweated or rejected by competitive industry, we have been changing our opinion; and it may be said that the doctrines that were preached by Cobden and Herbert Spencer now survive only in Free Trade and Free Immigration. The pendulum has swung far in the opposite direction, and no one will now dispute the authority of the State to lay a moderating hand upon the power of those that are uppermost in the struggle for life. Indeed, the characteristic of the present day is a growing acceptance of socialistic principles. Socialism is the negation of free competition, and the Hindu system may give us some idea of its fruits.

The penalties of artificiality.

It is hard to fight against Nature. She might not break through the protecting circles of the Caste and the Village. But she attacked them insidiously from within. By an increase of population for which there was no outlet, each compartment of society became congested with humanity. The practice of infanticide was a desperate effort for breathing space. Energy was stifled, and from the minute subdivision of the land and of its produce there resulted extreme poverty and hosts of unemployed. In India these are a legitimate burden upon the industry of their relations. It is no disgrace to live in idle dependence, and the weight of the incubus of family charity is to us as surprising as the cheerful resignation with which it is borne. You may devise a scheme which will regulate the distribution and the terms of employment, but your rules will not create employment as increasing multitudes demand it. You may limit the number of the rich, but the poor will be as poor as ever—only more numerous than Nature intended them to be. And worse still, the spirit of enterprise with which Nature has endowed us will not live in captivity. It takes flight, and custom lies upon the people—

> 'with a weight
> Heavy as frost and deep almost as life.'

Lessons from India in social politics.

May we not then conclude that there is no fixed guiding star in social politics? There are indeed beacons marking dangerous rocks on either hand; but they show what to avoid and give no clear direction for the setting of the compass. Scylla is the unhappiness of the individual; Charybdis the decadence of the race. Between these perils the ship of State painfully labours, compelled by an adverse wind to tack first towards one danger and then towards the other—to risk national decay by over-protection of the individual, to risk misery of individuals by over-deference to the strong. Statesmanship must, then, consist, not in vain search for a principle and in devotion to it, but in knowledge of the moment when a change of course is necessary, and in ability to bring the ship round upon another tack.

ix.—Domestic Life.

IF you would see the man that typifies India, picture to yourself the cultivator. It is an evening in October, and he is returning from a hard day's work sowing his wheat. Dark-skinned, wiry, stripped save for a loin-cloth and a turban, he steps behind his bullocks slowly but erect, and with a certain dignity of carriage. He wears a moustache but no beard, and through the folds of his loose turban you may see that his head is shaven, save for a single lock on the crown. His bullocks are yoked by a wooden frame passing over their necks and resting against their large humps. They drag the plough on its side along the ground: it is the simplest form of grubber—wooden, with an iron spike as its share. On either side of the dusty path are small unfenced fields, resembling our allotment grounds: some lying open, freshly ploughed for the cold-weather crops, others standing thick with cotton and millets, ready for harvest. The millets are higher than his head, but across the ploughed fields, or the cotton, are views of dark-foliaged trees, with glimpses here and there of brown villages and white temple spires. Before him, partly hidden by trees, are the mud-walled houses of his village. Over them hangs a light veil of smoke, which strikes out in flat streamers over the fields. There is the chill of cold weather in the air, and the smoke hangs

The cultivator: a type of village life.

low. Housewives are cooking the evening meal, and as he draws near his home the air is acrid with the smell of burning fuel. He passes below a large fig-tree overshadowing some rough idols; and, through a doorway in a blank wall, he drives his cattle into a yard. Round the yard are grouped the little cottages which shelter his family and his bullocks.

Amongst the first things you would notice is a number of thick, flat, brown cakes, stuck on one of the house walls, and apparently drying there. These are for fuel. They are made by the women from cow-dung mixed with water, and their manipulation is a part of every day's work. In densely cultivated tracts there is no firewood, and the cultivator is obliged to use for fuel the manure that his land requires of him.

In the village all but the very poorest have courtyards into which, across low verandahs, the house-rooms open. There are generally two sets of rooms, in separate buildings, one appropriated to the women-folk and the other open to men. They are in fact separate houses. The former is closed in rear by the courtyard wall. The latter opens on to the village street through a little balcony. Save for this balcony and for the cattle gate, the courtyard presents a frontage of dead wall to the outside world.

The houses.

This scene is from the northern India plain. The houses are here constructed of kneaded mud, with flat mud roofs supported by crossbeams. The house enclosures are crowded close together, so that each village presents the appearance of a little town. The flat roofs of the houses possibly indicate the influence of Muhammadan invaders from central Asia: but they will be seen only where the rainfall is moderate. Towards the foot of the Himalayas, with a heavier rainfall, tiled roofs come into use, and flat roofs yield to ridged roofs as we enter Bengal. The typical Bengali cottage has a high-peaked thatched roof, with the gables curved downward till they approach the ground. This shape affords resistance to the violent winds which sweep over the country from the Bay of Bengal. The cultivators of Bengal live near their fields, and the houses are scattered over the village area. This defencelessness is the result, not of immunity from attack, but of admitted inability to repel it. In the peninsula tiled roofs predominate. The village houses are less scattered than in Bengal, but stand in gardens of their own, the produce of which is an important asset of the family. In front of the street balcony there is sometimes a little yard, fenced with a low wall, in the centre of which is an altar, quite of classical form, supporting a plant of the sacred basil.

Cleanliness.

Indian houses are kept beautifully clean. Floors and walls are plastered from time to time by the women with a mixture of cow-dung and mud, which is for the purpose much more efficient than it would appear. There is little or no furniture beyond some rugs, some low rush stools, and a string bed or two. The housewife prides herself upon her collection of brass cooking and eating vessels, which are kept scoured to an admirable polish. China or glass is not in use, and meals are served in platters or saucers of brass and bell metal.

In the drier parts of the country, where rice is not

grown—that is to say, in the Indo-Gangetic plain, west of Patna, and in the western portion of the peninsula—the staple diet of the country is an unleavened cake of wheat, barley, or millet, eaten with vegetables, and with some description of pulse. The pulse may be served either dry and split, or as a soft mash. In rice districts every one eats rice: but as these districts are generally too rainy for the growth of pulse, fish is taken in place of it. Fish are, as a rule, abundant, and are caught in various most ingenious methods. On the large rivers nets are used. Smaller streams are blocked with a low dam in which passages are left, and cage traps are set in the passages. Sometimes a fishing-rod is employed, which is fixed in the bank and bent down by a string that is connected with a peg in the ground by a catch which is set to release at a certain pressure. Not till a good-sized fish is on the hook does the rod spring back and strike it; and sometimes several fish are caught in this way, one within the other, the catch not releasing till the due weight is complete. The hill tribes live on small millets, or upon a curious dwarf rice, the ear of which never emerges from its sheath. Its grain is made into gruel, which rapidly undergoes some alcoholic fermentation, and to assist this process, fresh gruel is poured upon old, the pot not being cleaned before it is replenished. A Gond was once pointed out to me by his fellows with admiration, as having kept his gruel-pot uncleaned for a quarter of a century. The grains of this plant sometimes ferment before they are gathered, and are a mild intoxicant when quite freshly cooked.

Diet.

For us meals are the cement of society: for the

Hindus they mark the distinctiveness of the individual. There are caste feasts at which men sit down and eat together; but generally, and especially when out of doors, or from home, a man eats alone, in silence, separated from his fellows. He clears a small square on the ground within which he places a little horseshoe-shaped hearth of burnt clay. He takes off his turban, upper garments and shoes, enters the square, and sits down to cook. The square cuts him off from the world: it is a sacred enclosure like the classical *templum* or *temenos*, and his meal within its circuit has the semblance of a religious ceremony. No alien foot must cross the boundary of the square: if the shadow of an alien falls across it, any food already cooked must be thrown away. Even within the home most wives do not eat with their husbands: they serve them and wait till they have finished eating.

Unsociability of meals.

Judged by a European or monetary standard, the people of India are very poor. Thirty years ago the wages of a field-labourer hardly exceeded the penny a day of the parable, which has struck all of us as surprisingly small. Wages have risen very greatly of recent years, and to-day a field-labourer can generally command at least twopence a day. His wife works off and on through the year, and her earnings will bring the family income to about eighteenpence a week. This sounds distressingly low. But, in the first place, food is very much cheaper than in England. Of the coarse rice, millet, or barley, which the labouring classes consume, a penny will purchase about two and a half pounds—two and a half times as much as a penny will purchase of wheat in

General view of incomes

—of the labourer.

England now. *Measured in food* the labourer's earnings are then equivalent to about four shillings a week. He pays no house rent. It is unusual to take house rent in Indian villages. Those who hold land occupy their houses rent free, and labourers are expected, in lieu of paying house rent, to render some small occasional services to their landlord. He requires no firing for warmth and no warm clothes. The tobacco he smokes is exceedingly cheap—often, indeed, grown in his own garden. His children catch some fish when the streams are in flood; and in abstaining from meat he does no more than the richest Hindu of the country-side. In these circumstances, supplied by Nature with so much that she denies in a temperate climate, a family can subsist on an expenditure of two or three pence a day. The poorest Italian families spend but little more than this. Except in time of distress or famine, the coolie and his family do not appear ill-nourished. All things said, however, he lives in great poverty, and it is surprising that he should be able to find some money for drink.

—of the tenant.

Coolie families frequently hold a little patch of land, and a number of families, who are classed in official reports as tenants, merely supplement labourers' wages by a plot of cultivation. But a social gap lies between them and those who look only to their land for support. The condition of the cultivator depends, of course, on the quality of the soil and on the density of the population. If his land is poor—as is, for instance, the case over much of the Deccan—no leniency of rent can redeem him from a life of hardship. If population is dense, rents are high, and high rents can neutralise, for the tenant, good land, although low rents cannot compensate for bad. But rents are not always high, even where competition is keen. A large number of tenants are secured by law at a statutory rent. A small cultivator in the closely cultivated plain of the Ganges, holding three or four acres of land, would be pretty well off if his income amounted to three-and-sixpence a week, of which six-sevenths would be the produce of his marketable crops, and the balance contributed by vegetables and the milk of a cow or some goats. His land rent would be sixpence a week. He would pay no house rent. He eats better food than the coolie, and his net income of three shillings would be equivalent in food-purchasing power to about six shillings in England. With an income of double this amount, and paying a rent of one and fourpence a week, a cultivator would in popular estimation be quite well-to-do. In more sparsely populated tracts the holdings are larger and the rent proportionately lower. A fairly prosperous man in this locality would hold ten or twelve acres and enjoy an income of six or seven shillings a week, of which less than a shilling would go in rent. Looking at these figures one can hardly believe that there is any margin for saving. But there is undoubtedly a margin: were it not so, cultivators could not borrow as readily as they do. With the thriftiness of the French peasant something could be put by. But the Indian cultivator, though frugal in the extreme, is not thrifty, and he expends upon family ceremonies such as marriages and funerals sums that would convulse the imagination of an English peasant. A cultivator will think nothing of spending six months' income on a marriage:

Marriage extravagances.

if he holds at a low rent he will spend as much as a year's income. It sounds incredible that a man making three shillings a week should spend four pounds on a marriage. But it is the case, and this remarkable propensity to periodical extravagance is more injurious to the Indian peasant than the unkindness of the seasons. When holdings are fairly large and rents low, a tenant will commonly spend the equivalent of eight years' rent—or £15—on a single marriage. For him, be it remembered, this sum is equivalent to double its amount in English money. It is on the father of the bride that marriage expenses usually fall, and one can easily imagine the disappointment with which a baby-girl is received and the apprehension with which a man watches the growth of his budding daughters. For to waste these large amounts is really compulsory. There is some question of choice in spending rather more or rather less; but one can rarely escape the disbursement of half a year's income at least in marrying off a daughter. Marriages and funerals are caste festivals, and a man's position in his caste depends upon the manner in which he acquits himself of his caste obligations. To the extravagant these caste ceremonies bring ruin: to the careful they bring debt and embarrassment. Very little of the money is spent upon presents for bride or bridegroom. It is laid out in providing a feast—or a series of feasts—for the caste, the members of which attend in force, and sit down to a heavy meal enlivened with music and sometimes ending with a small display of fireworks. The little bridegroom—generally quite a small child—is dressed out in bright clothes, crowned with a tinsel diadem, and is carried in a gaily caparisoned bullock chariot to the bride's house, attended by all his father's friends and relations and preceded by a band. He is received at the bride's house by her relations and the ceremony takes place. Boy and girl take seven steps, hand in hand, round a fire altar, and their union is symbolised by tying their skirts together. But the bride is hardly out of babyhood, and the only substantial feature of the wedding is the meal that follows it. The little married couple part and do not, as a rule, meet again till the girl is of marriageable age. This, sad to say, is put at nine or ten years. And there are also funerals. These are such as the Irish 'wakes' and cost much money.

Indebtedness.

For the cultivator to be indebted is merely to be true to his traditions. Under Native rule—and till lately in some of the existing Native States—it was customary that the Government should demand payment of its land revenue before the cultivator could harvest the crops that were to provide it, with the idea of safeguarding the State from being cheated by a man who should sell his produce and abscond without payment. The land revenue could then only be paid by borrowing, and the assistance of the money-lender was as essential as the rain and sun which gave the harvest. He lent at high interest, and was assisted by the State in recovering his dues. He was, in fact, employed as a State bailiff with usury as his remuneration. No such hardship continues in British India, and revenue is not now demanded till men have had time to realise by sale of their produce. But custom dies hard, and a visit to the money-lender is as natural as in England is the visit of the family doctor. Men will even borrow at high interest in preference to touching their savings. Rates of interest are falling, and substantial cultivators can now generally borrow in cash at 12 per cent. But on grain loans—and a large proportion of the seed grain is annually borrowed—interest remains at its traditional rate—25 per cent. on such grain as wheat, and 50 per cent. upon millet—for a single season. Compound interest is charged, and with a run of three bad seasons a loan of wheat seed is doubled and a loan of millet is more than trebled. But the money-lender has his better feelings. As a general rule he is honest in his accounts; and when times are very bad he will display liberality, and has been known to remit debts altogether if his debtor will in his name free a heifer or offer Ganges water at the temple. Where, however, land has become very valuable and money-lenders are tempted to get possession of it, distressing cases of extortion occur. In one that came before me two brothers who were in debt to a money-lender decided to make over their land to him on usufructuary mortgage, and to spend five years in making pilgrimages. On their return they were offered accounts to show that the money-lender had lost by his farming, and that their debt was actually larger than before. In despair they fell upon him and killed him. They were sentenced to death. But the fear of such desperate remedies is undoubtedly a salutary check upon growing dishonesty. The value of produce has risen very greatly, and cultivators should have benefited. Their expenditure has increased, but so has their indebtedness; and over the majority 'hangs the grip of the usurer and the shadow of the Civil Courts.'

Cultivators of the 'twice-born' caste will, as a rule,

not touch the plough: they farm by hired labour, and it is sometimes a mystery how they make a livelihood. By a very general custom, however, they are permitted to hold at lower rents than the ordinary. The working peasant is, on the other hand, exceedingly laborious. He works slowly and without pressing, and is as careful against over-exertion as some English gardeners. But like them, he is all day at it. He keeps his land remarkably clean and free from weeds, and in localities where the land is irrigated from wells, he is at the well-head, emptying the bucket as the bullocks drag it up, all day long,—and sometimes, when the moon assists him, all night long. Each time the bucket comes up he sings a little phrase, and of moonlight nights one may hear all around the creaking of the well gear and these snatches of song. Their lot is hard, but the people bear it cheerfully, and their patience in misfortune is admirable beyond words. They are exceedingly pertinacious, and will spare no trouble and shrink from no discomfort to enlist assistance. One morning as I rode out I noticed a suppliant at my gate: he told me that he had been ejected from his land and begged my intervention. Inquiries showed that he had been ejected by his landlord in due process of law, and he was told that any interference on his behalf was impossible. But he stayed on. We left on a tour by road which covered twelve hundred miles and lasted four months. He made friends with the servants and accompanied us throughout, never repeating his complaints, but merely taking care to be in evidence each morning, and to offer his salutations. Finally, I sent word to the landlord asking whether nothing could be done. He realised the situation and

Industry in cultivation.

very kindly restored to the man some of his land. To sit fasting at a man's door is a customary method of enforcing a claim against him: if the suppliant dies of this 'hunger strike,' his death is upon the head of him he has supplicated, and it has actually been necessary to penalise in the criminal law this method of compulsion.

Truthfulness.

In his home and in his village the Indian villager is exceedingly truthful: I have hardly ever known a man lie when surrounded by his fellows. Formally confronted with the State—in its courts—he has a different code of morality. A tradition has come down through centuries of oppression that the State is an alien and unintelligent force, overriding the caste and family which represent the real government of the people—a force whose peculiar actions it is lawful to oppose by every method possible.

The position of women.

The Hindu woman is married very young. But it is part of her religion to love her husband, and literally to adore him. She goes veiled, like the Muhammadan woman; and, if the family can afford it, she shuts herself up in apartments of her own. But this practice was adopted from the Muhammadans, and is not in accordance with ancient Hindu custom. In the heroic days of the Hindu epics, women married when of adult age, and actually chose their husbands. Family life is generally happy, and though polygamy is authorised, it is only amongst the rich that a wife shares her husband with others. But until the British Government intervened on her behalf, her life was haunted by the spectre of a dreadful martyrdom. On her husband's death it was her duty, as a pious wife, to be burnt on the pyre with him: she accepted her destiny, and the many accounts we possess of these human sacrifices very rarely mention any unwillingness on her part. When the flames touched her body there might be irrepressible screams: these were drowned by the beating of drums and the shrieking of trumpets. Some observers relate a horrible detail—that Brahmins stood around, pressing the woman down upon the fire with long bamboo poles, and so concealing the involuntary spasms of anguish. These sacrifices were known as 'satis,' or devotions. They were of common occurrence: in one year seven hundred were celebrated in the province of Bengal. In some parts of the country *sati* memorials abound on the outskirts of villages—small headstones engraved with two hands, standing upright, side by side, palms outwards. Our imagination does no discredit to human affection in depicting the anxiety with which a wife who was under such a doom watched over the health of her husband, seeing the shadow of her own death in the least of his ailments. The practice was made criminal by Lord William Bentinck in 1829. But from time to time there still occur attempts to revive it: beyond all doubt it is popular, and would be restored immediately if our influence were withdrawn. And if the British have saved the Hindu widow from one sacrifice, her caste still demands of her another. She may not be remarried: with hair cut short, in mean attire, the drudge of the family, she suffers the penance of a convent without its dignity, its repose, and its consolations. There are in India four millions of widows who are under thirty years of age, of whom nearly half a million are under sixteen, and (hard to believe) 20,000 are

L

children under six. Scandals, ending in murder or suicide, are the frequent and natural result. For the last thirty years widow remarriage has been championed by Hindus of enlightenment, and some have actually married widows. But it is uncertain how far most of them will hold to their convictions. An Indian magistrate of my acquaintance, prominent among the advocates of this reform, claimed and recovered damages from a newspaper because it hinted that he proposed to carry his principles into practice. The prohibition of remarriage is certainly gaining ground in the lower castes: it marks the desire of a caste to rise in the world, and it is, of course, a relief to the fathers of unmarried girls that widows should not compete in the marriage market.

Family affection.

The affection of a father for his children is touching to witness: he is not ashamed of showing it, and it is a pretty sight at a fair to watch a little family party out for a day's enjoyment, the mother carrying one child astride on her hip, the father another on his shoulder, and perhaps leading a third. To a Hindu his son is everything. Upon him he relies for the performance of ceremonies at his funeral, and afterwards, that will affect very greatly his future existence. To be sonless is the very worst of misfortunes, and a man in such a case will in desperation endeavour to earn merit by planting a grove or digging a well. He may also safeguard himself by adopting a boy, and heirs are frequently provided in this way, especially amongst the rich, to whom children often fail. But this is the expedient last invoked: only when it is clear that the goddess of Fecundity is indifferent to his wife's entreaties and oblations. In propitiation of this goddess religious fairs or 'stations' are held, attended of course only by women.

Life is by no means devoid of amusements. Most villages have a sort of club-house, in which men of the better castes can of evenings find variety from the society of their wives. There are marriages and funerals. There are frequent caste meetings, which, when rules have been broken, become convivial with a meal at the offender's expense. The country fairs are something to look forward to and to be enjoyed. Amidst the distractions of side-shows—and amongst them in these days are gramophones—you may see husbands and wives eyeing with anxiety the wares that are offered in the shop stalls, and making their purchases with immense deliberation. They will minutely discuss the prices all the way home. There are, moreover, the interests which Nature offers to those who live near her, in a climate that is never too rigorous for outdoor life. One sees things as they are. The shawl which the housewife is wearing has been watched by her since it grew as cotton in the fields: the weaver, the dyer, all work in public: the things in daily use have a life-history which the manufactures of civilisation altogether lack. Without endowing the peasant with fine sensibilities we may be sure that he appreciates the brightness of the Arcadian life—the gleam of sunrise upon the dew of young herbage, the rustle of leaves in the light breeze of midday, the yellow and purple of the afterglow landscape—such impressions as England rarely offers to any of us, and never to the workers who live in towns. And man lives very close to the animals around him. They are

Amusements.

Intimacy with animals.

treated, not so much with kindness, as with the consideration that is due to members of the family: the cultivator addresses his bullocks as 'my brothers.' Domesticated animals are extraordinarily tame: one of the sights of the country is a little child of five or six, sun-blackened, stark naked, with serious eyes, driving afield a pair of huge buffaloes that meekly obey him. It is pretty to see the absolute understanding between a little girl and her flock of goats. Birds are favourite pets, and in the houses of the very poorest you will find a tame parrot or partridge. Indeed, in one district, every other man carries a bamboo perch on which is seated an Indian nightingale (bulbul). But it must be confessed that partridges and bulbuls are desperately combative, and that fighting-matches between one bird and another provide such amusement as in some English circles is derived from singing-matches between cage-birds. No one teases animals in India, and birds' nesting is unknown. On the other hand, an animal that is past work suffers pitiable neglect, and it is sad to see a bullock dying unnoted, except by the crows that surround it expectantly. And the feelings of cabmen and cart-drivers are not more sympathetic towards their beasts than in other countries where they have not been controlled by the watchfulness of protective societies.

Childhood.

There is little discipline of children in an Indian home. They are seldom punished: a father who regards his son as the priest of his soul can hardly be expected to chastise him. But sons are educated by constant association with their fathers. As in the early days of Rome, boys are their fathers' companions in the business of life, and acquire, when mere children, much gravity of demeanour. It is rare in the plains of India to see children playing noisily together. They all seem oppressed with the seriousness of life. From time to time childhood is impressed by solemn ceremonies. The most important of them is, in 'twice-born' castes, the investiture of a boy with the sacred thread. This is a loop of thick, nine-stranded cotton-string, made by Brahmins, which passes over the left shoulder and hangs down across the body to the waist. The 're-birth' which it originally marked was into an apprenticeship of asceticism. The thread is never put off, and it enables you at once to detect a man of the privileged orders.

When the son grows up he takes partnership with his father, who is bound to provide for him, but has the sole management of affairs. On the father's death the eldest son steps into his place, and the brothers live as a joint family under his administration. They can separate by a formal dissolution and partition. But in orthodox families they generally remain united under a system which denies younger brothers the least initiative in domestic affairs. A Maratha Brahmin in Government service up-country, far away from his home, will regularly remit to his elder brother such of his pay as he does not actually need for the purchase of his daily food: he will not purchase clothes for himself, but will wait till they are despatched to him by the head of the family. Throughout life the family is a living obsession: it controls extravagance, but deadens initiative.

The joint family.

Within the family circle creep a tribe of poor relations. Towards them the Indian is extraordinarily charitable. A young clerk of mine provided sixteen persons with food and raiment—his wife, his widowed mother, four younger brothers (for whose education he paid), two widowed sisters with young families, and a cousin out of employ. No man rises in the world but a crowd of dependants cling to him, who find shelter in his house, share his food, and in return do little but offer him compliments. His home is an asylum for the widows and orphans of his family: it is also a refuge for the idle, for whom his tolerance is sometimes as demoralising as to us it is astonishing.

Poor relations.

So, when his last day comes, the householder may count upon a united band of relations to accompany him to the pyre. They will not bear him thitherward: it would be pollution to touch the corpse, however indirectly; and some low-caste men are hired to carry the bier. Amidst the tears and cries of the women the procession sets out: it approaches the pyre—a rectangular heap of wood, carefully adjusted by the Brahmins, encircled and cut off from the world by a shallow trench. Within this trench the bearers step, and lay the body on the fuel. The eldest son takes a torch, approaches the pyre and sets fire to it, hastily retiring from the contact. When the fire has burnt down, the ashes are collected to be thrown, if possible, into the Ganges. The mourners hasten off to cleanse themselves, by bathing, from their association with the dead.

Death ceremonies.

To the Hindu life appears as a calm, overhung by the mysterious and the terrible. He likens it to a peaceful stream which flows beneath frowning precipices, and ends in an unseen cataract.

x.—Some People of the Hills.

The head-hunting Nágas.

THE north-eastern frontier of India is haunted by the spectres of rapine and bloodshed, and by the pitiful cries of women and children. The country is mountainous, and our boundary follows the course of streams that flow through deep valleys. From their outposts on one cliff our officers can sometimes watch the destruction in a night-raid of a village on the opposite slope, which has become a familiar feature of the landscape. The sound of tumult comes across the valley; flames shoot up, and in the firelight the people can be descried fleeing from the warriors that, spear in hand, pursue them, and endeavouring to reach the stream across which there is the sanctuary of British territory. We are in a country of head-hunters. No man can expect a nice girl to marry him unless he can show her a ghastly trophy; and, so brutalised are human feelings, that heads of women and even of little children count for as much as the head of a warrior; indeed they count for more, as to kill a woman or child a man has to venture himself well inside the land of the hostile village. Heads taken by ambuscade are as honourable trophies as those won in open fight. We realise the extraordinary fact that man stands almost alone among the animals in delighting to prey upon his own species—and this, moreover, from no desire of food. For these people are not cannibals.

These tribesmen are related to the Tibetans on one side and to the Burmese on the other, and are collectively spoken of as Nágas. A considerable portion of their territory has been annexed, and constitutes the British district of the Nága Hills. It was only by advancing into their country that we could check their brutal raiding of the plains. The effect of our control has been marvellous. With a population of nearly 200,000, not more than two or three murders are committed annually. One year we attempted to ascertain the number of persons who were killed across our border and within a few miles of it. They amounted to between 200 and 300. Within our boundary the warriors still regret the loss of their customary excitement. But they are growing accustomed to the decoration of their houses with pumpkins in lieu of human skulls.

Nága customs.

Their villages are perched upon hill-tops, built of substantial wooden houses, and roughly fortified with wall and ditch. The country is densely populated for its resources, and almost every peak, ridge, and spur is crowned by a village, as conspicuous on the skyline as a hill-town of Italy. Below the houses the fields stretch down the hillside: with some tribes they are mere clearings in the jungle, cultivated with axe and fire; with others they are elaborately terraced out of the hillside and skilfully irrigated for the cultivation of rice. *Mutuo metu separati et montibus* the people have developed an extraordinary diversity of language. Seven distinct tongues are spoken within the British district, which, though alike in origin, are entirely different in vocabulary, each being wholly unintelligible to men that speak another. Nor is it sufficient that one tribe should hate another: two villages of the same tribe will often be at perpetual war—nay, one quarter of the same village will invade the other, or will admit alien marauders to levy from it a toll of heads. On the war-path the warriors are dressed in such brilliant and fantastic costumes as we associate with the Red Indians of Fenimore Cooper's romances. There are differences of costume between tribe and tribe, and between village and village. A typical warrior covers his head with a casque of plaited bamboo, carrying an enormous halo of black and white feathers. In front of the casque an elaborately puffed *toupet* of false hair overshadows his forehead. His ears are decorated with rolls of white and scarlet cotton. His chest is crossed by bands of goat's-skin with hair dyed scarlet. He wears a kilt of striped cotton, and a sporran adorned with white cowrie shells. A belt round his waist carries a tail of scarlet and white hair, which sticks out behind, finely arched, with an effect irresistibly comic. His legs are cased in gaiters of finely-plaited bamboo. He carries in one hand a long spear, decorated with tufts of scarlet hair, in the other a huge oblong shield of bear-skin, from the top of which project two long black plumes. A man's tribe and village is indicated by the pattern of his kilt and sporran: these hillmen share with the Scotch the ideas that have led to the elaboration of the tartan. The men delight in war dances, which, with warriors thus attired, are very remarkable spectacles. Those who live above the fever line (about 4000 feet above sea-level) are of very fine physique, and have shown much courage in resisting the attack of regular troops. Savages—and bloodthirsty savages—as they are, their life is complicated by customs and fashions which are more onerous and detailed than those of civilisation. They possess a quick intelligence and very keen trading instincts. Numbers of them descend every cold season into the plains, selling curiosities of their hills, and find their way to Calcutta and even to Bombay. Of recent years text-books have been written in the tribal languages and village schools have been opened. The children show quite as much aptitude for arithmetic as English children, and some of them make astonishing progress. Beyond a vague animism the Nágas have no religion. Their robustness of character offers a field for missionary endeavour which is more promising than the philosophic anæmia of the plains.

British control appreciated.

Five years ago it was decided, in the interests of humanity, to extend the limits of British territory, since, as our own tribesmen settled down, we could increase our responsibilities without adding to our police force. The occasion was celebrated by a gala meeting on the parade-ground at the district headquarters. Tribesmen of the newly annexed area appeared in force, and there also came large contingents of warriors from villages that were previously under British control. In all there were some 1500 warriors, dressed in full war-paint, and the ground was a whirling mass of different war dances. A regiment of military police was serried in the background, watchful lest spears, brandished in the dance within the village circle, should be turned in sudden attack against the circles on either side of it. The dances were over: the warriors had defiled before me, when five men in the garb of suppliants rushed forward and threw themselves on the ground at my feet. They were the headmen of five villages which had been left unannexed because of their distance from the existing frontier, and they implored that their villages might also be taken over, so that their women might go down to fetch water from the spring without the torturing fear that, through the bamboos on either side, their steps were watched by an ambuscade of head-hunters.

The Khasis.

To the west of the Nága country the Assam hills run out into the plains in a long promontory rising to 5000 feet above the sea. The higher levels are inhabited by a people known as the Khasis, who are in some respects the most interesting of the hill tribes of India. They have no connection with Tibetans or Burmese, and are an isolated remnant of an ancient race that was formerly widespread in India and Burma, but now subsists only in this people and in a few scattered tribes of Burma and Cambodia. They possess a peculiar language which, though largely monosyllabic, in the hands of skilful translators renders the Scriptures, and even the English hymnal, with much literary force. Having no script of its own, it has adopted the letters of the English alphabet. Two generations ago these hillmen were well known in official literature as the 'truculent and bloodthirsty Khasis,' and their forays into the plains of Assam were a frequent subject of complaint. But they are on quite a different plane to such tribes as the Nágas: they are not head-hunters: they are more courageous, better sportsmen, and they have developed forms of government which illustrate with singular force the universality of human tendencies—which indicate how much there may be in common between Greece or Italy and a remote district in the hills of Assam.

The matriarchate.

The Khasis offer to us what is, perhaps, the most complete existing specimen of the matriarchate—the social arrangement which, according to some philosophers, was man's earliest attempt at domesticity. All property belongs to the women. A man marries into his wife's family, or, if he prefers to continue in his own, he visits his wife only on occasions, and undertakes no responsibility for the care of his children. The term for a husband is simply 'he who causes conception.' If he accepts a more permanent arrangement and joins his wife's family, his earnings go to her family also. The head of each family is the grandmother. It is a common practice to style oneself after the name of one's daughter, and men constantly subscribe themselves in private letters after such a fashion as 'Your sincere friend, the father of Mary Anne.' One would have supposed that so peculiar a social system would have changed very profoundly the relations of the sexes. But human nature cannot be strangled by bandages. The men do the fighting and the heavy work of life. They relieve their labours by fishing or hunting, to which they are much addicted, and to one who has been used to the quietude of Indian life, it is curious to see on holidays a large party of men and women joyfully going off to the moors with bows and fishing nets, or to find a clerk doing a morning's fishing with rod and line before his office opens. The women mind the house and the children, and are prudent managers. They are decidedly good-looking in something of the Japanese style, and are perhaps inclined to make the most of their freedom. But it may be in a nasty spirit of cynicism that the men have decided that when office or status passes by heritage it is a man's sister's son and not his own son that succeeds him, so that he may be assured that his heir is at least a blood relation.

Costume.

The national costume is exceedingly picturesque. On festal occasions the men are richly dressed in coloured silk coat and loin-cloth, with turban surmounted by a tall waving plume of black tipped white feathers. They are adorned with breastplate and broad belt of chased silver, and carry a long sword in one hand and a plume of goat's hair in the other. The women wear a petticoat of yellow silk, a white bodice with a lavender shawl which passes over the head and is fastened round the neck after the fashion one may often see in Ireland. Both men and women wear heavy bead-necklaces of coral and gold. The beads are sometimes an inch in diameter, and the necklaces are very valuable possessions. Dances are ceremonial performances connected with religion: the women take part in them, wearing for the occasion small gilt crowns.

Pigs and potatoes.

If the women's dress reminds us a little of Ireland, the reminiscence is strengthened by ever-present pigs and potatoes. Most households keep a pig, which, together with some fowls, is on terms of great familiarity. Potato patches are everywhere: the crop was only introduced sixty years ago, and its rapid adoption speaks for the intelligence of the people. There is a large export trade in potatoes to Calcutta.

From the vague beliefs and apprehensions of their

religion three ideas emerge with distinctness. The Khasis are peculiar amongst hill-people in burning, not burying, their dead; but they do not believe that fire ends the life, as it consumes the body, of the individual, and they regularly offer food to the spirits of their ancestors. Connected in some measure with ancestor-worship are the stone cromlechs and menhirs with which the grassy downs are dotted—sometimes standing singly and of great size, sometimes arranged in great circles like miniature Stonehenges, and sometimes in a very characteristic grouping—three or five tall head-stones disposed in a straight row, each having before it a stone slab altar raised on short stone supports. The uprights present male ancestors (but on the female side), the altars represent female ancestors. In some cases these memorials are connected with funeral rites, and mark stages in the process of transferring the calcined bones of the departed from temporary resting-places to the family vault. In other cases they are simply monuments to keep alive the memory of the dead, and are in fact attempts to record history by a people that possess no written alphabet.

Religion.

The Khasis believe in divination, and by inspection of the entrails of slaughtered animals search the future in a manner which brings them curiously near the Greeks and Romans. A cheaper and more popular means of divination is, however, by the breaking of eggs, which indicate by the position of the fractured egg-shell whether a proposed undertaking will fall out prosperously or not.

Divination.

A third idea that is peculiar to them is that of a

huge, ghostly snake, the mysteries of which are known to certain priestesses and which they alone can propitiate. It occasionally needs offerings of human blood: from time to time wayfarers are found murdered, and, if the ends of their fingers and toes are cut off, it is known that they have been sacrificed to this demon. Such dread does this cult inspire that even in the British station of Shillong people are very unwilling to go out at night alone. Twenty-five years ago, when the survey of the Assam valley was undertaken, it was necessary to import trained measurers from Upper India. One of them, a Muhammadan of Rohilkhand, yielded to the attractions of a Khasi girl and kept house with her. It was told me by a friend of his that, one day, having learnt that his mistress was a snake-witch, he insisted upon being shown her familiar. She opened a small circular box in which there lay curled what appeared to be a thick horse-hair. Placing the box on the ground she made passes over it: gradually the hair swelled and grew till it became an enormous snake which reared itself erect with crest expanded. The man was terrified: the woman laughed and made some reverse passes: below them the snake shrank and dwindled, till it could again be shut down below the lid of its box.

Snake-worship.

Quite half the Khasi Hills district is administered by a number of little indigenous governments under the general control of a British officer. There are twenty-seven of these small States with constitutions that illustrate very strikingly the extraordinarily close correspondence which sometimes occurs between the mental evolution of

Political ideas.

widely separated and widely different races of mankind. The belief that the future can be discovered in the bowels of an animal is a remarkable link between the Khasis and the Greeks: not less remarkable is the classical tinge of Khasi ideas in regard to forms of civil government. For a warlike race male leaders are essential, and matriarchal ideas have so far given way as to permit the chief of each State to be a man, though he succeeds to office on the strength of his female ancestors. The headship of the largest State is, it is true, vested in an hereditary priestess. But she is represented in secular matters by a male chieftain; the State is formed by a voluntary confederacy of smaller States, and her function is to bind the component portions together. The chief of each State is assisted by a council which he is bound to consult. He holds office, not in simple hereditary right, but by election, being chosen from amongst those who are qualified to succeed by relationship to a particular female line. The method of election varies in different States, and its diversity indicates the tendency of mankind to substitute secular for priestly authority. In some States the electing authority is a college of augurs who belong to a priestly clan: in others secular electors, such as the headmen of villages, have secured representation along with the augurs, or have even displaced them: in others, again, election is by general plebiscite. One State which has acquired (probably by conquest) the hegemony of some smaller States, has conceded to the latter electoral rights which are less in degree than those enjoyed by its own citizens—has, in fact, granted to them a position which has something akin to that of Athenian *metoikoi*.

Spread of Christianity and its effects.

But the most striking feature of the Khasis is the zeal with which they are embracing Christianity and the material benefits that follow conversion. There is much similarity between the scenery of the Khasi hills and that of Wales, and it is curiously appropriate that these people should have been evangelised by Welsh missionaries. Sixty years ago a Welshman established a small school in the hills. He met with very little success, but in appreciation of his labours the chief Government official recommended that a small grant of Government money should annually be made to him. The Governor-General (Lord Dalhousie) demurred to a formal arrangement of this kind, but permitted the recommending official to allot a sum from the amount that was at his disposal for miscellaneous contingencies. From this small beginning the Mission has grown until now almost a sixth of the population is avowedly Christian, and Christian influence extends over a much larger proportion. Two of the chiefs have accepted Christianity. In 1829 the ancestor of one of them treacherously killed two British officers: his descendant now reads the lessons in church. There are churches in all the larger villages, and on a Sunday, riding about the hills, one may hear church bells tinkling in all directions, and may meet groups of neatly dressed men and women on their way to service, Bible and hymn-book in hand. The Mission has fitted the English alphabet to the Khasi language, and has formulated (and perhaps embellished) a Khasi grammar. It has opened more than two hundred village schools for teaching in the vernacular, and in partnership with the State maintains a high school at the district headquarters in which English is taught. It was to be expected that Welsh missionaries should have brought with them their national aptitude for singing in parts, but it is surprising that the Khasis should have taken so readily to an accomplishment which can find no roothold in Oriental music. Hymn-singing in parts is a prominent feature of church service, and school children sing glees and catches with sweetness and accuracy. The humanising effect of Christianity is evident on all sides. The houses of Christians can be picked out in a village without a moment's hesitation: in neatness of construction and cleanliness they stand apart from the others, and little flower-gardens and rose-covered porches indicate a living appreciation of the beautiful. Inside the house the rooms are frequently neatly panelled and prettily decorated. The people have undoubtedly a natural turn for the artistic, and the children easily learn to draw and colour. But the development of this talent is entirely due to Christian influence.

Progress of conversion.

There are those who are inclined to suspect the gifts that Christianity can offer to India. I would that they could see what it has bestowed upon the hills of Assam. The Welsh Presbyterian Mission has no doubt enjoyed some special advantages. It has not had to fight its way against the dominant influence of the Brahmin priesthood. Hinduism actually gained a footing in the hills some sixty years ago: in the largest of the Khasi States a temple was dedicated to the 'Great Mother' of the Hindus, who was propitiated with human sacrifices. It was the continuance of these sacrifices, in defiance of the prohibition of the British

Government, that led to the downfall of the chief, the annexation of the State, and the strengthening of British control over the Khasi hills. The temple lost its worshippers and Hinduism its foothold, leaving Christianity confronted, not by the rigid opposition of an organised hierarchy, but by a vague mass of floating superstitions. The missionaries, themselves of narrow means and of no very high education, have enjoyed substantial financial support owing to the generous bequests of a wealthy fellow-countryman, and have at all times been sufficiently numerous to fill any vacancies caused by death or ill-health. Moreover, they were first in the field with the establishment of village schools, and have been permitted to retain them in their management, assisted by a Government subsidy. Religious teaching is subject to a conscience clause, but, when once Christianity began to spread, parents showed no great desire to remove their children from its religious teachings.

Causes of its spread.

The Mission has thus enjoyed very substantial advantages. But these do not of themselves suffice to account for the rapid spread of Christianity, and for the large number of adult conversions, amounting to at least a thousand a year. The missionaries, men and women, have displayed to the full the zeal and self-sacrifice that are expected of them. They have also displayed great prudence: adult converts are not welcomed until they have shown by a period of probation that they are earnest in their submission to new standards of morality, so that conversion has come to be considered not a concession, but a privilege. And the method in which church administration has been organised has made Christianity appear, not an exotic cultivated by foreign teachers, but a growth firmly acclimatised in the people's thoughts. The administration of affairs is in the hands of councils or presbyteries which mainly consist of Khasi members. There are, of course, missionary members who can offer advice as well as opinion; but in a fine spirit of self-abnegation it has been decided that a missionary shall not be president. There have, of course, been disappointments. A new church, drawing itself together from a society of lower ideals and laxer morality, cannot always safeguard its circle against unworthy intrusions, and there have been presbyters who have been false to the obligations of their office. But it has proved wiser, at the risk of some scandals, to foster an expansive vitality, than, in dread of them, to cramp the young church within a hard-shell cover of protective authority.

Interesting developments.

Born of a Welsh mother, the Khasi church has taken the complexion of the Khasi hills. Needing, and receiving, careful guidance, she has been stirred by the consciousness of independent growth, and by some features of her development she assists us in realising the condition of the early Pauline churches. The missionaries are her prophets: subject to their exhortation her affairs are her own. There is a spirit of active charity: I have known between £40 and £50 subscribed by school children on behalf of their parents—generally quite poor people—for the relief of distress in Khasi villages. Religion is not a Sunday cloak: it is a burning subject of thought and discussion. Riding alongside of you, your Khasi subordinate will eagerly take any opportunity of talking of it. Three weekly newspapers are published in Khasi: in two of them the leading article is generally religious, dealing with a question of scriptural interpretation. Heresies are amongst the natural fruits of this vitality, and they continually exercise the persuasiveness and the arguments of the missionaries. Upon minds of such fervency great was the effect of the religious revival which stirred Wales six years ago. Its excitement was reflected throughout the Khasi hills with extravagancies that at one time threatened to pass beyond proper control.

The lesson it gives to missionary endeavour.

It must not be supposed that in India the Khasi church is unique in its display of Christianity as a civilising and social as well as a religious force. There are other springs of similar vitality; but we shall rarely find them breaking through the compacted strata of Brahminical Hinduism. They are on the outskirts—as in the Himalayas near Darjeeling, in the hill-country of Bengal, and amongst the low-caste people of southern Madras. The appeal which Christianity makes to the poor and rejected hardly touches those who have settled with pride in the niche that the caste system has allotted them. To pride of caste Christianity is a stumbling-block: Hindu speculation sees in it but foolishness; to the eyes of Islám it appears too similar a faith to be worth the trials of conversion. We may regret that missionary endeavour is so largely occupied in a direct conflict with these forces—in educative and argumentative work at the centres of Indian society, while so much ground remains untouched which can promise a more grateful harvest. While missionary effort applies itself to the secular education of youth in Dacca and Calcutta, the Nága tribes (for instance) are left in darkness. St. Paul's appeal on Mars Hill to philosophic intelligence was an exceptional incident in the early history of Christianity, and leaves it a fact that the Gospel spread from the uncultured to the cultured—from the fringe of society to the mass of its material. Why should we imagine that in India it will follow a different course, striking its first roots, not in the houses of the poor, but in college lecture halls? Energized by Christianity, those whom Hinduism now despises will effectively compete with it. Already Khasi magistrates, engineers, and doctors are taking places under the State that formerly were appropriated by educated Bengalis. Perhaps, when once this is realised, the older cults will not need the authority of a Constantine to change their attitude.

xi.—Agriculture and Irrigation.

India's typical products.

In the classical days of Greece and Rome three products of India attracted the notice of curious inquirers—a 'tree from which the Indians made cloth'—'a reed from which a sweet juice was expressed'—and a plant yielding a dark-blue dye known as *indicon*. The first was the cotton-plant, the second the sugar-cane, and the third (with name almost unchanged) indigo. These plants were not known to the ancient agriculture of Egypt and Mesopotamia, possibly because they are summer products, and during the summer the lands of these river valleys were too deeply flooded to be cropped. The peoples of these countries, as well as the Greeks and Romans, used linen for light wear, and sweetened their dishes with honey. The cultivation of cotton and the sugar-cane was introduced by Arab conquerors into the Levant, and from the Levant the sugar-cane found its way to America and the West Indies. Out of cotton modern Egypt has woven its prosperity, and the West Indies subsist upon their sugar culture. India has found herself surpassed by both countries in growing crops that were peculiarly her own. In Egypt the cotton-plant produces fourfold, in the West Indies the sugar-cane produces nearly threefold, the return that they yield in India. And the cultivation of indigo now appears to be doomed by the manufacture of artificial dye in German laboratories.

If the soil contain sufficient moisture, crops can be cultivated in India all the year round. Of crops that mature rapidly two and sometimes three can be harvested from the same land in the course of twelve months. In some parts of India three crops of rice are taken, and double cropping is frequent in the northern Indian plain—wheat following maize or indigo, peas or beans following rice, and a crop of rape following cotton, if it be sown amongst the cotton-plants while they are still bearing. In this manner a cultivator may double or even treble the area of his holding. The crops that are cultivated during the summer months are everywhere tropical, such as cotton, millet, or indigo. During the winter months, north of the tropic of Cancer and for a distance of about a hundred and fifty miles south of it, only temperate crops, such as wheat and barley, can be cultivated. The tropic passes across the north of the peninsula, just above the Satpura hills, and wheat can only be grown for a short distance south of this range. Further down the peninsula there is less distinction of temperature between summer and winter, and tropical crops are grown in both seasons.

The agricultural seasons.

India may be divided into three regions, according as the typical food-crop is rice, wheat, or millet. Rice is the crop of Bengal, east of Patna, and of the eastern third of the peninsula. Wheat typifies the agriculture of northern India, that is to say, of the Indo-Gangetic plain west of Patna, and of the country extending southwards down to and just across the Satpuras. Millets of various sorts predominate in the western two-thirds of the peninsula. In the Rice country rice stands almost alone. In Bengal tall fields of

Agricultural geography.

jute break the dead level; but elsewhere rice takes possession of the land. North of the tropic it is often followed by a catch crop of peas, beans, or linseed during the cold season. South of the tropic rice follows rice. In the Wheat country conditions are more varied. During the summer months millets and cotton are largely cultivated: wheat is the cold-weather crop, sharing the land with barley and a species of pea known as gram.[1] It increases in importance from east to west, attaining its maximum area in the Panjáb, and it may be that wheat was introduced by the invaders who came from central Asia, and that this is the reason why, like Muhammadanism, it decreases as one passes eastward from the north-west border. In the Millet country various kinds of millet are grown: some very tall, with round pendulous heads of grain weighing sometimes a pound each, or with spiked heads like bulrushes: others of low growth, chiefly cultivated on the highlands, the principal of which is the bird's-claw millet that is the main crop of Mysore. Rice appears again in the strip of low country which borders the Arabian Sea, below the hills that overlook the western coast-line.

These crops provide the people with cereal grain. Something more is needed to take the place of the meat diet of European nations. In the wheat and millet countries this is supplied by pulses such as peas, beans, and lentils. In the rice country the people eat fish.

Diversity of Indian crops.

There is an extraordinary variety of crops—a greater variety than in any other country in the world. Of cereals, in addition to such well-known crops as wheat, barley, and oats, there are maize—the 'mealies' of South

[1] The *garbanzo* of Spain.

Africa—and nine species of millets. There are twelve kinds of pulse. Of oil-seeds there are nine. Narcotics include tobacco, opium, and the hemp that produces the drug—a species of nettle. Two other kinds of hemp, falsely so called, yield fibre from their stalks. Cotton and sugar-cane have already been mentioned. Of vegetables there is great variety, including all the better-known vegetables of Europe. Lastly, there are four crops that practically are only grown for export—jute, tea, indigo, and coffee. The areas which are covered by some of these crops are as extensive as good-sized countries. The area under rice is very nearly equal to the total area of the United Kingdom—119,000 square miles. There are 33,000 square miles under wheat, and, if other temperate crops are included, the area cropped during the cold weather extends to 60,000 square miles. Millets of kinds cover 75,000 square miles. One of the Indian pulses—the *lathyrus* or chick-pea—is remarkable for possessing for mankind poisonous properties if eaten in quantity. It is grown chiefly for cattle-food; but its cheapness commends it to the poorer classes, and if consumed in small quantities along with other food it is not injurious. But if for any length of time it constitutes the sole diet, it paralyses the lower limbs, apparently by the action of a poison which has, however, not yet been isolated. When rain fails this crop is largely sown, since it can make shift with less moisture than any other; and times of famine leave a distressing mark upon the population in the paralysis of large numbers of persons who have been reduced to live upon its grain. The paralysis has baffled all attempts to cure it. Curiously enough those that are afflicted by it, and drag themselves about on crutches, are noticeably cheerful—more cheerful, indeed, than their more fortunate comrades.

Methods of cultivation.

Each of these crops is cultivated in diverse methods in different parts of the country. Rice is sometimes sown broadcast; more frequently seedlings are transplanted from a seed-bed; in some places the broad-casted rice is ploughed up when a few weeks grown, so as to thin out the crop and destroy the weeds that infest it. The condition of the crop when so treated appears hopeless; but the number of seedlings for which there is space right themselves, and in a fortnight one would not know that they had been disturbed so violently. Wheat in the Indo-Gangetic plain is most carefully cultivated: in preparation for sowing, the land is ploughed again and again, occasionally twenty times over. In black-soil areas, so much care is not needed: before sowing, the land is twice roughly scarified by a bullock hoe. Cotton is in some places drilled in lines, in others sown broadcast. Generally, any two provinces of India differ very markedly, not only in the character of cropping, but in the methods of cultivating the crops which are common to both.

Some noticeable products.

Sugar is, as is well known, the juice of the sugar-cane, pressed out in a mill and boiled down till crystals form. The simplest process of refining it is by straining off the treacle, or uncrystallisable molasses. It is curious that India, the home of the sugar-cane, does not seem to have discovered this process, since, although there are now many refineries in the country, refined sugar bears names which indicate its importation from Egypt or China. Jute is the fibre of a tall plant, for the growth of which Bengal practically holds the world's monopoly. Formerly it provided the poorer classes with coarse wearing apparel. They now use finer and more expensive material, but the fibre has come into universal demand as material for the sacking in which grain and other raw produce is packed for consignment. The exports of jute, raw and manufactured, bring to the province an income of £24 millions a year. Indigo is obtained by steeping the plant in water: the extract, when oxidised by violent beating, throws down the dye in flakes of dark blue. The drug hemp may be in the form of the dried leaves (bhang), or the female flowers of the plant (gánja). Opium is extracted from the seed-head of the poppy: the capsule is scratched with a comb and a milky juice exudes which, when refined and pressed, is the opium of commerce. We have grave prejudices against hemp and opium, because we take alcohol instead of them. To use a hackneyed quotation, we

> 'Compound for sins we are inclined to
> By damning those we have no mind to.'

Consumed in excess, both are exceedingly injurious. So also is alcohol. But in moderation they are not harmful, and are taken by thousands of sober-minded Indians. Their use probably reflects in some measure a particular need of life or environment. Opium is of special value for bowel complaints. These are particularly common and severe in the moist, forest-clad province of Assam, and the consumption of opium in Assam is, per head of population, eight times as large as that of any other province. The unhealthiness of the Assam valley varies with distance from the hills, being at its worst near the hill-slopes, and least evident near the river Brahmaputra; and careful inquiries have shown that the consumption of opium varies in like manner, the inhabitants of the sub-montane tract consuming, man for man, almost twice as much as those of the central tract, and three times as much as those that live near the river.

Use of leguminous crops as fertilisers.

Until comparatively recently it was believed that plants could not use the atmospheric supply of the nitrogen they require. It is now well known that plants of the leguminous (pea) order can absorb nitrogen from the air, not by any action of their own, but by the assistance of bacteria which infest them and form nodules on their root-fibres. The people of India have, time out of mind, been aware of the fact, though not of its explanation; and by growing leguminous crops along with cereals, they assist the latter to make shift without manure. These mixtures of crops are very numerous and varied. Gram and peas are commonly sown with wheat, and tropical pulses with the tall millet. Lines of high-growing pulse are frequently drilled through cotton-fields. By associating crops together the cultivator secures another purpose, most useful to men of small means, to whom a failure of harvest may bring ruin. Weather that injures one crop may spare the other, and the combination acts as a species of insurance.

Manure.

There is probably no land in the world which needs manuring more urgently than the land of India, or which receives so little of the manure that is available for it. The fertility of the soil is drawn upon very heavily by the close and frequent cropping that is needed for the support of a dense population; and it is annually diminished by the violence of the surface-drainage that results from the falling of heavy rain upon an exposed surface. On the other hand, much of the manure that is required to replenish these losses is used for fuel in the lack of wood; and popular prejudice against touching anything that is unclean hinders the proper care of manure and the use of many forms of it. The women handle cow-dung in the making of their fuel cakes; but the manure heap, that contains what is left over, lies uncared for on the outskirts of the village. And generally, none but the very lowest castes will have any concern with sewage.

Injurious effect of surface-drainage.

The loss of fertility by surface-drainage is very serious. In the higher reaches, Indian rivers have cut their courses deep below the level of the country. The deluge of the monsoon falls upon land that is parched up and unprotected by vegetation. The rain streams off the the surface, down towards the river channel, loaded with the finer particles of the soil and with the fertilising nitrate salts that have been drawn up to the surface by evaporation during the hot weather. Year after year the fine soil that has disintegrated in the sun's heat is washed down into the rivers; and no one can have watched the muddy torrents which, in heavy rain, rush across the fields without reflecting upon the loss that the country is sustaining, and which surely must be lessening its fertility. Egypt and Mesopotamia are similarly unprotected by a covering of natural vegetation. But they receive no rainfall to speak of, and India stands almost alone amongst inhabited countries in being drenched with rain when the fields are uncovered. In the days of their formation the river valleys must have been protected by a dense growth of grass and jungle. They have lost it, and are losing their soil also: they are contributing to the formation of new provinces which are rising from the bottom of the sea around. In Bengal and along the littoral of Madras, where in a moister climate vegetation is more persistent and the drainage slope is gentler, the country suffers much less severely from the corroding effect of rain. Up-country, in the Indo-Gangetic plain, land that is perfectly flat suffers but little. But rivers and streams are very numerous, and the slopes that lead down to them cover a large area, bearing crops which are often so poor that an English farmer would not think them worth harvesting. In the black-soil country of the peninsula there is little flat land, and the loss by denudation is very heavy. Efforts are made in some tracts to check it by embanking the fields. Rice-fields are always embanked, as it is necessary that water should stand in them at an even level; they suffer but little from erosion, and, moreover, in the moist conditions of the rice districts the onset of the monsoon finds the land less dry than elsewhere.

Limited use of manure.

Rice responds generously to manure, but will, as a rule, yield pretty well without it. In the black-soil area, manure is hardly used at all, except for irrigated garden land. Unless it be irrigated, this soil generally profits little by being manured, and its irrigation is difficult and expensive. In the upper portion of the Indo-Gangetic plain, the fields which lie around the village site are well manured: manure can easily be carried to them, and they are benefited by the daily offices of the inhabitants. But the ring of manured land encloses an inconsiderable portion of the total. Where, as in Bengal, the houses are scattered over the village area, and are not grouped together, manure is better distributed, and there is a distinct gain of produce.

A curious method of manuring land, which is practised in the hills throughout the country, is effected by fire. The hillside jungle is felled and burnt: in the ashes seed is dibbled, and the resulting crop is, during the first year, magnificent. As a rule, a variety of crops are sown together; maize, millet, cotton, and rice clustering together in a dense mass of vegetation. But in the second season the produce decreases greatly: in the third season it almost reaches vanishing point, and is choked by weeds. The cultivator moves on to another patch, and does not return for several years. This method of cultivation by the axe and fire is, of course, very destructive of the forests, and is discouraged by the Government. Where the rainfall is light the forest takes years to recover itself—may, indeed, never be restored—and in western India long ranges of hillsides have been laid desolate for all time. In the dry season they are a stony wilderness; during the rains they bear grass which, when burnt, will occasionally provide nourishment for a poor crop. With a heavy rainfall, as in eastern India, the forests grow again rapidly, but in a changed character, bamboos taking the place of the original trees.

Manuring by fire.

Taking the country as a whole, one acre in seven

is irrigated. The subsoil water is drawn upon by wells: surface-drainage is collected in tanks: rivers feed irrigation canals. The character and extent of the irrigation depends upon the soil. The Indo-Gangetic plain is, as has already been stated, formed of the débris of the Himalayas. These mountains are composed very largely of shales and slates, and the soil that is derived from them is of poor natural fertility, but responds liberally to manure and water. In Bengal, at the eastern end of the plain, irrigation is not required. Elsewhere in the plain every drop of water is utilised. Wells are sunk in thousands, sometimes of masonry costing from £50 to £60, sometimes mere holes in the ground, lined with basket-work, or unlined, costing a few shillings. Water is lifted from ponds and streams by baskets swung to and fro by a couple of men, catching the water on the upstroke. Huge canals intersect the country. In the Panjáb two-fifths of the area is irrigated: in the United Provinces (between the Panjáb and Bengal) between a quarter and a third.

Extent to which irrigation employed

—in northern India.

In the black-soil country of central India and the Deccan irrigation is used practically for garden crops only. The land is retentive of the moisture which it receives from the rain. Owing to the deep cracks into which it opens when dry, its irrigation is difficult and expensive; and, if unaccompanied by manure, artificial watering adds but little to the produce and appears to increase the danger of rust.

—in central India and the Deccan.

In the crystalline area of the peninsula—that is to say towards its east and south—irrigation again

—in the south and east of the peninsula.

comes into prominence. A quarter of the land in the Madras presidency is watered. In the uplands, the land of this region is too poor to be irrigated: a large portion of the Mysore plateau grows nothing but a small millet. But in the lowlands, where the detritus of these rocks has accumulated, the land repays careful farming; and in the river deltas, along the Madras seacoast, it is very productive indeed. Wells are numerous, and the country is dotted with tanks, most ingeniously constructed wherever there is a depression or a valley in which water can be impounded by cross-embankment. The deltas are watered by canals, which are fed by rivers, the surface level of which is raised by a másonry dam or anicut.

—in Sindh.

In the extreme west of India the province of Sindh consists, for agricultural purposes, only of the area which is irrigated by the river Indus. Like Egypt, it is entirely dependent upon the river for its productiveness.

Sources of irrigation.

There are between one and two million wells in India which water 13 million acres. Another 15 million acres are watered from tanks or from the small private canals. An area of 17 million acres is ordinarily watered from canals that have been constructed and are maintained by the Government. The State then itself provides more than a third of the total irrigation of the country. It has tapped seven of the large rivers that flow into the dry area of the Indo-Gangetic plain, by constructing enormous canals that are large rivers in themselves. The Chenáb canal in the Panjáb waters two million acres, and has a discharge six times as great as that of the Thames at Teddington. These canals draw off the river water above a masonry dam which is constructed across the river channel and holds up the water; and as their bed-slope is flatter than that of the river, they gradually raise the water to a higher level, and ultimately deliver it at the surface level of the country. During the cold season the dams divert the whole of the river supply, leaving the channel below them dry. But water springs up into the river bed again; and some way down its course there is a fresh supply, which may again be impounded and taken off into another canal. In this manner three canal systems are fed by the Jumna and two by the Ganges. Not only do these canals increase prosperity: they create it. Two of the Panjáb canals literally have converted desolate uninhabited plains into thriving countries. Along the banks of the Chenáb canal now stretch fields and villages inhabited by a million people, where twelve years ago a few nomads wandered over a desert of parched earth and camel-thorn. The State irrigation works of India are, of their kind, the greatest and most beneficent triumphs of engineering that the world has seen.

Seasons of irrigation.

Even during the monsoon season rice is benefited by an occasional watering. But generally the crops are watered during the cold and hot seasons. During the monsoon the wells are unused, and the river floods overtop the canal dams and flow seawards down the river channels. In tracts, however, such as the western Panjáb and Sindh, which are rainless or nearly so, water is needed at all times; and here the flood waters of the rivers are led off on to the land by canals which need no river dam to fill them.

The agricultural implements of the country are

simple in design and rough in construction. Holdings are generally so small that there is little object in appliances for saving labour. The plough is a single-tyned grubber—heavy when for use in black soil, but in the rice districts so light as to be easily carried on the shoulder. Where crops are drilled, three tubes of bamboo, meeting in a cup above and below connected with a light three-tyned grubber, serve the purpose. For lifting water from short depths men employ the lever lift that is so familiar to those who visit Egypt. A long pole is hinged to the top of a post, one arm being longer than the other. The long arm carries a rope and bucket, the short arm is weighted so as to be easily pulled down when the bucket at the other end of the pole is full. In Madras attention is attracted by the curious sight of a man balanced upon the short arm, and raising and depressing the long arm by walking up and down his end of the lever. Where the depth is greater the Persian wheel is used, and from still greater depths water is raised in a leather bucket to which bullocks are roped. They drag up the bucket by rushing down an inclined ramp, of length approximately equal to the depth of the well. In some places the bucket empties itself, on reaching the well-head, through a tube which then opens automatically: in other places it is emptied by hand. Sugar-cane is pressed in some tracts in a wooden vertical roller-mill, sometimes with two, sometimes with three rollers; elsewhere in a huge pestle and mortar, the pestle being turned round the mortar, pressing against its sides, by an ingenious application of bullock power. Generally, close inquiry will reveal circumstances which have led to the adoption of one form or another;

Field implements.

and the variety of Indian farming implements could furnish a text for a discourse upon the ingenuity of man in adapting himself to his environment. Bullocks tread out the corn, not assisted, as they are in Egypt, by any mechanical contrivance.

The laws of Manu which, with the Vedas, form the most sacred portion of the Hindu canon, discourage the pursuit of agriculture by the 'twice-born' on account of the risk of killing earth-worms, and of the hardships suffered by plough-bullocks. In these circumstances one would not expect to find cultivation as zealous and as thorough as it is in Egypt or China, and much of the Indian land is very carelessly farmed. But the lower castes take a more practical view. Generally they are exceedingly industrious—their fields are indeed cultivated like gardens—and they have at their fingers' end the simple rules of experience which vary from place to place and contribute quite as much as science to successful farming. Their ploughing may be light, but it is repeated over and over again until the soil is ground into the tilth of a garden seed-bed. They probably obtain from their land all that it can yield without an expenditure on manure which is beyond their resources. It is possible that cultivators may be assisted very greatly by the co-operative movement which was initiated during the days of Lord Curzon's viceroyalty. The Government has lent its influence, and the services of many of its most capable officers, towards the establishment of co-operative loan societies on the general lines of those by which Raffheisen and other reformers have revolutionised the life of the peasant farmers in parts of Germany, Italy, and France.

Character of husbandry.

Co-operative banks.

India possesses already nearly 2000 of these societies with a membership of 185,000 and a working capital of half a million sterling. They are at present under close supervision, and it remains to be seen whether the movement can gain sufficient vitality to progress under the moderate control which the State could afford to give, if it extended itself greatly. In the suspicious atmosphere of the East a few cases of misappropriation and bankruptcy would probably set it back very severely. But this new development offers most hopeful possibilities in a country that lacks capital; and by introducing into Indian society a new principle of union it may assist in dissolving the prejudices which so rigidly circumscribe the life of the people.

Yield of the land.

For a densely populated country with much alluvial soil, India does not yield generously to her cultivators. Where wheat is manured and irrigated, it will give twenty-four bushels to the acre, or rather more: if irrigated without manure, the crop will rarely exceed twenty bushels; and over the large area which receives neither water nor manure — quite one-third of the total — the average is only ten or eleven bushels to the acre. So small a return may suffice for profit on the prairie farms of Canada and America. But it allows a very meagre subsistence to a man farming eight or ten acres. Indian cotton, on an average, certainly does not yield 100 lbs. of cotton lint per acre: this is less than a quarter of the average produce of Egyptian cotton-fields. One field with another, an acre of sugar-cane does not yield as much as a ton; in the West Indies the average produce approaches three tons. Although India is the home of the sugar-cane, she is obliged to import sugar for her own consumption. A very large portion of the Indian soil appears to have been worn down by continuous cropping to a condition of impoverished stability: it contains no stock of soluble plant-food, and the crops are supported by the quantity that can annually be freed for them. In these circumstances they cannot be expected to yield well, though they may be able to yield without diminution for long periods to come. The improvement of agriculture is, of course, an urgent question. For many years past it has received the attention of Government. But, until recently, finances have not sufficed for the establishment of agricultural departments on an adequate basis with a proper staff of experts. Here and there some improvements have been adopted: iron sugar-mills and ploughs have been purchased by the thousand. But it cannot be said that, so far, the State has succeeded in inducing the people to adopt crops or methods which are not recommended by long-standing custom.

Tea-gardens.

In telling the story of his adventurous journey from Tonquin to India—across the head-waters of the Mekong and Irrawaddy—Prince Henri d'Orléans mentions the astonishment with which, on emerging into the Assam valley from the dense jungle that veils the borders of southern China, he found himself suddenly transported into a European civilisation. For miles and miles tea-gardens extend, with their neat rows of flat clipped tea-bushes, intersected by well-kept roads, which at intervals run up to substantial homesteads—the tea-drying house, the engine-house, and the planter's bungalow. Every ten miles or so, a grassy clearing amidst the tea, with a little thatched club-house, testify to the planter's devotion to polo. Sixty years ago these gardens were all under thick tropical jungle or high grass, through which one could pass only by following the tracks of wild buffalo or rhinoceros. Now tea-gardens extend down both valleys of Assam on the slopes of the hills that fringe them. They have been opened in north Bengal at the foot of the Himalayas: they extend up 7000 feet into the Himalayas, and in the hills of the Madras presidency they afford glimpses of an industry which, across the sea straits, has clothed with an entirely new vegetation the hills of Ceylon. Tea was introduced from China, but the tea-tree was subsequently found growing abundantly in the hills of Assam, and Assam seed has been substituted with advantage for the Chinese variety. The English capital invested in Indian tea-gardens is about 20 millions sterling, and the exports bring a return to the country of £6 millions annually. India supplies more than half of the English consumption: of the balance three-quarters is provided by Ceylon. A few educated Indians have taken to tea-planting, but speaking generally, the industry is in European hands, and tea is grown practically for export only. Less than a twentieth of the produce is consumed in India. The gardens are worked almost wholly by imported labour, and in India they provide work and subsistence for half a million persons of the coolie class who, but for this new opening, would have been pinched for a livelihood, and by their competition in the labour market would have pressed others. A very large proportion of them settle down near their garden and take up plots of rice land. The hospitality of the tea-planters, and the open-air geniality of their lives, recall features which Thackeray has associated for us with the Southern States of America.

xii.—Famine.

Failure of rain: immensity of the disaster.

For a century past the British Government of India has from time to time been assailed with the bitter criticism with which Englishmen are wont to requite the achievements of their kindred; and some of its denunciators have not scrupled to avow that it is responsible for the famines which afflict the country so terribly. It is hardly to be supposed that these critics attribute to the Government the failure of rain which causes famine, though their charges sometimes appear to be coloured by some vague implication of this sort. Their direct contention is that the Indian people succumb to famine only because they are poor, and that for their poverty the British Government is to blame. But if once the nature of an Indian famine is realised it becomes a marvel that the people should support so tremendous a catastrophe as hardily as they do. The failure of a year's rain means that fully two-thirds of the population are out of employment for a year, and that their difficulties are aggravated by a sudden rise in prices. Let one endeavour to realise what would be the condition of our great industrial centres if afflicted by such a calamity—if all factories were closed down for twelve months, and if the price of a loaf rose to a shilling. Can it be supposed for a moment that in such a case hundreds of thousands would not perish unless relieved by the State or by charity organised on an enormous scale? And what of the wreckage of civil government, of the riots, of the armed repression that would ensue? In India the people suffer in silence, and bravely do their best to meet their misfortunes. It never enters their heads to force the State to assist them. For one thing, their ancient traditions give them no reason to expect such assistance.

Endurance of the people.

The failure of a single harvest is equivalent to six months' unemployment. But this misfortune does not ordinarily entail the grant of State famine relief. The people sustain it with such assistance as is given by suspending the collection of rents and land revenue, and by the making of recoverable advances: they do not starve or lose condition unless the preceding harvests have been unfortunate. That a poor country should have this power of endurance is very remarkable. It is due in the main to the efficacy of the family and the caste as institutions for mutual relief. There is no man but has some one to turn to in misfortune—some one who, having this world's goods, cannot repulse him without moral offence. Indeed it might perhaps be argued that caste owes its extraordinary development to apprehension of famine. Caste certainly establishes some such responsibility for relief as was thrown upon English villages by the Poor Law settlement. It may then be said that, so long as losses are limited to a single harvest, the Indian people relieve the distress of individuals by private charity: it is only when confronted by a more serious calamity that they throw themselves upon the hands of the State.

Without doubt the people of India would suffer less

severely, when rain fails them, if so many of them were not dependent upon the land for their support, if a larger proportion were engaged in manufacture. Industrial enterprises are steadily advancing. Mills at Bombay, Dehli, Cawnpore, and Calcutta maintain over half a million of the poorer classes in permanent employment: the tea-gardens which British capital has opened out have placed another half-million coolies out of reach of famine. But from the beginning of its history India has been an agricultural country, and it is absurd to suppose that the British or any other Government could have changed its character within the compass of a century.

Too many subsist on the land.

In treating of the Indian rainfall we have indicated some reasons for the opinion that the Bombay branch of the monsoon should not be regarded as one of the unchanging forces of nature, and that its strength and direction may not improbably have suffered material alterations during the past twenty centuries. But there is no reason whatever for believing that its character has been permanently changed within the last two or three hundred years. Certainly during the past thirteen years it has shown less steadiness than during the thirteen years preceding. But from the time of Joseph it has been noticed that fluctuations of weather commonly occur in cycles; and there is nothing which might lead us to apprehend that, the lean years once past, fat years will not succeed them. The historians of Moghal rule were interested in the fortune of dynasties, not in the fate of peoples; but incidental references leave us in no doubt as to the occurrence in their days of famines of lurid intensity,

Famines not increasing in frequency.

driving mankind even to acts of cannibalism. Two centuries before the establishment of British rule a Dutch writer mentions a famine which absolutely depopulated the rich province of Gujarát in the Bombay presidency. The careful researches of the Famine Commission of 1882 showed that no less than seventeen severe famines, affecting the crops of twenty-one years, had occurred in one part of India or another during the preceding century, and that somewhere in the country a famine must be expected in one year out of five. The ten years 1891 to 1900 were extraordinarily unfortunate; during four of them famine overspread large tracts of the country. But the decade 1861 to 1870, a generation earlier, was similarly unfortunate. And in the earlier famines, owing to difficulties of transport, food supplies actually ran short, so that no expenditure of money could save the people from starvation. Fifty years ago there were only 300 miles of railway in India; the mileage is now a hundredfold greater; and since no famine extends over the whole of the continent, there is always grain available for the famine-stricken and means to bring it within their reach. Should India fail, Burma can come, and has come, to her assistance.

Famine weather.

When the monsoon rains fail they rarely fail from the beginning. Sufficient rain usually falls to enable the people to sow their crops—and suffer the loss of seed grain as well as of harvest. Then the clouds withdraw: the sky loses its blue in a thick haze: the wind grows dry and hot again, and the crops wither. Never can the skies be assailed with such concerted longings as when the millions of India look upwards for the rain-clouds that are failing them. But some hope still remains. The summer crops may be past saving; but, should rain fall in October or November, the cold-weather crops will be sown—and on a greatly extended area—and hardship will not deepen into severe famine. If the autumn rains also fail, famine descends upon the country and prices leap upwards. Those whose land can be irrigated are safe—indeed they profit by the rise in prices—and the cultivators strenuously exert themselves to procure water, digging wells where possible, baling water out of village ponds and streams, and often conducting it long distances to their fields in earthen channels. The most prudent of them sow catch-crops, such as carrots, which need but a few weeks to come to maturity. By December unmistakable signs of famine appear in wandering beggars, emaciated and in rags, who flock into the towns and to the railway stations, and make pitiful appeals to casual charity. So deep is their distress that they will eat any food that is given them; and one of the surest indications of the pressure of famine is the disregard by the poorest of their ordinary caste rules. These are the paupers of the village communities—persons that are ordinarily supported by the charity of Hindu households, which are now compelled to refuse alms in defence of their own children. Until within the last ten years the appearance of these vagrants was regarded as the earliest indication that the time had come for the initiation of State measures of relief. Works were then opened for the able-bodied, and poorhouses for indigent beggars. But when distress has become so acute as to drive thousands from their villages, heavy mortality is unavoidable; and the

Signs of famine—wandering beggars

present policy is to ascertain the existence of famine by careful local inquiries, not to await ocular demonstration of its effects—to relieve the village paupers in their villages, and to regard the need of poorhouses rather as a sign of administrative failure. These poorhouses were indeed terrible studies in human misery and degradation. In a single district there might be four or five of them, each containing from a thousand to two thousand refugees. Whatever care be taken, it was difficult to enforce discipline and the rules of sanitation on a crowd of people who had been brutalised by suffering. It was noticeable that in this extremity of degradation women retained less sense of decency than men, and gave far more trouble to the superintendent. They also showed beyond doubt far more capacity for resisting hardship, and for recovering from its effects. When inspecting a poorhouse one almost invariably found that the women were putting on flesh much more rapidly than the men. Few poorhouses escaped violent outbreaks of cholera, and sometimes the cemeteries attached to them were almost as crowded as their wards. A peculiar difficulty was occasioned by the necessity of providing for hundreds of little children who were orphaned or had been deserted by their parents. Under the pressure of want mothers will desert their children—will even sell them. The sufferings of children in famine time are especially pitiful. One cold-weather morning I came across two little boys sitting crouched over a fire they had kindled by the roadside. I told them that they would warm themselves quicker if they took a run. 'If we ran,' one replied, 'we should get

—formerly relieved in poorhouses.

Orphans and deserted children.

hungry.'[1] Hundreds of these children are taken charge of by charitable Mission associations, but hundreds remain on the hands of the State during the period of the famine. On the return of prosperity most of them find homes again in their villages. The discovery of their belongings—often a tedious and difficult business—is the last action of a famine campaign.

It is not an ordinary function of the State to provide food at a month or two's notice for millions of people, and the principles and procedure of famine administration cannot be elaborated offhand or without much experience. Since 1882 three Commissions have studied the subject, and it is only within the last eight years that the State has finally elaborated a policy which can be trusted to save life without much needless waste of public money. It does not ask the feeble-bodied to leave their villages and flock to relieving centres: it offers them subsistence at their homes; and, if this concession may occasionally admit to State charity those who do not really need it and would not walk some distance to obtain assistance, it forestalls much hardship that would end in mortality. To obtain trustworthy information, and to distribute home-relief, an effective village agency is needed, and fortunately in most provinces such an agency is available in the village accountants that have already been mentioned as included in the village staff of communal servants. It has always been the business of these accountants to keep a record of the holding and leasing of land, of rents due, and of rental pay-

Evolution of present system of relief.

[1] My wife took charge of these children and brought them up till they could be put out into the world.

ments—in fact, to serve as petty notaries public. During the past thirty years they have been systematically trained in these duties (which are essential to the efficacy of legislation for the protection of tenants), and have also been entrusted with the recording of areas cultivated and cropped, and with the submission of periodical information in regard to the character of the season. They have thus become State as well as Village officials, and the Government has accepted responsibility for their remuneration. Without such a staff the grant of relief to the afflicted at their homes would have been almost impossible: with its assistance the only difficulty to be met is that of effective supervision.

Relief of incapable paupers.

As soon, then, as reports make it clear that famine is impending, a list is prepared for each village, showing feeble-bodied paupers who have no definite claims for maintenance upon any well-to-do family, but who are usually supported by general charity; and, when famine descends, the first step is to grant these persons fortnightly allowances, sufficient at the current price of grain to provide them with subsistence. Wandering is prevented, and there is no need of poorhouses except for those who flock into British territory from the Native States. These States undertake to relieve famine more or less on the lines followed in British India; but their resources are in many cases slender, and their staffs too weak to support a sudden strain. Famine-stricken people cross their borders in thousands and add very seriously to the responsibilities of British relieving officers.

For children it is necessary to make special provision. Unwelcome though it may be to those who idealise human nature, it is a fact that motherly love dissolves under the stress of privation, and that, even when women are granted relief for their children and themselves, they will stint the children in their share of the bounty. Experience has shown that if children are starving they must be relieved directly and not through their parents—that is to say, by the distribution of cooked food, not of cash allowances. A children's relief-kitchen is opened within walking distance of each village, in the charge of a village schoolmaster, of the police, or of a private individual who will give up his time to its management. Arrangements are of the simplest: the food is a mixture of boiled rice and pulse, which is distributed by measure according to the size of the child. The children fashion for themselves leaf-cups and platters, and about meal-time one may see them trooping to the kitchen from all directions, with their tin tickets of admission slung round their necks, and, as often as not, wearing their leaf-cups on their heads. Ordinarily, about a hundred children are fed at each kitchen, but the numbers sometimes rise to seven or eight hundred, when the fair distribution of the food is no light task. Indian children easily conform to rules of discipline and quietly take their seats in orderly rows. In the famine of 1899 it was not unfrequently the practice for the children to rise before they commenced eating and cry out 'All hail! Queen Victoria.' There is a popular saying that children have no caste, and Hindu prejudices are not offended by their eating food cooked by strangers. But there was, nevertheless, to begin with, some feeling against it, and this served a

Children's relief-kitchen.

useful purpose in discouraging from attendance all but the really necessitous. But the feeling wore off, and care became necessary to exclude the children of families which could afford to support them. As a rule, the manager, whether schoolmaster, police-officer or private individual, used his knowledge honestly and intelligently. Only Brahmin cooks were employed: but their ministrations were by no means always accepted, and I have seen low-caste children that were brought to the kitchen starving and emaciated, weep bitterly when told to eat the food set before them—even when encouraged to eat it by their own caste people—and only yield when its smell was too much for them. But these suspicions soon gave way, and the children's kitchen became quite the most popular of the relief measures undertaken by the State. Human nature is at its best when concerned with children, and, considering the opportunities that offered, there was surprisingly little peculation. Sympathy was strengthened by a text which says that 'the sacrifice of cooked food draws down rain,' and evidences of gratitude were more than usually conspicuous. The year after the famine, talking to the people of a village which had suffered heavily, I noticed the children coming from school, and remarked that they looked well enough. 'They are yours,' the village headman exclaimed; 'had it not been for the kitchen they would all have died.'

Relief-works for the unemployed.

But when numbers are concerned, village pauper relief and children's kitchens are of much less importance than the relief-works which provide employment for the able-bodied. During a famine the Indian Government concedes to the needy the 'right to work' that is so earnestly upheld by the English Labour party; and, forthwith, it finds itself confronted with two perils — that of wasting public funds, and demoralising the people, by giving relief to the undeserving, and that of denying assistance to those in want by overscrupulousness of administration. It is necessary to impose tests: that the people should come some distance to obtain work, that they should leave their homes and live on the works, that their wages should suffice for subsistence only, that a daily task should be performed. But these tests cannot always be trusted to eliminate the unworthy: near every relief-work there are numbers of villages the inhabitants of which can attend to work but sleep at home: a subsistence wage which just suffices for an individual is more than sufficient when it is paid to each member of a large family: when people crowd to a relief-work in thousands the enforcement of a proper task is at the outset impossible. Nor are these tests of constant value: when the people are unaccustomed to relief measures they may be too strict; when the people become habituated to them (as, for instance, when one famine succeeds another at a short interval) they may be too lenient. Famine-relief administration is then an arduous struggle to avoid extravagance on the one hand and mortality on the other, by the use of standards which are of imperfect application and of fluctuating value: and, when called to the bar of the various Commissions which have been appointed to consider its results, it has been accused at one time on the first, and at another time on the second of these counts. But it is, at all events, free from one great difficulty. It is not complicated by the objections of trade unionism to the grant of less than a full market wage; and the great success which, on the whole, it has displayed is entirely due to the freedom it has enjoyed in fixing the rates of famine wages. These wages are paid to each man, woman, and child separately: they are calculated to meet the needs of individuals, not of families. A male worker has no surplus after feeding himself; but his wife and children earn wages with him, or, if they are unable to work, are relieved gratuitously as dependents. The applicants for relief are graded according to their physical capacity: for the men, women, and children of each grade a task is determined, on the performance of which they receive a money wage, sufficient at the prices of the day to provide them with a full working diet. The wage is altered from time to time as prices fluctuate. And what if they fail to perform the appointed task? Till eight years ago they were, nevertheless, entitled to receive a 'minimum' wage which was sufficient for bare subsistence. The object of the State being to save life, in principle no famine-stricken person, however disinclined for work, should receive less than subsistence. But large numbers took advantage of this rule to supplement their private resources by idly hanging round a relief-work, and, under the recommendations of the Famine Commission of 1901, it has been abrogated. As matters now stand, a man who fails to perform his task is paid only in proportion to the work he has performed, those incapable of work remaining, however, entitled to gratuitous relief. The terms upon which workers are now paid resemble those of ordinary contract—the amount of wages depending on the amount of work accomplished—except that no person may earn more than the famine wage. If this limitation were not imposed a man might earn enough to keep his wife and family, while throwing them on to the care of the State—and this, too, by work which is generally not of much public value. For the only business upon which famine workers can be employed is earth-work—the making of roads, or the excavation of tanks. The localities in which these improvements are undertaken depend not upon the public need of them, but upon the areas that are afflicted by distress, and much of the work that is performed is practically useless—may indeed be worse than useless, as it may burden local finance with the upkeep of roads that are of no real public utility. And a further restrictive measure has been necessary. A relief-work may adequately meet existing distress by providing for (say) a fifth of the population of the tract which it serves. But from villages that are situated in its close vicinity it frequently attracts half the population or even more. Most provincial governments have therefore reserved discretion to exclude persons whom local inquiry shows to be in no need of relief—a development of the system of local investigation, as opposed to automatic check, which has proved so helpful in dealing with the needs of village paupers and young children.

The numbers on a relief-work are ordinarily limited to 5000, but in times of stress they may rise to double this number or even more. For two or three miles across country there extends a long-drawn swarm of humanity, the men digging earth on either side of the new roadway, the women and children carrying it on to the road

Management of a relief-work.

embankment and consolidating it. Behind the lines of borrow pits are the rough grass shanties in which the people take shelter at night. At intervals there are booths where boiled or filtered water is distributed, and where grain dealers expose their wares. Areas set apart for sanitary purposes are carefully flagged off. There is a hospital and a children's kitchen. There may be twenty or more of these works in a single district. Indeed the responsibilities of the Indian Government in time of serious famine are staggeringly heavy: during the famine of 1899 the number of persons on its hands reached at one time four millions, and over large areas it supported a fifth of the population. The most active supervision is required to maintain the observance of rules and to prevent peculation. In India there is no reserve from which European agency can be drawn for particular purposes. Some British officers are borrowed from the army, and it is difficult to rate too highly the energy and resourcefulness of these young Englishmen in dealing with circumstances that are quite new to them. But the control of relief operations practically falls upon the ordinary staff of Government officials, in addition to their normal duties, and almost every Englishman lives in the saddle. The native officials—a large proportion of them in merely temporary employ—work as a rule with zeal and integrity. But money is being spent abundantly; ordinary account rules are relaxed, and not a few subordinates yield to temptation. In addition to this danger there are others which result from the reluctance of native officials to accept responsibility. I once came across a work on which starving people had received no pay for several days because the officer in charge—perfectly honest and well-meaning—found himself some rupees short in balancing his account, and was afraid to spend more before he reconciled the discrepancy. And during the hot-weather months there is the overshadowing dread of cholera. Few relief-works can expect to escape it entirely. Hunger is less terrible, and the people abscond, to be collected elsewhere with difficulty; or works are broken up and the relief camps shifted, with desperate trouble, to other localities. Whatever be done great mortality from cholera is unavoidable. Arriving one morning at a work on which several thousands were employed, I found that they had all run away, leaving between two and three hundred dead or dying on the ground. It had been impossible to organise a special hospital here, and all that we could do was to administer doses of brandy and chlorodyne to those who were alive till means of transporting them to hospital could be arranged. Such an experience is by no means an infrequent incident of famine duty. To localise the effects of such outbreaks endeavours are made to employ the people, when possible, on minor works in their villages, especially during the hot-weather months. Relief may in this case become too attractive: but in some provinces successful endeavours have been made to exclude the undeserving, by limiting admission to ticket-holders.

Incidental measures of relief.

The efforts of the State to provide food and employment are supplemented by special measures which put heart into the people as well as strengthen their resources. Amongst the many activities of the Indian Government is that of an agricultural land bank: it makes advances to cultivators at low rates of interest for the construction of wells or tanks and the purchase of seed and plough-cattle. In ordinary years this loan business is not very considerable, the advances aggregating less than half a million sterling, but in years of famine it expands to three or four times this amount, and, although the advances are supposed to be recoverable, a large proportion of them is, as a matter of fact, remitted. Advances are made under special rules to the large community of hand-weavers, whose fingers would lose touch for their looms if hardened by the use of spade and mattock. Famine-stricken India owes much to the charity of the English people. During the two great famines which occurred between the years 1896 and 1900, no less than a million and a half sterling was subscribed, mostly in the United Kingdom. It was spent to the immense advantage of the people in the provision of clothing, of extra medical comforts, and in grants for seed, grain, and bullocks to ruined cultivators. The collection of the Government land revenue is suspended, and much of it is ultimately remitted altogether. In 1896-97 the State relinquished in this manner over a million sterling. Under the existing law suspension or remission of land revenue obliges landlords to suspend or remit their rents, so that the concession finds its way to those who are most in need of it.

Success in saving life.

In its struggles with the two severe famines which occurred during the decade 1891-1900 the State spent over eleven and a half millions sterling, excluding the cost of such indirect measures of relief as remissions of revenue and of advances made to the cultivators. What success did it attain in preventing mortality? The registration of births and deaths in India is at no time very reliable. In rural areas it can only be based upon the periodical reports of illiterate village watchmen. In famine times this agency is necessarily disorganised, and little trust can be placed upon the published statistics of current mortality. A better indication is obtained by comparing the census figures for the beginning and end of the period. These show that the population of the British districts that were affected by famine decreased by over two millions. In Native territory the decrease was very much larger—close upon five millions, in spite of an expenditure on relief measures (assisted by loans of over £2 millions from the British Government) which drove many States to the verge of bankruptcy. But if we regard not the dead but the living, and inquire how many lives were saved by the £11½ millions expended, we shall gain a better idea of the obligations of the people to the State. Had the population of British districts suffered as heavily as that of the Native States, their mortality would have amounted to at least 7 millions, instead of 2¼ millions. If, making some allowance for relief that at times reaches the undeserving, we take credit for the lives of only those that were a full three months on the hands of the State, the number of lives saved is 3 millions in the first, and 3½ millions in the second famine—no unworthy return for the money expended.

Rapid recovery from famine.

The mortality that occurred, severe though it may be, is really trifling compared with that which attended famines a generation ago. It is evident from the reports of those days that large tracts of country were depopulated, and for several years lay desolate. At the present time nothing is more marvellous than the rapid recovery of famine-stricken districts. The British districts that suffered between 1891 and 1900, in two years recovered their full area of cultivation, and by a phenomenally high birth-rate the population strives to restore its numbers. In former days the young and strong perished along with the old and the weak. Those who now succumb are confined to the latter classes, owing partly to the generous distribution of relief, but partly also to an increase in normal resources. There are proofs that in Upper India the lower classes of the population have gained strength to withstand distress. Wages have risen greatly, owing in a measure to expanding industry, though also no doubt to the diminution of numbers that has resulted from past mortality. The extension of irrigation has for thousands of square miles rendered famines profitable (in increased prices) instead of disastrous; and the great enhancement that has occurred in the value of land enables the cultivating classes to borrow more readily to meet exceptional misfortune.

Famine indebtedness.

Their debts remain as a depressing heritage. Successful attempts that in the Central Provinces were made to lighten this burden are worth mention to illustrate the enormous influence for good that is possessed by the Indian Government, and the benefits which it can impart by exerting it courageously. In these provinces the effects of two successive famines had been aggravated by virulent attacks of rust and blight in the years preceding; and, owing to one cause or the other, many districts had, over a period of seven years, only gathered half their normal produce. The mass of the tenants had naturally fallen into hopeless bankruptcy. Crops having failed them, they had borrowed, mostly in grain for sowings and for subsistence, at from twenty-five to fifty per cent. compound interest, and were so overwhelmed with debts that improving harvests merely gave occasion for mortgagees to foreclose or for landlords to eject. The situation was desperate, and the Government took courage to apply a special remedy. If private creditors would consent to abate their claims to amounts which the tenants could pay off within a reasonable period, the Government offered to submit its claims for arrears of land revenue and cultivating advances to a similar abatement. These claims were not inconsiderable, but were trifling compared with those of private creditors. For each group of villages an arbitration board was formed, composed of three or more non-officials, who had a general acquaintance with the circumstances of those who came before them; and creditors were invited to submit their claims to these tribunals and to agree to their arbitration. Fortunately for the success of the operations, it was determined to make no attempt to settle the precise amount owed by each debtor—an inquiry which would have provoked endless wrangling. The function of the board was, after roughly determining the indebtedness of each man, to settle how much he could pay within a period of from seven to ten years, and to distribute the instalments among the creditors, the Government included. It may be imagined that it was only after long and patient negotiation that creditors were induced to accept this procedure. Most tenants were in debt to more than one person, and if one of the creditors stood out, proceedings were blocked. In the end, to the lasting credit of landlords and money-lenders, the arbitration was accepted by practically all of them. The awards were cast in a form which gave them legal validity, and the general result was that in the five districts that had suffered most acutely, debts amounting to some millions sterling were written off, and thousands of families were rescued from degradation.

The people not pauperised.

When good rain falls, employment is again available, the relief-works are closed, and assistance is gradually withdrawn from the weak and helpless. In a couple of months the people settle down to their former habits, and one may ride about the country unassailed by the complaints of a single beggar. It is immensely to the credit of Indian famine administration that it does not demoralise the people. It is absolutely uninfluenced by the false sentiment that relieves itself by granting charity—and hopes for gratitude. In its campaign against famine the Indian Government achieves one of the dreams of socialist enthusiasts—but only because it is logical, disinterested, and despotic as well as benevolent.

xiii.—Manufactures and Commerce.

THE trappings and furniture with which we surround ourselves are collected for purposes rather of ostentation than of enjoyment. It is in town life that the desire of display and feelings of rivalry have their most effective opportunity, and it has always been to towns that artificers and artists have looked for their customers and their patrons. In the country, released from these influences, men cheerfully revert towards barbarian simplicity. Nine-tenths of the Indian people live in villages, and their wants are practical, not sentimental or artistic. They are, moreover, generally too poor to afford expenditure upon luxuries. The manufactures of India are then, on the whole, severely utilitarian, and, apart from craft-implements and coarse earthen pots, mainly consist in the weaving of cotton-cloth, the shaping of metal vessels for cooking and eating purposes, and the making of rough shoes.

Limited needs of rural community.

In some parts of India cloth-weaving is a domestic industry. In Assam most families possess a small portable loom on which the women employ their spare time, keeping the web stretched for the passage of the shuttle by fastening one end to a peg in the ground and the other end to a band passing round the waist. But generally in northern India weaving is a separate trade, and is in in the hands of one of the Hindu low castes and

Cloth-weaving.

a particular community of Muhammadans. There is in most large villages a weavers' quarter. Looking through a small doorway you will see the weaver sitting at his loom in a little chamber, the floor of which is sunk well below ground level: the village roadway outside is encumbered by long warps, stretched for sizing, that are suspended horizontally between low supports. Weaving has been practised in India from immemorial antiquity: labour is cheap, and the country is the home of the cotton-plant. But by an extraordinary transplantation of industry the centre of weaving has been transferred to Lancashire, where manufacturers have to pay high wages, and to fetch the raw material from thousands of miles across the sea. So long as the Suez Canal was unopened and the Indian railway system undeveloped, the Indian hand-weavers could hold their own—at any rate for the coarser fabrics. They are now being driven out of employ by the cotton-mills of Lancashire, and by the mills which have been established in great numbers in Indian cities. The spinning of yarn by hand is now a dead industry: all the hand-weavers use mill-spun yarn. The imports of English cotton stuffs into India are sufficient to provide seven yards of material a year for every man, woman, and child of the population; another yard is added by the manufactures of the Indian cotton-mills. It is obvious that very little room is left for the hand-weavers' industry. No census of its production has been possible; but assuming that the weavers only use mill-spun yarn, the stuffs made by them annually supply about three yards of cloth per head of population. There has obviously been a very great displacement of labour, though it must be remembered that some portion of the imports is absorbed by increasing consumption.

Metal-work.

The manufacture of brass and copper vessels for cooking and eating is one of India's characteristic handicrafts. The raw metal is imported, since no copper-mines have been worked in India for many years past. In former days, families, with any pretence at respectability, prided themselves on their array of brightly scoured brass and copper, and only the poorest would use iron or white metal. Fashion is changing, and there is now a large import of ready-made white metal plates and dishes. The consumption of raw brass and copper is stationary, at the value of about a million sterling. But the fashioning of brass and copper vessels remains an extensive and flourishing industry. Brass is preferred by Hindus and copper by Muhammadans. The elegantly shaped water vessels in general use are cast: cooking-pans and eating-platters are hammered. Each process is in the hands of a separate trade caste. No native of India travels but carries with him a small metal jar with which he drinks, and, by pouring water on his hands, performs his ablutions. To illustrate the fanciful origin of many human habits, the vessels used by Muhammadans are fitted with spouts, like teapots, in deference to a verse in the Korán which enjoins that ablutions should be performed in running water.

Shoe-making.

Leather-dressing and shoemaking are in the hands of one of the very lowest castes, since the touching of cattle hides is abhorrent to Hindus. There are shoemakers in every village: in towns whole streets are occupied by them, but in the larger cities Chinamen are successfully competing in the industry. India exports hides in enormous quantities, and circumstances appear to favour the establishment of large leather factories for export manufacture. Two have been successfully founded, the pioneers having been given the security which a nascent industry requires (and which Free Trade refuses), by a large Government army contract. An export trade in boots and shoes has sprung up with Egypt and South Africa.

Urban demands.

The urban handicrafts of India, however interesting and artistic, are but small industries, and do not add materially to the wealth of the country. The most characteristic of them are cotton- and silk-weaving in coloured patterns (sometimes with an admixture of gold thread), dyeing, plain or in patterns, and embroidery in silk or in gold thread.

Fine Indian fabrics.

Since her trade first penetrated to Europe India has been renowned for her fine muslins and coloured calicoes. They are mentioned as imported by the Red Sea route at the commencement of our era, and they contributed largely to the trade which the Arabs, and almost every nation of Europe, have, in turn, struggled to capture. Less than two centuries ago the use of Indian calicoes threatened so seriously the English weaving industry that their importation was formally prohibited by statute. Laws may hasten or delay the defeat of a handicraft by machinery, but can scarcely affect the ultimate result. India has now lost her monopoly, and the manufacture of these fabrics is stagnant or declining. In former days she exported fine materials: at the present time her exports, though of infinitely greater value, are confined to plain fabrics for China and Japan. It is now difficult to procure the famous Dacca muslin, and no pieces are made such as, according to the traditional fineness, would pass through a ring. The home of cotton, India was also the home of the dyes that were employed to colour it—carthamine, Turkey red, lake (lac), turmeric, and indigo. They are all being displaced by the chemical dyes that are manufactured in Germany. But it should be remarked that, for the glaring colours that are now supplanting the more subdued tints of the East, public taste is responsible, since it is possible to dye artistically with chemical products.

Art wares.

Indian silver-plate, enamels, damascene-work, wood-carving, marquetry, and lacquer-work are familiar to the English public. Their manufacture generally flourished in the environment of Native courts, and their artificers subsist in places which were once the capitals of kingdoms. Our public galleries show that ancient work was often exceedingly beautiful, and that in present days very admirable specimens can be produced. Indian art manufactures generally show, however, a lack of neatness in finish which distinguishes them very markedly from those of China or Japan. Of late years some of these industries have been encouraged by the purchases of tourists, or by a limited demand for export; but the necessity of cheapness has demoralised craftmanship, and in modernising their patterns the artisans do not show the taste that would guide a living artistic skill.

While, however, the ancient industries of India are fading beneath the influence of modern competition, others of a more useful though less interesting description are rising to take their place.

Indian factories.

Fifty years ago there were only 10 cotton-mills in India: there are now 227, employing 225,000 hands. At that time no jute was woven in the country: the jute-mills which line the banks of the river at Calcutta now employ 187,000 hands, and produce goods worth £11 millions a year. If India is losing her silk-weaving industry, she has learnt to manipulate leather, manufactures of which at Bombay and Cawnpore are annually gaining in importance. The country possesses large resources in coal, iron-ore, and manganese. With the progress of railway construction coal-mining has developed and now employs 100,000 persons. Iron-works on any large scale have still to be established: hitherto this enterprise has been repressed by the competition of imported manufactures, but now, in the hands of an Indian capitalist, it has determined to try its fortune. Mica and manganese are quarried for export to the value of nearly a million sterling a year. On a general review it may be concluded that industrial undertakings are making steady if gradual progress, although as yet they hardly affect the export trade, except in manufactures of cotton and jute. During the last ten years the number of industrial establishments (including mines), employing 50 hands or over, has more than doubled, and the number of employés has increased by 60 per cent. Apart from cotton- and jute-mills and mines, most of these concerns are of a petty discription—brick and tile yards, saw-mills, cotton gins, and the like. But amongst them are six woollen-mills and nine paper-mills.

Indian commerce in its present development is

very largely the product of the Indian railways. Fifty years ago there were only 300 miles of railway in the country, and the total value of the sea-borne trade was less than £40 millions. The railway mileage is now over 30,000, and the value of the export and import trade has risen to £200 millions. Apart from the internal commerce which feeds the stream of exports or distributes the arriving imports, the railways have developed a traffic between the various provinces to an aggregate annual value of £90 millions. There is a coasting trade which is valued at £70 millions, and a trans-frontier trade by road of a value of £10 millions. Some of the railway-lines are of little but strategical importance, but taking all of them together, they not only pay interest on their capital, but in favourable years earn a handsome profit for the State. They carry grain at the extraordinarily low rate of a halfpenny per ton per mile. A passenger can travel ten miles for a penny. Their finances have not been burdened with heavy charges for land compensation. The Government takes up land at an equitable valuation, which can be called in question in the civil courts, but which is assessed in independence of influences that have made land charges so heavy an item in the capital expenditure of English railways. Influenced by facilities of inland transport, by the opening of the Suez Canal, and by the substitution of steam-vessels for sailing-ships, the trade of the country has grown enormously, and has completely changed its character. Formerly India exported valuable goods of small bulk: she now supplies the world with cheap raw produce. In part-payment

Effect of railways.

Growth of Indian trade.

she absorbs large quantities of gold and silver. But this has always been a peculiarity of the country. Pliny complains of the annual drain of specie to India, which in his time amounted to about half a million sterling. In the days of the East India Company—in 1834—it had risen to over nine millions. It is now nearly double this amount. Taking the exports at £115 millions, £80 millions are paid for by imports, £17 millions by treasure (imported privately), and £18 millions by disbursements made by the Indian Government to meet its Home charges—the expenditure, that is to say, for which it is responsible in England. Merchants who owe money in India, to pay for goods consigned to them, purchase from the Secretary of State bills on the Indian treasury. These Home charges were the immediate cause of a change in the Indian currency which must have touched very acutely the resources of the people.

Its peculiarity.

Forty years ago the value of the rupee in gold was approximately the tenth of a sovereign, or two shillings. Owing to the increased production of silver and to currency legislation demonetising it in Germany and elsewhere, the value of the rupee fell rapidly, and became subject to violent oscillations. The Home charges must be met in gold, and the Indian finances were dislocated by the rapid and irregular increases in the amounts of rupees that were required to provide the gold. By 1894 the rupee had fallen to thirteen pence, and the decrease in its gold value which had occurred during the past twenty years was annually costing the State the equivalent of three-quarters of a million sterling. Nor was this all. The continual

The Indian currency.

fluctuation of exchange value hampered commerce, since merchants were unable to foresee the gold value of their Indian obligations; and it checked the investment of British capital in India. It was accordingly decided to adopt measures to fix the value of the rupee as the fifteenth of a sovereign (1s. 4d.). They included the closure of the Mints to the coinage of silver on behalf of the public, the acceptance of sovereigns as legal tender, the unlimited exchanging by Government of rupees for sovereigns (and of sovereigns for rupees as far as practicable), and the establishment of a special Gold Currency Reserve. They have been quite successful in their object. But the closure of the Mints to the public depreciated silver still further, and the rupee which is now worth sixteen pence as a coin, as a piece of silver is worth ten pence only. This depreciation must have caused heavy losses to those whose savings were in the form of silver ornaments; and unfortunately these are with the poorer classes a favourite means of hoarding. On the other hand, the relief afforded to the State finances by standardising the value of the rupee undoubtedly saved the country from fresh taxation.

A token coinage: possible effect upon prices.

The rupee is now a token coin: it cannot without great loss be melted down or converted to jewellery, and there is a risk that the currency will fail to adjust itself to the actual requirements of the country, and that prices will be inflated by an overabundance of rupees. The Government has been unable to concede to the public the unlimited exchange of gold for silver: on the other hand, to meet urgent demands during the export season, it has been adding rupees to the currency at the rate of about £4 millions a year. During the last five years there has been a very extraordinary rise in agricultural prices, which has caused much hardship to families who live on fixed incomes. Prices fluctuate in India very widely with vicissitudes of seasons ; but until recently in years of good harvests they fell to a level which did not exceed by more than a quarter the height of a generation ago. But since 1905 they have steadily risen to more than double this height. There have been failures of crops in some provinces ; but they should not have sufficed to produce throughout the country a rise in prices so steady, so general, and so pronounced, and some authorities are of opinion that the cause is to be found in a redundancy of rupees. Others consider it to be merely an illustration of an upward tendency of agricultural values which is of world-wide extension The change has been of great economic importance, since it has had the effect of transferring very large sums of money to the country from the towns. It may account for some of the unrest which is now disturbing urban society.

The export trade.

The Indian export trade may be likened to the flowing of a reservoir of raw material. Taking its total annual value (exclusive of treasure) as £115 millions, no less than £70 millions consist of raw produce which is grown without much capital expenditure—cotton, jute, hides, grain, seeds, and wool. Tea and coffee (which require a heavy capital expenditure) contribute £8 millions, opium £6 millions, dye-stuffs (including lac and indigo) £4 millions. There remain £27 millions unaccounted for. Mill-made cotton yarn and piece goods (mostly exported to China and Japan) and jute cloth and bags make good £20 millions of them, leaving

£7 millions only for all other articles. Silk, which in the days of the East India Company was an export of much importance, is now imported in infinitely larger quantities than exported. The ladies of Europe no longer affect Indian silks, and the weavers of India have been impoverished by European competition. But in their day they have inflicted a like calamity on others. The competition of Indian silks ruined, for instance, the silk industry of Canterbury, which during the seventeenth century flourished exceedingly in the hands of Protestant refugees from the Netherlands and France, who found in England employment for their skill and an active sympathy for their religious convictions. The records of the Walloon and Huguenot Church of Canterbury exhibit copies of petition after petition in which these men bitterly complained of the cheapness and popularity of Indian silk goods. The Government responded with edicts prohibiting import or consumption. But the law was evaded, and by the middle of the eighteenth century the industry was practically extinct. The Indian silk trade has suffered less severely, since a good deal is still manufactured for the local market. Silk-growing is, however, an exotic in the country, if we omit from consideration the wild or semi-wild silks that are indigenous in central India and Assam. That the sugar trade should have suffered similar reverses is much more surprising, as sugar was for many centuries an exclusively Indian product. India no longer sells sugar: she buys it, and to a very large amount.

It must not, of course, be imagined that this export trade is not exceedingly profitable, though in the main it provides employment for agricultural labour only. Indeed its effect in distributing the profits of trade throughout the villages of the land is, from one point of view, beneficial for a poor country. But it does not offer much encouragement to the growth of town as opposed to country life, and leaves the people but little affected in their habits by their introduction to the commerce of the world.

Exports and employment.

The import trade is of a much less simple character. Its amount (exclusive of treasure) may be put at £80 millions. By far the most important items are cotton fabrics and metal goods, which contribute respectively £27 and £14 millions. A leading feature of the metal trade is the outstripping of iron by steel. Their imports are now of about equal value, at £2½ millions: thirty years ago, when iron was imported to the value of a million, the trade in steel was quite insignificant. It speaks satisfactorily for the growth of Indian manufactures that the country's requirements of unwrought metals should have increased sevenfold during this period. But the unwrought metals which India purchases are still equivalent to only one-eighth of those she takes in manufactured condition. It must be realised, moreover, that railway material constitutes over a quarter of the metal imports, while cutlery and hardware contribute only a seventh. Sugar is imported to a value of £6 millions, and silk goods to a value of £1½ millions. Other items of importance are apparel and woollen goods, £3½ millions; kerosene oil, £2 millions; liquors, glass-ware, and jewellery, a million each; paper and matches, half a million each; umbrellas and toys, half a million between them. These heads account for

The import trade.

three-quarters of the imports: the balance consists of a great diversity of petty luxuries, many of which find their way to every little mart about the country.

Treasure.

Gold and silver are imported, in approximately equal values, to an amount of £17 millions. This is exclusive of the value of the treasure exported (chiefly consisting in gold produced at the Mysore mines), and is in fact the net amount which annually finds its way amongst the people, and is hoarded by them.

Countries sharing in India's trade: Exports.

In her export trade India is a market for the world. She offers raw produce of kinds that are needed in most countries, that in some cases she alone can supply, and that are accordingly excluded by no hostile tariffs. The supplies that are purchased from her by the United Kingdom are about a quarter of her total exports, and show no marked tendency to increase. Amongst her other customers Germany is the chief, taking 11 per cent.: the United States and China follow, each with 8 or 9 per cent., France with 6 per cent., Belgium and Japan each with 5 per cent., Austria and the Straits Settlements each with 4 per cent. There is a steady market for cotton in Japan, for jute in France, Germany, and the United States, and for opium in China. Oil seeds are pretty regularly exported to Germany, Holland, Belgium, France, and Italy. For the rest, the Indian produce which each country desires varies each year with its own conditions and the Indian prices. Indian wheat finds its way on occasions over the whole of western Europe. Her rice may be despatched in large quantities to Argentina, Arabia, or Japan, as well as to Austria, Germany, and Holland.

Of the import trade into India the United Kingdom has always held and still holds the lion's share.

—Imports. British manufactures form two-thirds of the imports, and they have risen in value steadily if not very rapidly—by 18 per cent. during the last ten years. But they do not maintain a steady level. In 1898 they were less by 8 per cent. than in 1894. During the last ten years imports from Germany and Belgium have doubled, owing chiefly to sales of cheap metal goods. There has also been a large increase in imports from the United States; but they chiefly consist in kerosene oil, and have developed at the expense of supplies from Russia. Making, however, every allowance for these increases, the market which any country but the United Kingdom secures in India remains inconsiderable. Germany and Belgium do the largest business; but their contribution to the import trade is only 4 per cent. each. The share of no other country is much above 2 per cent.

It seems clear that had India been able to offer capitalists the security of a protective tariff she would have profited by a more rapid development of industrial activity, and could have advanced her manufactures beyond cotton stuffs and gunny bags. In some respects her conditions are precisely those which the most earnest free-traders will admit as justifying the nursing use of a tariff. Her people are poor, because they are crowded in the fields: she has to her hand raw material for manufacture, with an abundant supply of labour which is extraordinarily cheap if of rather poor quality. From time to time efforts have been made to establish new industries. Cotton-weaving

India and free trade.

has succeeded after many reverses. Jute-weaving has been encouraged by very special natural advantages. Other large manufactures have been attempted, but have been driven from the field by the cheapness of the imported goods that compete with them. It may be urged that Indians are not ready to engage in manufacturing enterprises, and that a tariff would have raised prices for the many without creating better employment for the few. But this can be said no longer, for there are at present evident signs of a desire for industrial employ. Technical schools are crowded with boys of good caste who, a few years ago, would have scorned instruction that was not literary. Why (for instance) should India import half a million's worth of matches from Sweden and Japan, toys and umbrellas from Germany to the value of another half a million, a million's worth of glass-ware from Austria? She could assuredly make these articles for herself were her youthful industry assisted against adult competition. Admitting that a tariff should not be employed to redistribute profits within the Empire, there remain many industries which would flourish on Indian soil if their growth was protected against competition that has its sources outside the Empire's limits. It is urged that countries which find their sales decreasing will purchase less, and that a protective policy would diminish India's export business. But trade is not barter: Indian produce is purchased because there is profit to be made with it, and to remit goods in exchange is, of course, not the only means of payment. As a matter of fact, few countries trading with India attempt to balance their purchases by their sales. Germany, for instance, receives in value of goods four times as much as she despatches.

xiv.—The Government.

The 'district' system.

THE Government of no large country can hope to administer its territory except by the establishment of local centres of authority, which will bring its influence home to the people, and will relieve its headquarters of business that can only be transacted efficiently on the spot. These local centres of administration may be entrusted to hereditary magnates, as under the feudal system; to elected committees such as our county and borough councils, or to salaried officials. The British Government of India could only make use of official agency. The policy of the Moghal empire was opposed to the growth of feudal authority. Bernier, at the court of Aurangzeb, remarked that the nobles of the empire were maintained by grants of money, never by landed estates. When we took over the country we found that, apart from chieftains who had been left undisturbed in their hills, the only persons of any local consequence were the contractors who, at periodical auctions, had engaged to collect the revenue. The idea of elected committees would have struck an Oriental with much surprise. We therefore followed the Moghal system, under which each district was committed to the charge of a salaried official who (as under the Moghals) was at once chief magistrate and chief fiscal officer.

An Indian district may be compared with an English county. Its area on an average will be that of Devonshire, and its population a million. General Some districts contain two million inhabitants descrip- or more, and one (an extreme case) four tion. millions. The officer in charge of the district (styled in some provinces Magistrate and Collector, in others Deputy Commissioner) in his magisterial capacity exercises no larger punitive authority than other full-powered magistrates. The district staff of magistrates will include four or five full-powered officers (of whom only one will be a European), and about twice this number of officers who have been invested with less than full powers. There will also be at least a dozen honorary magistrates—private gentlemen who have undertaken duties such as are in England committed to justices of the peace. Over this staff the District Magistrate has general powers of control, which do not, of course, extend to interference with the judgment of any magistrate in deciding upon the merits of any particular case before him. But the District Magistrate distributes criminal work amongst the various courts: he can transfer cases from one court to another, and he keeps himself informed of the progress of the work, sees that hearings are not unnecessarily delayed and witnesses inconvenienced, and, by the occasional examination of decisions that have been delivered, satisfies himself that particular officers follow correct procedure. He also hears appeals from the decisions of such of the staff as have not been invested with full magisterial powers. On the fiscal side, he is responsible for the collection of the land revenue and the income tax, and has under him for this purpose a large staff of Indian officials.

In some provinces cases between landlord and tenant are dealt with in the fiscal (or exchequer) courts and not in the civil tribunals, and in this case there are special rent courts which transact this business under the general control of the District Officer.[1] At the district headquarters there will also be the Superintendent of Police, the Civil Surgeon (in charge of two or three hospitals, and 30 or 40 rural dispensaries), the Executive Engineer (in charge of roads and buildings), and the Forest Officer, if there be State forests in the district. These offices are generally held by Europeans, but Indians have been appointed to some of them, partly by promotion from subordinate rank and partly by entering the superior services through competitive examinations in England. These 'departmental' officers all receive orders from the Government through chiefs of their own; but their correspondence, if of importance, is seen by the District Officer, they consult him in matters of difficulty, and in urgent cases defer to his judgment. In regard to the Police his control is more detailed: the Superintendent of Police keeps him informed of all occurrences of importance, and takes his advice in investigating serious or difficult cases. It will strike us at once as anomalous that the District Officer should concern himself with magisterial and with police matters, with the trial of criminals as well as with their arrest. But as a matter of fact he tries himself but few criminal cases, being occupied with his duties of control and burdened with multifarious work of all kinds. He is for the people and for the Government a referee upon almost every conceivable

[1] A convenient title for the District Magistrate, as it covers his multifarious non-judicial functions.

question that arises in connection with his district, and may at one time be exerting himself to compose a private quarrel which threatens to ruin a family of position, and be inditing a report to Government upon the fish supply of his district. And an effective check has been provided upon any temptation to strain his dual authority over the magistracy and the police. By his side there is the District and Sessions Judge, equal in rank and distinct in authority, who is under the control, not of the Government, but of the High Court. Appeals lie from the District Magistrate and all full-powered magistrates to the Sessions Judge, and all really serious cases are committed for trial to the Sessions. Moreover, the High Court can, at any time, interfere with magisterial proceedings, send for the record, and pass what orders it pleases. Under the District Judge there will be seven or eight Civil Courts.

Judicial and Police functions.

All things said, however, the exercise by one man of magisterial and police functions is of course open to logical objections, and reform in the name of the 'separation of the judicial from the executive' is strongly urged by the advanced school of Indian politicians, especially by those of Bengal. Any such change would be a grave misfortune. It is true that cases have been known to occur in which a magistrate has impressed both his police and his magisterial powers to secure a conviction. But they are, happily, very rare; and the appellate courts are open. There is no department of the Government which needs stricter control than the police: it is only before the magistrates that police misconduct comes effectively to light, and the direct connection between the magistracy and the police is a most salutary check upon the latter in the people's interests. If the police were under separate control, a magistrate's censure would lead to recrimination rather than to reform, and it would be necessary to spend large sums of money in increasing the European police personnel. At present the District Superintendent has at most one European assistant. Moreover, in India, friction is easily set up between two separate departments which might seriously jeopardise the conduct of criminal work. We cannot afford to run such a risk. That the general control of magistracy and police should be in the same hand is deep-rooted in the convictions of the people. It shortens criminal trials, and lawyers may object to it. It strengthens executive authority, and is naturally disliked by those whose sympathies are anti-British. But there has been no such change in the habits and intelligence of the general population as to warrant us in abandoning an arrangement which is supported by all the forces of tradition and custom.

Local self-government.

An innovation upon popular ideas in a direction where failure was perhaps not threatened by so great a risk was the transfer to boards or committees of the charge of such purely local matters as are included in the term 'municipal,' such as the maintenance of roads and bridges, sanitation, water-supply, primary education, and the collection of rates imposed to provide for these purposes. Outside the presidency towns this policy was not effectively initiated until forty years ago. It was given very great extension during the viceroyalty of Lord Ripon in 1882. Every town, down to the smallest, has been equipped with a municipal committee, the members of which are largely, and in some provinces chiefly, appointed by the votes of ratepayers. The local affairs of rural areas have similarly been committed to boards, the constitution of which is largely elective. In some provinces the chairmen of committees and boards hold office by election, so that larger scope is afforded to popular wishes than in most countries of Europe. If public spirit exists, it has been given full opportunity for showing itself: ratepayers can influence very greatly the management of their towns, and individuals can serve the public by working as its representatives on committees and sub-committees. The results have been at once satisfactory and disappointing. The affairs of some towns are exceedingly well managed. But where there has been success it is due not to the diffusion of public spirit, but to individual capacity, and has been gained by the efforts of one or two citizens who have a taste for administrative work, and whom the general public are willing to accept without question as municipal despots. Where men of this class are not forthcoming, passably good administration has only been secured by close Government control. The capacity of a community to govern itself depends not upon the ability displayed by its leading men, but upon the practical interest which is taken in public affairs by the mass of its citizens. Judged by this standard, very few districts or towns have responded to the opportunities that have been afforded to them, and the burden of the resolutions in which provincial governments annually review the progress of local self-government is the difficulty of inducing committee men to attend meetings, of getting the ratepayers to take the trouble of voting at elections. In

England local government not infrequently leaves much to be desired: money is wasted, men will not sacrifice themselves by serving on committees, public affairs fall into the hands of cliques. But in such cases the ratepayers feel themselves aggrieved, and at least grumble freely. In India they do not: they do not expect effective administration from unpaid agencies. To them, government is an art which requires special training and knowledge, and merits remuneration. It is still a strange doctrine that public affairs should be conducted not by officers of the State, but by the tax-payers who provide their salaries.

The central authority.

At the head of the central government is the Governor, Lieutenant-Governor, or Chief Commissioner of the province, with a staff of secretaries and under-secretaries, who demand from District Officers an unremitting stream of letters, returns, and reports. In Madras and Bombay a Council of two members is associated with the Governor. Each member has a separate portfolio, but they meet under the presidency of the Governor for the decision of important cases. In other large provinces the Lieutenant-Governor's control of revenue administration is delegated to a Board of two members. But they are subordinate to the Lieutenant-Governor and do not sit with him. Between the secretariat and the district officials of each department there intervenes the head of the department—a Commissioner to every five or six District Officers, an Inspector-General for the Police department, a Sanitary Commissioner for the Medical department, and so on. These act as intermediaries between the central government and the district staff; correspondence passes through them, and they add very materially to the labours of the men on the spot, owing in part to a natural tendency to seek through the post for information which they would do better to obtain by inspection. The burden of correspondence presses heavily: it ties the District Officer to his desk, and leaves him with but little time for making acquaintance with the people of his district, and exhibiting to them the sympathetic side of the Government. These quasi-political functions are amongst the most important of those committed to him; but they cannot be formulated in rules, their results cannot be tabulated in reports, and they are the first to suffer when time presses. The central government and the heads of departments must without doubt maintain a watchful eye: District Officers and officers of other departments are not all of equal ability: promotion cannot be rigidly limited to those who are really capable—indeed there has perhaps been too much tenderness in superseding the unfit. Close supervision is needed for some officers; but when exercised through the post it too often extends to all ot them. The necessity of limiting correspondence has been recognised from time to time, and efforts have been made to control the stream. But they cannot be effectual so long as the secretariats are permitted to grow at a faster rate than the executive staff. They have grown very much more rapidly, and cost now half as much again as thirty years ago. So long as there are secretaries to write letters, letters will be written, and the only effective method of setting back the flood of correspondence is to reduce the staff of the secretariats to the lowest possible limit. Such a reform would involve no loss of practical administrative efficiency, for at present a great mass of correspondence that is addressed to the head of the provincial government actually does not penetrate beyond the office of an under-secretary.

The supreme government.

Above the central governments of provinces there is the supreme government—the Government of India—which consists of the Viceroy and of his Executive Council of six members. Through the supreme government India is touched by a side stream of the current of English politics, for the Viceroy represents the views of one or other of the two great political parties of England, and, apart from official correspondence, he is, by private letters and telegrams, in close communication with the Secretary of State. It is by this channel that the breath of Liberal doctrines has found its way to India, and has inspired the Government with ideas that could hardly have originated in the conservative environment of the East. To this source India has owed the substitution of English for Oriental education, the liberty of the press, the delegation of local government to elective committees, and the association of elected representatives of the public in the work of legislation. The leading function of the Government of India is to lay down principles of administration and secure their observance. But, reserving to itself the power of controlling the provincial governments in a multitude of questions of detail—especially in respect to finance—and being itself obliged to make continual references for the orders of the Secretary of State, it maintains a voluminous correspondence with the Indian provincial governments on one hand and with the India Office on the other.

As has already been stated, the scheme upon which the British Government is modelled was inherited from the Moghals: it offers the people a system to which they are accustomed, and which is in conformity with their ideas; and it has accordingly been successful. But in one important matter we have not been content with the simplicity of Oriental conceptions of the State: we have drawn a distinction between the executive and the legislative functions of government, and have provided that, when making laws, the Governors of provinces and the Viceroy should act, not alone, but in association with a Legislative Council. These Councils were at first small committees, composed mainly of English officials, but including a certain number of representative Indian gentlemen who were nominated to the Council by the Government. In 1892—during the viceroyalty of Lord Lansdowne—a departure was made of far-reaching consequences. The municipal and rural boards to which the management of local affairs had been committed were authorised to nominate a few members to the provincial Legislative Councils, and their nominees on the provincial councils were empowered to nominate representatives upon the Viceroy's Legislative Council. A like privilege was conceded to Chambers of Commerce and to the Universities. Public opinion was thus definitely given an official voice in law-making; and the members of the Councils were, moreover, permitted to interpellate the Government on matters of executive administration. They also discussed the annual budget, but only after it had been prepared and issued, so that their comments could only affect the financial arrangements

Legislation.

for following years and not those of the year under discussion. Further changes of great moment have been introduced by the recent reforms that are associated with the names of Lord Morley and Lord Minto. The size of the Councils has, roughly speaking, been trebled; they are no longer small committees, but include from forty to fifty members. The number of members that hold office by election has been more than trebled: not only are local administrative bodies permitted to elect; the privilege has been conceded to representatives of the land-holding and commercial communities, and to special Muhammadan electorates. A certain proportion of non-official Indian members continue to be nominated by the Government; but it has been provided that on provincial Legislative Councils the non-official members, elected and nominated taken together, will be more numerous than the official members, so that they will be able to outvote the latter if they combine. The authority of the members, apart from the discussion of projected laws, has been widened very largely. They will have a voice in the preparation of the budget of the year, and not merely in criticising it: they can move resolutions affecting the executive business of Government, and they are permitted to ask supplementary questions. There are safeguards. The Government can veto the election of a member who is altogether undesirable: the members who are elected by local administrative bodies must be serving or have served on these bodies, and cannot, to use a vulgarism, be 'political carpet-baggers': the Government can decline to answer questions if it consider it very inexpedient to do so; and certain functions of the executive government are definitely excluded from discussion. But the powers of the elected members will remain very great. If they can effect a combination with the non-official nominated members (and, in Bengal, if they simply combine amongst themselves) they will be able, on the provincial Legislative Councils, altogether to block any legislation that is proposed by the Government. By questions and supplementary questions they can put officers of the Government not merely into the witness-box, but into the pillory, and it is probable that, in a contest of wits, the official members of Council, who have but little training in the art of debate, will fare indifferently at the hands of astute Indian lawyers, and that sometimes the worst may appear the better cause. Two results are certain. The Councils will be, in fact, little parliaments: their proceedings will occupy a very large portion of the attention of Government, and questions of reform will involve not merely careful consideration on their merits, but the anxious balancing of non-official opinion and negotiations to secure a preponderance of votes. Secondly, the elected members, in so far as they are representative, stand for the educated and well-to-do classes only: they naturally will oppose any measures which will protect the poorer classes at the cost of middle or upper class interests. The poor will have as their spokesmen only the official members of Council, and, when confronted with the risks of bitter opposition, the official members may be pardoned if they feel that the cause of the poor appeals to them less insistently than heretofore. It is significant that within recent years two measures which had for their object the protection of peasant proprietors from the temptation to borrow money recklessly on the security of their estates (and which have proved most beneficial) were opposed by the whole weight of the non-official members, and would certainly not have been passed had the Councils then enjoyed their new constitution. A third result may be expected. Indian public opinion will speak more loudly and insistently than in the past, and it will become increasingly difficult for the Secretary of State, or the British Parliament, to over-ride the wishes of educated Indians.

The future depends upon the reasonableness of the attitude of the elected members. If, like the Irish members of the British Parliament, they resolutely decline to use their opportunities for improving the government of their country; if they are so obsessed by their aspirations as to despise any attitude but that of uncompromising hostility which would rather forgo reform than be indebted for it to the co-operation of the Government; if they should employ their influence, not for the benefit of the people, but to secure further emancipation from British authority, and to organise agitation against its continuance, the difficulty that always confronts an alien rule may be aggravated by storms which may necessitate the laying of the ship on a new course at whatever risk. If, on the other hand, they realise the danger of courting a revolution which would be a sanguinary welter of confusion, lit by no guiding star, and directed by no programme, and are content in the interests of their country to turn to legitimate purpose the powers that have been granted them, it may well be that these reforms will gradually bridge the gap that now divides the European from the Indian. They will certainly increase the estimation in which Indians are held by Europeans, and will remove a grievance which is none the less acute because it is of a sentimental character. The most hopeful feature of the reforms is that they enlist the co-operation of the land-holding and commercial classes as well as of the journalists and lawyers, whose intelligence, even when disciplined and patriotic, is liable to appreciate too clearly the advantages of fishing in troubled waters.

Apart, then, from the more or less elected committees which administer purely local affairs, and from the provincial and imperial Legislative Councils, we have a hierarchy of four governing authorities—the Government of India, the provincial governments, the heads of departments, and the district staff. How far are the natives of the country represented in this hierarchy?

Share of Indians in the Government;

In the lowest of the four grades—that is to say the district staff—which, being nearest to the people, represents to the masses for all practical purposes the government of the country, natives of India are in the vast majority. If the district possesses twelve stipendiary magistrates, at least ten of them are Indian, who, if qualified by ability and experience, exercise a punitive authority equal to that enjoyed by the English district magistrate: ordinarily four or five of them are invested with these full magisterial powers. Of the rent courts, all but one or two are similarly committed to Indians. There may be eight civil tribunals: all of them are presided over by Indians,

—on the district staffs;

save that of the District Judge, and two or three of them exercise powers which are substantially equal to those of the District Judge. The district Police staff is wholly Indian, save for the Superintendent and (perhaps) one assistant: so also is the Medical staff, the Engineering staff, and the Forest staff, save for the one English official at the head of each. The Educational department is still less influenced by English control, since several districts share the supervision of an English inspector of schools. Speaking generally then, the executive and judicial staff of the country is Indian, with an Englishman as senior official in each department of the district administration. The pay of Europeans in responsible office is naturally much larger than that of their Indian confrères, partly because their expenses are so very much heavier. Their salaries range in the several departments from £600 to £1750 a year, the latter representing the emoluments of the District Magistrate and the District Judge. The salaries of the senior Indian officials range from £300 to £800 a year.

In the higher grades of the official hierarchy, English officials are more conspicuous. The heads of departments are, as a rule, English: so are the secretaries and under-secretaries of both the provincial governments and the supreme government. Their clerical staff is, of course, wholly Indian or Eurasian. The provincial governorships are all in English hands, and so, until lately, have been all the memberships of Executive Councils, whether in the Bombay and Madras presidencies or in the supreme government. Recently an Indian has been given the

—in higher offices of control.

legal portfolio on the Viceroy's Executive Council, and Indians have been admitted to the Executive Councils of Bombay and Madras. It can no longer be said that the Indian people cannot pass behind the veil which screens the deliberations of the highest executive authority of their country.

Considerations affecting employment of Europeans.

Only half a century has passed since Indians were given an opportunity of acquiring by education the knowledge, the ideals, and the morale which are required for the direction of public affairs on modern lines. In the East ideas change slowly, and, if we were to do our duty by the country, it was necessary that for many years the public services should be under English control. A generation ago the morality of the Indian services, including the judiciary, was very low, and complaints of bribery were frequent. There has come about a vast improvement in this respect, partly no doubt owing to the development of a strong Indian bar, but due also in great measure to the higher ideals which have sprung up from our schools and colleges, and to the growth of the scruples which we designate collectively as 'good form.' But these scruples are of recent origin, and it may perhaps be doubted whether they would maintain the probity of the public service were they not strengthened by a leaven of European example. With every appreciation of the merits of native Indian officials, it may be stated that they do not, as a rule, possess the energy or initiative of Europeans. And in one respect they work at a serious disadvantage. Being connected with the country they are liable to personal influences from which alien officials are absolutely free; and, moreover, whether they resist these influences or not, they are generally suspected by their countrymen of yielding to them. And when this suspicion is intensified by racial or religious prejudice, as is sometimes the case between Hindus and Muhammadans, most men in the minority would, beyond a shadow of a doubt, rather have an Englishman in authority over them than one of the rival party. Our policy has then been to reserve for Englishmen a proportion of posts in the public service which, though small in itself, suffices in number and in character to secure English guidance and control. Each department of the superior public service is divided into two branches, imperial and provincial. All posts of control are classed as imperial: others, whether executive, judicial, or subordinate, are classed as provincial. Appointments to the imperial branch are made in England by the Secretary of State—that is to say, are limited in intention to Europeans. The superior provincial service is recruited in India by the appointment of natives of the country. It includes over two thousand native officials, whose emoluments, as judicial or executive officers, contrast favourably with those allowed to similar functionaries in any European country, except, perhaps, England. But this sharp distinction between the provincial and imperial services is softened in three directions. In cases where admission to the imperial service is determined by the results of competitive examinations held in England, natives of India can enter themselves for this competition, and can, by success, win their way into the service. A considerable number of Indians have in this manner been appointed to the imperial medical service, and into the imperial Indian Civil Service (about 1200 strong),[1] sixty-five Indians have gained admission, and can command prospects equal to those that are enjoyed by Europeans. With advancing education and morality, it is unjust and undesirable that Indians should be absolutely barred by race from any share in the appointments that are classed as imperial. The London competitive examinations offer them an avenue of admission. But it is rather a back door than an avenue. It is indirect, unfair, and capricious—indirect, because the examination is framed to test the acquirements of Englishmen, not of Indians, so that the young Indian competes under difficulties which, if not actually intended to exclude him, place him at an immense disadvantage compared with English competitors; unfair, because the examination room offers success only to the most quick-witted Indian races; and capricious, because the number of Indian students that succeed varies very greatly from year to year, so that the proportion of Indians to Europeans depends not upon the requirements of India, but upon such uncertain facts as the character of the question papers or the general capacity of the candidates in each particular year. There are, moreover, serious objections to an arrangement which obliges Indian students as a necessary condition, not merely of success, but of attempt, to cut themselves adrift

[1] Only 687 of these officers hold offices of control: 268 are young men who are being trained by working in less responsible posts, and 289 represent the reserve that is required to fill the vacancies that result from the grant of sick-leave or furlough.

from their families, to encounter the unaccustomed temptations of a strange land, and to incur expenditure which not seldom permanently cripples their families.

Recognition of exceptional ability in the provincial service.

There is, however, another avenue by which Indians can attain to controlling authority. To afford an opening for men of conspicuous ability, 51 posts out of the 687 which are reserved for officers of the imperial service have been thrown open to members of the provincial service. They include seventeen headships of districts and twenty-six district judgeships. But officers of the provincial service who are advanced to these posts draw very much less pay than would be enjoyed by European incumbents. Economy affords a logical reason for this restriction. The cost of living in India is much higher for a European than for an Indian, and a salary which might just suffice for the one would be very liberal indeed for the other. But the saving that is effected is not considerable, while the distinction which it emphasises cannot fail to seem invidious.

The High Courts offer a third opening which is fettered by no such limitation. For some years past Indian lawyers of repute have been held qualified for appointment to judgeships in the High Courts on equal terms with Europeans, and the provincial High Court benches include at present fifteen Indian judges.

The English officials of the Government represent the inspiration and the guidance which the West can give the East in civil administration, and it is in the highest degree important that they should be men of character as well as of ability, and should be equipped with that knowledge of the Indian languages, customs, and ideas, from which alone can spring a true understanding and sympathy. The qualities of character that are most required are those that are gained by a public school education — self-control, self-reliance, and the art of influencing others—and in the interests of India the best method of recruiting the Indian services would have been by selection in competitive examination from candidates nominated by the headmasters of public schools—taking the term in its broadest possible sense. Such a scheme would, however, have appeared too restrictive to the British democracy, and in the interests of the British public, competition for Indian service has been left absolutely open, with a test that is purely intellectual. Fortunately there is a widely diffused type of national character, and men who have failed from lack of morale have been comparatively few. But India can complain with reason that her officers are sent out untrained. The East India Company maintained special colleges for the training of its civil and military officers. These were closed when selection by open competition was introduced, but for many years youths who were appointed to the Indian Civil Service were prepared for their career by a two-years' course of special training which included jurisprudence, law—English, Roman, Hindu, and Muhammadan—Indian history, political economy, and two, if not three, Oriental languages. The course was an excellent one. It has been abolished in the

Selection and training of English officers.

interests of general university education, and probationers for the Indian Civil Service now pursue their studies for the ordinary university degree, and go out to India one year after their selection most imperfectly equipped for their responsibilities. They learn no law worth the name, a little Indian history, no political economy, and gain a smattering of one Indian vernacular. In regard to the other branches of the service, matters are still more unsatisfactory. Young Police officers are sent out with no special training whatever, though for the proper discharge of their duties an intimate acquaintance with Indian life and ideas is essential. They land in India in absolute ignorance of the language. So also with Forest officers, Medical officers, Engineers, and (still more surprising) with Educational officers. Men are sent to India as school inspectors who may be absolutely ignorant of the history, religion, and language of the people whose schools and colleges they are to supervise. It is hardly too much to say that this is an insult to the intelligence of the country. It may be argued that men can best learn in India on the spot, that they should pick up their special qualifications after landing in the country. But this assertion is contrary to experience, and would be made by no one who was familiar with the customs of Anglo-Indian society. Speaking generally, from the month of an officer's arrival in the country, he is caught up in the meshes of heavy routine work, the obvious relief from which is offered by bridge, polo, and the English society around him. Unless he has already crossed the threshold of Oriental studies, he will seldom turn to them in hours of leisure, and there is some ground for the suspicion that the English officials of the Government are less in touch with the country than were their predecessors twenty-five years ago. There can be no real sympathy without understanding, and no understanding without knowledge. Hardly a day passes in which a member of the Indian Civil Service, of the Educational, the Police, or of the Forest services, has not an opportunity of gaining or losing for us popular esteem. It is, of course, essential that he should be able to converse idiomatically in the language of his district. But this is not sufficient. He should know enough of the feelings of the people to be able to judge of his actions from their point of view. He should be sufficiently acquainted with their sentiments and customs to be able to understand their life and to enter into it. Nothing wins the regard of an Indian so easily as a knowledge of facts connected with his religion, his prejudices, or his habits, which are all-important in his domestic life, though they may not influence his relations with the Government.

It is desirable that every young man appointed to India—in at all events the Civil Service, the Police, the Educational and the Forest departments—should undergo a special course of instruction in Indian subjects, apart from the technical training which is to fit him for his particular work. This course should comprise Indian history, economics, customs, philosophy, and religion, and at least two Indian languages. Preferably it should be pursued at a special college established for the purpose in India, in an atmosphere and amidst surroundings which would conduce to the assimilation of Indian subjects.

The cost of establishing and maintaining such a college would be repaid many times over in the increased efficiency of our English services, and in the increased respect which they would command from the people.

XV.—Taxes and Land Revenue.

In England the expenditure of the State is almost wholly met by taxation. The Indian Government subsists only partly by taxation properly so called: it relies very greatly upon the proceeds of the share which from immemorial antiquity it holds in the proprietorship of land, and upon the profits which it makes in various State undertakings. The income which it derives from the land may be likened to the tithe which in England has for a thousand years past been appropriated to the maintenance of a State Church. The receipts which may be classed as profits are drawn from enterprises in some of which it has anticipated the recommendations of socialism. Taking its total revenue as £48 millions, £18¼ millions are raised by taxation, £20 millions represent the annual proceeds of the State's share in the land, and £9¾ millions can be described as State profits. The incidence of actual taxation per head of population is only 1s. 7d. To this we must add 2½d., representing local and municipal rates. In the United Kingdom local rates increase taxation by 45 per cent.; in India they add only 13 per cent. to the obligations of the people.

Taxation not the only source of revenue.

The taxes include an Excise levied on salt, spirituous liquors, and drugs, a Customs duty and an Income tax from which agricultural profits are exempt. A poor man who clothes himself and his family in country-made materials and does

The taxes.

not indulge in spirit or in drugs, pays nothing to the State but the salt duty, the incidence of which is only 3d. per head. Salt is a necessity, and its taxation in India has excited criticism. But by the construction of railways its price has been reduced, for millions of people, by at least the equivalent of the duty. On the opening of the railway the price of salt in the Central Provinces fell from three-halfpence to a penny a pound. At that time the rate of duty was about a halfpenny a pound, and it continued at this figure until recent years. In the course of the last half-century, with increasing prosperity, the consumption of salt per head has doubled. But in comparison with its actual cost it has been taxed almost as highly as is tea in England; and during the viceroyalty of Lord Curzon, and subsequently, three successive reductions have been made which have now lowered the duty to one-fifth of a penny per pound. Stimulated by these abatements, the consumption of salt has increased by more than 20 per cent. during the last eight years.

Salt.

The most productive of the Excise duties are those on drugs and spirits: they now bring in £6½ millions a year. Spirits are consumed very largely by the inhabitants of the hills and jungles, and, until recently, no complete accounts were maintained of the actual consumption by this class of the population, since distillation was effected in these localities in little pot-stills, the proprietors of which paid licence fees, but no still-head duty. But it is known that spirit drinking has increased very largely indeed, in spite of enhancements in the rate of taxation. The Indian Government has watched this development

Excise.

with concern, and the keynote of its policy has always been the minimum of consumption with the maximum of revenue. But the increased consumption of spirits results from a change which is in itself the reverse of disquieting—the increased spending power of the lower classes. To a coolie a glass of spirits is one of the few material pleasures that is offered by life; and if some of these hard-working men drink less for the taste of the liquor than to become cheerful and to forget, drunkenness is very much less evident in India than in some towns of the United Kingdom.

Customs.

Customs are levied, generally, on goods imported by sea at an all-round rate of 5 per cent.;[1] but in the interests of Lancashire the imports which would produce most duty have been left only partially taxed, cotton yarn being admitted free of duty and cotton piece goods being taxed at the reduced rate of 3½ per cent., an equivalent excise duty of 3½ per cent. being imposed on piece goods manufactured in Indian mills. This concession, which is hailed by some persons as a rightful sacrifice to Free Trade, is really a bounty offered at India's expense to Lancashire manufacturers, and it is resented very acutely by Indian mill-owners.

Income tax.

The Income tax produces no more than a million and a half: it is levied only on industrial, commercial, and professional incomes, and the difficulty of effecting a proper assessment is, in India, exceedingly great. Another million and a

[1] The customs leviable on silver, tobacco, wines and spirits, and kerosene oil have just now been enhanced very largely. Silver will pay at 15 per cent., tobacco and spirits at 100 per cent. or over, and kerosene oil at 25 per cent. These enhancements are expected to add about a million sterling to the revenue.

half is yielded by Stamp duties, to which certain documents are liable.

State profits.

The most important of the receipts which are classed as *Profits* is the income that is derived from the export of Indian-grown opium to China. This trade has offered India an opportunity of securing from China a contribution which has been of great assistance to her finances. The receipts have fluctuated considerably, and at present amount to £4 millions a year. But in order to assist China in making good her expressed intention of checking the consumption of opium, the Indian Government, during the last three years, has reduced the export by over a fifth. It remains to be proved that the Chinese Government is in earnest, and is effectually restricting the cultivation of the poppy within its own territories. Another item which may be classed under this head is £3 millions that are derived from the fees which are levied upon litigation. In India, for a poor country, lawsuits are extraordinarily numerous: they offer the people the excitement which in other countries is afforded by horse-racing or lotteries. The fees that are levied upon them may be regarded rather as a charge for services rendered (by the maintenance of a very costly judicial establishment) than as a tax in the proper sense of the term. State railways and canals may ordinarily be expected to yield a profit of £2 millions after paying all expenses, including interest upon capital. Forests belonging to the State yield it a net revenue of three-quarters of a million.

We now come to the consideration of the income (called Land Revenue) which the State derives from its share in the ownership of the land. This is the most important and the most interesting of its receipts, and the most difficult to explain to the comprehension of English readers. It is to us a strange idea that the State should hold a part ownership of the land of the country, though it is a familiar doctrine of latter-day socialism that the State should be proprietor of the whole of it. Yet one arrangement is logically as possible as the other. The English Government holds outright Crown lands which yield a revenue of half a million a year: it can be imagined as surrendering these rights in return for a share in, or rent charge upon, a much larger area. The tithes illustrate a dual right in land: they have been circumscribed by limitations which have reduced their proceeds in England to about £4 millions a year. If they had been maintained at a tenth of the produce of land, and were held not by the Church but by the State, they would afford a good parallel to the land revenue of India—in amount as well as in character, for the Indian land revenue at present approximates pretty closely to a tenth of the agricultural yield of the country.

Land revenue.

In the days of Hindu supremacy the State generally collected its land revenue in kind, by actually taking a share of the cultivator's produce. The laws of Manu (*circ.* 200 A.D.) set the king's share as a sixth, an eighth, or a twelfth, according to differences of soil and the amount of labour necessary to cultivate the land: in some cases it might apparently be as much as a fourth. In graduating the share according to the quality of the land and the cost of cultivation, the writer showed understanding of the subject. Tenants growing

Under Hindu rulers.

wheat without irrigation or manure can pay their landlord as much as half the produce: such rents are actually paid in some parts of India as well as in South America. On the other hand, a valuable crop such as sugar-cane can with difficulty bear a rent that is equivalent to a tenth of the produce. When historians mention a single uniform share as taken by the State they must be supposed to refer to an average, not to the collections actually made on particular areas. Their estimates are frequently very misleading. Megasthenes, writing at the court of Asoka in 320 B.C., states that the Raja took from the people three-quarters of their produce: on the strength of a brief visit to India a like statement has recently been made regarding the British Government by a prominent Labour member of Parliament. Both writers are ludicrously incorrect: in no circumstances could agriculture sustain such a burden. But the former may be forgiven his mistake as he had access to no accurate information: the latter has no such excuse. That the revenue of the State was a share of the produce is noted by the Chinese pilgrims who visited India in the fifth and seventh centuries of our era. One of them gives the average share as a sixth. But its actual amount must in reality have depended upon an annual contest of strength and wits between the people and the Raja's officials. In some Native States the revenue is still collected in kind, and traces of this custom survived until lately in a few backward localities in British territory. We have then been able to watch the procedure. The cultivators are obliged to collect their grain on public threshing-floors: the Raja sets watchmen over the grain-heaps till the officials arrive and divide the produce by actual measurement or by estimate. The people leave no stone unturned to defeat the exchequer. A trick which came to my notice was to dig a pit under the threshing-floor and cover it with a cartwheel, plastered over with mud. When the grain was heaped above, the cultivator, without exciting the watchman's suspicions, could with a stick poke out the mud between two of the spokes, making a hole through which grain would trickle into the pit and escape division. It is worth mention that in one of these localities the share of the State varied with the caste and standing of the cultivator, being one-third for newly settled men, one-fourth for men of standing, and only one-fifth for Brahmins. One might suppose that the cultivators would prefer a system under which their liabilities depended upon the character of the harvest, to the payment of fixed money rents. This was not the case: when asked to vote, they elected almost unanimously for the latter alternative. Fixity of payment gives security against official rapacity, and relieves men's minds from the worry of the annual struggle on the arena of the threshing-floor.

Labour in lieu of produce.

In early Hindu days there was little coin in the country: when at peace with its neighbours the State had no use for large quantities of grain, the collection and storage of which must have offered great difficulty. Accordingly it seems to have taken labour in place of some of its grain dues, and to have received a portion of its revenue in the form of a corvée. The Chattisgarh tract, isolated amidst the hills and jungles which form the watershed of the Mahanadi river, and the province of Assam, at the extreme north-eastern corner of the country, were almost the only areas that escaped Muhammadan domination, and have handed down to us unbroken the customs of Hindu rule. In both these localities, which lie so very far apart, we found a regularly organised corvée, the State exacting services, whether for the cultivation of the Raja's demesne, the maintenance of a primitive militia, or the making of roads and river embankments, which had been substituted very largely for its claims upon produce. In both tracts the revenue paid by villages to the State was surprisingly low, equivalent to only two or three pence per acre. But judging from the people's complaints, the Raja's demands for labour had been no trifling burden, and they thankfully accepted their conversion into cash revenue. Circumstances were very similar in the remote Native State of Manipur, situated between Assam and the province of Burma.

Great changes occurred under Muhammadan rule. For the maintenance of a brilliant court, the con-

Under Moghal rule.

struction of splendid public buildings, and the prosecution of endless wars, money, not grain, was needed. Coins were minted on a liberal scale, and the State's demand of produce was converted into money payments which were assessed at

Cash demanded in lieu of produce.

area rates varying with the soil and the locality. This revolution was completed in the reign of Akbar. The rates were supposed to be settled for a term of years, but under the military exigencies of the Moghal empire the revenue was enhanced from time to time till it left the cultivators nothing but bare subsistence. The cash revenue which Aurangzeb exacted from the provinces of northern India was considerably in excess of the land revenue now paid by them, although at that time there were no canals, no transport facilities, and much less cultivation than at present. Moreover, compared with the present time, twice as much grain was then required to purchase a rupee, and it has been calculated that in the Panjáb, the United Provinces, and Bengal, the Moghal revenue, measured in grain, was actually three times the present demand of the Indian Government. Nor were the people better off in southern India. The Hindu rajas in Madras expected to receive from two to three-fifths of the produce: the Mahrattas went even further, and endeavoured to extort a half. The memoirs of the European travellers of those days make pitying references to the misery of the cultivators. Four of them note expressly that the land throughout the empire was considered to be the property of the sovereign—the theory which has been the foundation of such crying abuses on the Congo. In fact, to quote the dictum of a Muhammadan lawyer of that time, 'there shall be left for every man who cultivates his land as much as he requires for his own support till the next crop be reaped, and for that of his family and for seed. This much shall be left him: what remains is land revenue, and should go to the public treasury.'

Collection through contractors.

The Muhammadans introduced another change of far-reaching consequences. Foreigners like ourselves, they found it difficult to control a multitude of petty Hindu officials, and they adopted the expedient of farming the revenue to persons, who would engage to collect it for a term of years, in consideration of a small commission and what else they could extort from the people.

Some of these contractors were speculators; others were chieftains who had managed to retain a feudal status; others again were village headmen, representatives of a community of cultivators. The theory on which these contracts were made subsists to this day. In Upper India a man is under no legal obligation to pay the land revenue that is assessed on his land: he pays it in virtue of an agreement with the State, technically called a 'settlement.' He may refuse to contract, and is in this case excluded from possession during the period of contract, but is allowed a small rent charge. On the conclusion of the period he regains possession of his land if he then agrees to pay its land revenue.

Under the British Government.

On taking over the country the British Government, in Upper India, generally followed the arrangements of the Moghals, and dealt with the contractors whom they found in possession. In Bengal these were generally big men, holding contracts for very large areas. Similar conditions prevailed in Oudh: it was at first proposed to oust the contractors and deal directly with the villages, but the experience of the Mutiny was against such a reform, and the contractors were maintained in possession. In the remaining portions of Upper India the contractors were as a rule much smaller men—more closely connected with their villages. Indeed the village brotherhoods had very generally been permitted to contract directly with the State in joint responsibility. In the Central Provinces contracts were made with the village headman, or with outsiders who had secured from the Native Government farms of the revenue of villages or small groups of villages. In all these cases the contractor was permitted to appropriate during the period of contract any payments which he could secure for newly reclaimed land. In the Madras and Bombay presidencies a different course was followed. Contractors, where they existed, were generally set aside, and the Government dealt directly with the cultivators, paying through their headman. The cultivators had no concern with waste land: this was assessed by the State to revenue as it was taken up for cultivation. In all provinces the period of contract was gradually lengthened: the contractors or cultivators were at the same time permitted to retain an increasingly large proportion of their profits. In this way a valuable property in land was created which has been recognised by law as that of proprietorship. But in this process the cultivators, who originally held from the State, became the tenants of private landlords.

Creation of proprietary right in land.

The early years of British rule were spent in a vain and melancholy attempt to maintain the heavy assessments of the Moghals, which were only payable when the State returned its income to the people in profuse local expenditure. In Bengal, after some years of difficulty, it was decided to make a venturesome experiment, and to confirm the revenue contracts in perpetuity, subject to the condition that if a contractor fell into arrears his rights were to be immediately sold by auction. The contractors were at that time liable to render to Government ten-elevenths of the amounts due from the villages covered by their agreements, and the immediate result of this reform was that large numbers of them were ruined and sold up. But better times befell their successors: cultiva-

Early difficulties.

Permanent settlement of Bengal.

tion rapidly increased; the construction of railways and the expanding trade of Calcutta raised the value of produce, and at the present time the fixed assessment paid by the landlords of Bengal to the State is only a fourth instead of ten-elevenths of their income. This permanent settlement of Bengal costs the State annually about three millions sterling, which is the amount of revenue enhancement that would have accrued were the province settled temporarily on the terms that are applied elsewhere.

Temporary settlements elsewhere.

In the other provinces of Upper India a more cautious policy was followed. The period of settlement was lengthened to twenty or thirty years: greater care was taken in ascertaining or in fixing the payments of the cultivators to the contractors (now transfigured into landlords), and the share of these payments that the latter were allowed to retain was increased very liberally. The periodical revisions of the land revenue, technically called 'settlements,' are based upon a consideration of the 'assets' of the estate—that is to say of the rents paid by tenants *plus*, in some cases, a reasonable enhancement, and of the rental value of the landlords' own demesne lands. Rents are not infrequently understated, and to check fraud of this kind, and also (in cases where rents are enhanced) to ascertain what would be a fair enhancement, the fields are surveyed in detail, elaborately classed according to their productiveness, and a searching comparison of areas and rents is instituted between village and village. These operations generally occupy three years in a single district, under the superintendence of a specially selected English officer. When the 'assets' have been determined, a share of them is fixed as payable by the landlord during the succeeding period of settlement. This share was, a century ago, nine-tenths, or even more than this. It has been lowered by the successive reductions till it now stands at about a half, and in many districts is considerably less than a half. By these reductions the State has created in the interests of landlords an exceedingly valuable property.

'Ryotwari' settlements.

In the Bombay and Madras presidencies the State deals with the cultivators direct, and here it has been necessary to follow a different system. In determining what could fairly be demanded from each of a multitude of small holders the only practical method is to proceed from aggregate to detail—to decide what the State can reasonably demand from a tract of country after considering its present payments, and the changes which have come about in local conditions (affecting prices, trade, irrigation, and the general circumstances of the people) since they were last fixed. A fair revised revenue having thus been determined for the tract, it is distributed over the holdings with careful reference to their area and productiveness. In the Madras presidency the results of this process are checked by comparison with calculations showing the net cultivating profits of each class of land, the profits, that is to say, that are yielded by it after making liberal reductions for cost of cultivation. Half these net profits are taken to represent the share of the State; but as a matter of fact the revenue hardly ever reaches this standard.

It would obviously be unjust and inexpedient to increase a man's payments because the productiveness of his land has been increased by improvements that he has effected, and care is taken to exclude from assessment any profits that have been secured in this way. In some provinces it has been laid down that land which has been improved is to be assessed for all time as unimproved: in other provinces it is not assessed on its improved value till an ample period has elapsed for the recovery of the money that has been expended.

Exemption of improvements.

Another concession is made that is less capable of logical justification. When the enhancement that is warranted is very large, it is lessened in order to mitigate to the landlord the effect of a sudden increase in his payments; or, the collection of part of the enhancement is postponed for several years. Logically, having enjoyed exceptionally large profits for many years past, the landlord should be in all the better position to render to the State its full share when the time for reassessment comes round. Practically, however, this is not the case. Indian landlords are not generally of the class that puts money by against a rainy day: they live up to their income, and to meet a sudden large increase in expenditure would be compelled to lower very materially their standard of comfort.

Special leniency for personal reasons.

The land revenue is fixed on a consideration of averages, and it is paid under a form of contract which supposes that the landlord will set good years against bad, and will punctually acquit himself of his obligations whether the seasons are favourable or the reverse. When seasonal fluctuations are not excessive, this arrangement works well enough, since the landlord's annual profits are sufficiently large to enable him to meet the land revenue without borrowing, even in a year

Concessions to alleviate seasonal disasters.

when they fall short of the average. But when, owing to great calamities, a harvest is nearly or wholly destroyed, thriftless men can only meet the demands of Government by borrowing, generally at high rates of interest. Moreover, it happens sometimes that, owing to various causes, estates suffer permanent deterioration. In this case the continued payment of the land revenue may involve a landlord in very serious embarrassment. During the viceroyalty of Lord Curzon special concessions were made to meet these cases: in the former, the collection of the revenue is suspended until seasons improve; in the latter, the revenue is permanently abated in anticipation of the expiry of the contract term. Under the laws in force in most provinces, the benefits of these concessions are passed on to the tenants. Few measures of the Indian Government have brought more welcome relief, and to a larger number of families.

Proportion of land revenue to produce.

It is exceedingly difficult to estimate the proportion in which the present land revenue stands to the gross produce of the land, since the average amount and value of the latter is not precisely ascertainable. The comparison does not throw much light on the actual pressure of the land revenue, the correct relation of which is, of course, to profits, not to produce. But as the point is not infrequently raised in discussions of Indian politics, it may be mentioned that careful inquiries instituted by the Famine Commission of 1901, and subsequently continued, indicate that over the poorer tracts of India—the Central Provinces and the Deccan—the land revenue is equivalent to considerably less than one-tenth of the produce: over large tracts it is equivalent to a tenth, and in a few very productive localities it rises to an extreme maximum of a fifth. Taking India as a whole, a tenth may be accepted as a fair average. That the demand is very moderate follows from the rates at which it falls per cultivated acre: they are extremely low, even for a poor country. In two provinces (Madras and Sindh) the incidence is just over 3s. an acre; it is 2s. 8d. in the United Provinces, 2s. 2d. in Bombay, 1s. 5d. in the Panjáb, and less than a shilling in the Central Provinces.

Is land revenue a rent or a tax?

A question of some theoretical interest is whether the Indian land revenue is of the nature of rent or of a tax. To English students it will appear to be a tax upon rent, but (as we have seen) its history is altogether against this conclusion. Rent has grown out of land revenue, not land revenue out of rent. The rent is in fact a share of land revenue that has been relinquished to the land-holding community. Were the Indian Government to abandon its land revenue altogether, prices would not fall, nor would the poorer classes benefit, for in the form of rent they would continue to pay it. It resembles a tax in that it is money that is taken from certain classes of the community to provide for the expenditure of the State; and, if the money would have been more productive in private than in State hands—if, left to the people, it would have grown and fructified in their pockets—the objections that apply to all taxation would apply to the land revenue also. But there is nothing to show that this would have been the case. The permanent settlement of Bengal has not stimulated the investment of capital in land improvement: the Bengal districts which adjoin the United Provinces display, neither in the condition of the land, the houses or the people, any signs of superiority; indeed, owing to the greater power of the landlords, the cultivators and labourers are decidedly poorer than in the United Provinces, and, when oppressed by famine, have needed relief no less urgently to be preserved from starvation. The rental profits which the State has relinquished have been absorbed in great measure by the most extraordinary process of sub-infeudation. A man whose land pays him well too often finds no higher ambition than to lease it and enjoy urban life on the profits. In some districts land is not infrequently let in this fashion many times over; indeed, cases are not uncommon where there are a dozen or more lessees one above the other. By relinquishing rent the State has not encouraged production; it has afforded a life of leisure to a large number of persons with ambitions that are literary rather than productive. The resources that it has spared to the people have, no doubt, encouraged education. They have also encouraged litigation, to the great advantage of lawyers. The greatest material advantage they have procured is perhaps the development and wealth of the city of Calcutta.

Land revenue and the 'unearned increment.'

From one point of view Indian land revenue administration has an interesting connection with modern English politics. For a century past it has had the effect of appropriating for public purposes a very large share of the 'unearned increment' of land. It seems doubtful whether, with Legislative Councils as now reconstituted, the Indian Government will be in a position to continue this policy, and to reassess periodically the growing value of the land. In England imposts on land are an ideal of popular politics: in India legislation that is popular will be strongly opposed to them. For, above the coolie class, the vast majority of the population holds land or cultivates it.

Protection of tenants—by legislation;

Taking one province with another, land now sells by private transfer at from fifteen to twenty times the land revenue. That is to say, by the moderation of its assessment, the British Government has raised the selling value of landlords' estates from next to nothing to over 300 millions sterling. This astonishing rise in the value of land has revolutionised village conditions. Formerly tenants were in demand: now the desire is for landed property or profit. Landlords are tempted to enhance rents and to eject tenants, and money-lenders use every endeavour to secure landed investments by enmeshing the agricultural classes in debt. Out of the moderation of the Government has sprung a new and instant danger for the mass of the people. Men who are poor, thriftless, and exposed periodically to losses of harvest, cannot resist the aggression of landlords on the one hand, and the advances of money-lenders on the other, and a very serious risk has arisen that the poorer cultivators would be gradually reduced to a position of serfdom. But the State has not hesitated to intervene and to use its proper functions of controlling and moderating the struggle for life. Tenancy laws have been passed securing the mass of the tenants in possession of their holdings at a fair rent. Nor has the magnitude of the problem deterred the Government from accepting a responsibility without which its efforts would have been useless—the responsibility of deciding what is a fair rent in individual cases of dispute—nay, more, in some provinces, of settling rents in detail at periodic intervals. Mistakes have no doubt been made: legislation in some cases has fixed its eyes too closely on the foreground, and, while protecting existing tenants, has not safeguarded from degradation the generations that are to come after. But it is impossible to deny that the law has been, generally, very beneficent and very efficacious, and that, in the simplicity of its motives, the directness of its methods, and the completeness of its efforts, it offers a striking contrast to past endeavours of the English Parliament to regulate the struggle between Irish landlords and their tenants.

—by the influence of Government.

Nor has the State limited its efforts on the tenants' behalf to the formal procedure of legislation. It has at times usefully employed its influence for their protection. At the last settlement of the Central Provinces, some seventeen years ago, it was discovered that the development of the wheat export trade had proved disastrous to those tenants—from a third to a half of the total number—who, being of comparatively recent standing, had been left unprotected by the law as it then stood. In their desire to secure wheat the landlords demanded rents in grain instead of in cash, and at such high rates as to be practically unpayable, the object being to gain control of the tenants' produce by the pressure of rent arrears. It was within the rights of the Government to assess its land revenue upon the landlords' rent rolls. The landlords objected that the rent rolls were fictitiously high. The offer was made to lower the demands of the State if the rent rolls were lowered to a realisable standard and fresh leases were issued. This alteration was, naturally, unpalatable, but after much negotiation it was accepted. Arrears were recalculated, with the result that thousands of tenants were set on their feet again. Some years later the Government took power by legislation to fix the rents of tenants who had hitherto been left outside the law—that is to say, to exercise by law the authority it had already exercised by consent. Practical experience had been so greatly in favour of this innovation that the landlords refrained from challenging it, and it was accepted as non-contentious by their representative in Council. A striking testimony to the benefit of the rent reduction, in enabling the tenants to withstand the effects of a subsequent famine, was given before the last Famine Commission by one of the largest landlords of the Province, who at the outset was strongly opposed to the interference of the State with his rent rolls.

To some the executive interference of the State in a matter of this sort may appear quixotic or indiscreet. But history has rarely afforded a more striking illustration of benevolent initiative and accomplishment on the part of officials.

xvi.—The Police and the Law Courts.

On the outskirts of one of the larger villages you will notice a house standing apart from the others, and distinguished by gabled roof and white-washed walls from the mud or bamboo cottages beyond it. This is the Police Station, and if you are an official and your visit is expected, a row of, say, a dozen men in dark-blue uniform will be standing to attention in front of it, under the command of a sub-inspector, who salutes you with his sword and then advances, full of information as to the state of the crops, the condition of the people, and the crimes of importance that have lately been committed. Over an area of eighty or ninety square miles of country the detection of crime and the arrest of criminals are in his hands. The district is mapped out into police circles, each having a Police Station as its centre. For the forty or fifty thousand people living in its circle the Police Station stands for the genius of British authority. The nearest magistrate may be thirty miles away or more.

The Police Station.

The Indian police have accomplished great things; but they offer an ever-present threat to laxity of administration. Considering the density of the population, its poverty and its diversity, crime is under very close control. One is struck with the number of little children wearing silver necklaces or waistbands (and little else besides) that play about the road in towns and

The police a credit—also a threat.

villages, with no one in charge, but in absolute confidence. Coolie women go from village to village with no fear for their silver bangles and necklaces. Houses are not closely shut up at night; their doors not infrequently stand wide open. A man can safely travel with a bag of rupees wherever his business takes him. On the other hand, the Police Station forces have many opportunities for evil. Their power is very great. They institute inquiries into crimes that are reported or heard of, and in cases where the offence is technically serious—including all cases of theft, however petty—they can arrest the suspected offender and march him off to the magistrate. Recruited from the people, they have the morality of their neighbours, which passes no very harsh judgment upon the taking of bribes. The State finances can afford them but small pay: the officer in charge of the Police Station is fortunate if he receive £60 a year, and the constables are paid one-tenth of this amount. Their English superiors—at most two in each district—with whatever activity, can exercise but limited personal control. The police have great temptations to take bribes and to oppress the people. And they yield to these temptations if they are not impressed by the strength and vigilance of the superior authority.

They have peculiar difficulties. They are confronted not only with individual criminals or small gangs of criminals, but with extensive associations for the commission of crime, which do not always trouble themselves to work furtively, but make open war upon society. Such associations spring up naturally in a country where unity and secrecy of purpose is so powerful a link

Special difficulties.

between man and man. Two generations ago, before railway travelling was dreamt of, the highways were infested by the members of a criminal fraternity known as *thugs*, who, using the most ingenious disguises, attached themselves to travellers, won their confidence, and, on a convenient opportunity, strangled them.

The thugs.

The fraternity included men of various castes; but they were knit together by a peculiar and secret form of worship, and before undertaking an enterprise, formally committed it to the favour of their goddess. They terrorised the country. So numerous were their victims that a special service of police was organised for their repression. Under Colonel Sleeman, whose name lives in India to this day, the secrets of the fraternity were discovered, its active members arrested and convicted, and their families brought under close control and set to industry. In a carpet factory at Jabalpur some old men—sons of thug leaders—were working till the other day. The thugs have disappeared; but their footsteps are followed (though in much smaller numbers) by professional poisoners who use the railways to pick up acquaintanceship with travellers, into whose food, when cooking, they drop the poisonous berries of a species of nightshade which stupefy, and sometimes kill outright. Solitary travellers offer them their best opportunity; but family parties are sometimes poisoned and robbed in this manner.

Dacoity.

Another form of organised crime is dacoity or brigandage. This openly preys upon society. A party of armed men attack a village and hold it up: terrifying the people by some acts of brutality, they pillage the houses, torturing any persons who will not show where their money is concealed. I have known cases where they have cut off the noses of women who have courageously refused to point out their husbands' property. The people seldom resist: a band possessing four or five guns will terrorise a village containing many times this number. The dacoits are not infrequently men of good family, who are impoverished or indebted; and they, as a rule, have behind them some man of wealth and position who provides them with funds and assists them in disposing of the property they have looted. It has happened before now that the man in the background was a local justice, or honorary magistrate. These predatory instincts are a survival from the days of the Pindaris, an association of outlaws, who in the declining days of the Moghal empire banded themselves together in central India, organised themselves in military form, and plundered the country from one side of the peninsula to the other. They actually founded a kingdom which is still subsisting, and they promised to become one of the ruling forces of the country, till in 1817 the British Government opposed them with an army of 120,000 men. Dacoity continued to be a scourge to the country during the early days of British rule. It is now generally under control, and most of the dacoities that are shown in the police records are simple gang burglaries, which are classed as dacoities because they are technically covered by the legal definition of the crime. They have very little in common with the violent outrages that are dacoities properly so called. But the crime is held down, not altogether strangled, and it springs up whenever there is a feeling of unrest in the country. During famine time there is not uncommonly an outbreak of dacoity, committed, not by the famine-stricken, but by brigands of respectability, who lead bands of their dependants against rival villages. One of the most significant fruits of the existing unrest in Bengal is the large number of dacoities that are committed by bands of educated young men, who, in order to gain funds for their political campaign, force the pockets of their own countrymen, and do not shrink from robbing by means of torture. This is quite a novel development in India, though it was experienced in Upper Burma after the annexation, when dacoits showed their dissatisfaction with the new régime by torturing and robbing their own people. But dacoity is not always a sign of local disorder. It is sometimes still committed by brigands from outside who in these days profit by the facilities of railway travelling. Not long ago a village in Assam was openly raided by a large armed party of Afghans, who confessed, when in custody, to having settled every detail of the enterprise at their homes beyond the Khyber Pass. Some of them had acquired a knowledge of the locality and of its richer inhabitants by having travelled as hawkers of cotton stuffs. Cases of this sort are, however, now uncommon, and dacoity is no longer a popular profession, though from time to time local Robin Hoods arise, who collect round them bands of desperadoes and are ready to offer pitched battle to the police. In their capture the Indian policemen have often displayed very signal courage. But there remain permanent associations for the commission of crime in the criminal tribes that infest some parts of the country. They have no means of livelihood but thieving, for which they have acquired the most extraordinary hereditary aptitude.

Criminal tribes.

To commit a burglary the men will enter a village at night disguised as dogs, playing the part, with extemporised make-up, much more naturally than it is presented in a Christmas pantomime. It is men of this class who are said to be able to steal a man's bedclothes off him. The tribes are kept under close supervision, and efforts are made to reclaim them, but without much success. The best use that can be made of men of this class is to enlist them as village watchmen. They are, as a rule, faithful to their salt, and they are exceedingly skilful detectives. They will trace a stolen bullock by its footprints for miles across country. In northern India a European staff of servants commonly includes a house-watchman. An acquaintance of mine, who had lived for some time in the cantonments of Cawnpore, shifted his residence to the civil station, a mile or two distant, and amongst his other servants took his watchman with him. A few days later, he received an anonymous letter pointing out that the watchmen of the cantonment were not of the same community as those of the civil station, and advising him to engage a new man. He thought little of it, so it was decided to use a more forceful argument. It was the hot weather, and, as usual, he slept out of doors. Waking one morning, he was amazed to see all his drawing-room pictures swinging from the branches of the tree above him: within the bungalow a party of 'ragging' undergraduates might have been enjoying themselves: the furniture was turned upside down. His bureau stood wide open. Money had not been touched, but his stock of postage-stamps had been taken, and was neatly disposed round the edge of the lawn, on each stamp a pebble, so that it might not be blown away. He made no more ado about changing his watchman.

In towns there are many professional criminals: but they are less closely associated, and in their antecedents and practices differ little from the criminal class of European cities. The police generally have them well in hand. The village population is honest and law-abiding. If there are thieves the people know of them, and keep an eye on their behaviour. The vast majority of the offences that are recorded as committed are of a very trivial character. Quite a third of them are thefts or attempts to commit theft, and in most cases the theft is of insignificant amount—a few shillings or even pence—and represent casual lapses to temptations that are strengthened by hardship. So far as the duties of the police are concerned, the law takes no account of the value of the property stolen: however small it be, the police are bound to take up the case and forward it for trial, because theft is classed as a serious offence. Thousands of men are arrested and sent for trial before a distant magistrate, charged with the commission of petty thefts which really do not call for police interference as a matter of course. Our legal definitions are too rigid to suit human nature in the East. As a matter of fact the village people could themselves deal with petty crime of this sort if they were permitted to do so. Moreover, it is open to any one whose property has been stolen to institute proceedings by complaint to a magistrate, who can order police inquiries and summon the offender before him to answer the charge. Were cases of this description withdrawn from the authority of the police, there would be very

Ordinary criminals.

much less scope for the misuse of authority, and the abuses which discredit our police administration would be materially lessened.

Misuse of police authority

Some of these abuses are due to the fact that the police officials are not more intelligent than we can expect them to be on the pay they receive. Riding across the country one day, I met a couple of constables who were escorting a respectable-looking man with all the precautions that are used with desperate offenders. He was handcuffed, and through the handcuffs there passed a rope, the ends of which were grasped by the constables. In the rear there followed an unhappy-looking coolie. I inquired what the offence was, and was told 'cattle-theft.' Looking closer at the prisoner, I recognised him as an old acquaintance, the landlord of a neighbouring village. Greatly surprised, I asked him what had happened. He told me that he had recently broken up some waste land: it did not bear well, and he had been advised to propitiate the local god by the sacrifice of a sucking-pig. He did not, of course, keep pigs, so had sent a servant round to get a pig from one of his low-caste tenants. The man was away from home: his wife refused to give the pig, so the servant took it. The coolie in the background was the tenant. I called him up and asked what he meant by charging his landlord with theft for taking a due which would be allowed for in the rent. His wife, he said, had hurried off in a temper to the police station, before he had returned home. The constables were merely carrying out orders, so, giving them a note to the magistrate, I rode on to

—due to unintelligence;

the police station. The sub-inspector in charge was apologetic, but urged that he had received a circular from the Inspector-General pointing out that cattle-thefts were increasing, and that cattle-thieves should be most strictly dealt with: they injured not only the individual, but the country, since a cultivator whose bullocks were stolen had perforce to leave his land uncultivated. I objected that one did not use pigs for ploughing. He brought out the circular. A stupid police-clerk had appended to it a 'List of Cattle,' copied apparently from the Cattle Trespass Act, which began with elephants and camels, and descended, through horses, buffaloes and bullocks, to goats and pigs. In this case, owing to the pedantry of a subordinate, a man of some local consequence was marched in handcuffs thirty miles along the public road. Had police interference with thefts been subject to a value limit this could not have occurred, for the value of the pig was certainly not above a shilling.

—due to anxiety to secure results.

The simplest and most obvious method of judging a police officer's work is by statistics—by examining the proportion of cases detected to cases occurring, and the proportion of convicted persons to persons arrested. This, and the sporting desire to run down criminals, constantly tempt the police to fabricate evidence. They not infrequently yield to temptation, though generally, I believe, to enmesh those whom they believe to be guilty, and with no deliberate intention of ruining the innocent. A good illustration occurs to me. It fell to me once, owing to the illness of the District Superintendent of Police, to raid what was said to be a den of coiners. We found no one in the house but an old man and his wife, who, naturally enough, protested their innocence. Close search brought to light a set of coining appliances, including dies which contained freshly-struck coins. The man kept a gambling-house, and was of notoriously bad character. Coiners were known to be about, and it was likely enough that he was associated with them. The case was committed to the Sessions, and he was sentenced to seven years' imprisonment. Some little time afterwards a private acquaintance hinted to me that the dies and coins had been placed in the house by the police, and asked me to compare the years of mintage that were inscribed on the dies and on the coins that were supposed to have been struck in them. This little point had escaped attention. I compared the years, and found that they disagreed. It was morally certain that the police had found some means of placing the dies and coins in the house, but before doing so, had omitted to make sure that their dates corresponded.[1] This illustration will explain the very profound and general distrust which the people have of police methods. There are few who do not think that to lose money by theft is a small matter compared with the worry of the police inquiry that follows. Petty thefts are only reported to the police because it is punishable to conceal their occurrence. At the same time the people fully appreciate the protection the police afford against serious crime, and a proposal to move a police station is commonly opposed by a petition from the villagers. 'Individuals may suffer from inquiries that are harass-

[1] It should be added that an appeal was instituted on the man's behalf, and he was acquitted.

ing and tortuous: but the community is relieved from apprehensions of violence; and if a theft has been committed in a neighbour's house, and his premises are in the hands of the investigating police, we watch his troubles philosophically and hope that a like misfortune may not befall us.

The people's unwillingness to assist.

It should, however, be observed that an attitude of detachment—an unwillingness to be involved in public affairs by giving assistance in criminal inquiries—is characteristic of the country, and does not need to be explained by any special distrust of the police. If a man sees a crime committed, his first impulse is to conceal his knowledge. He sees no reason why he should assist the State to do its own business; and by giving evidence he may incur enmity which may, at some time or other, provoke revenge. Moreover, a witness has to suffer much, to travel some distance to the court, to be detained, it may be, some days, and not improbably, under cross-examination, to be heckled in a fashion which to us is irritating, and to an Indian appears degrading. Such being the attitude of the people we may enter into the feelings of the police, and can understand how it comes that they press for evidence in ways that under lax supervision may easily degenerate into forms of torture.

Reforms.

Efforts are now being made to improve the police by increasing their pay, and by raising the status and emoluments of the superior officers. But it is doubtful whether any measures will succeed that do not strike at the root of the evil—the power which the police exercise of arresting persons upon petty charges. The principle should be to limit police interference as narrowly as is possible without a material sacrifice of the public peace and security.

By the time a case reaches the criminal court it is frequently overlaid with a tangle of false evidence.

Cases in the criminal courts.

In their villages the people are exceedingly truthful: were they not so, indeed, the complicated inquiries which precede a settlement of rents and land revenue would be quite impossible. But when a man is in the witness-box, in face, not of his village, but of the State, he thinks lightly of an oath to speak the truth. We can observe this levity in England also; but in unravelling falsehoods an Indian magistrate has experiences that are even more complicated than those of an English county court judge. If witnesses for the defence cannot be procured locally, they can generally be hired for a few pence in the precincts of the court-house. Prudent men do not trust to tutoring their witnesses: they dramatise the situation they wish to prove, and act it, so that the witness may testify to what he has actually seen, and may be better able to withstand the rigours of cross-examination. This expedient is, it must be confessed, not altogether unknown to the police: even if the incidents are to be correctly stated, it is safer to rehearse them, that the witness's memory may not slip. Apart from the police, a criminal charge can be instituted by a petition to a magistrate; the court fee is only eightpence, and a criminal complaint is very often employed as a means of harassing an enemy, or in order to settle a dispute that it would cost more to take to a civil tribunal. One very wet cold night, when I was on tour, my orderly informed me that an old woman was outside the tent and insisted on seeing me. When admitted, she threw herself at my feet crying for justice, said she had been cruelly beaten, and held up an arm which was closely bandaged and looked swollen and inflamed. She had come thirty miles through the rain to see me, was wet through, and a pitiful object. I asked where she lived, and the man who had struck her. They were next-door neighbours, and I happened to remember that there was bitter enmity between the houses in the matter of a front drain. Accordingly, before issuing a summons, I asked her to show me the wound. She protested with tears that the removal of the bandage would be too painful: she would indeed rather withdraw the charge. I insisted, and found that the swelling was caused by a very bad boil, which her relatives thought they might as well make use of for the confusion of their enemies.

Over-interference of the criminal courts.

The atmosphere of the courts being so destructive of morality, we must regret that cases of assault, trespass, and petty theft are brought before our criminal courts in thousands, instead of being dealt with on the spot. This is the more unfortunate in that Indian society is from ancient times accustomed to the jurisdiction of local juries or boards of 'dikasts.' The word 'panchayet,' meaning a jury of five persons, has passed into the English language—as spoken in India—to express an arbitration committee. Caste panchayets decide most quarrels that arise between caste-fellows; and it seems quite possible that, appointed under the auspices of Government to represent localities, they should deal with the quarrels which, between men of different castes, now develop into petty criminal cases. If they would sometimes act with less simplicity of purpose than the magistrate, they would always be assisted by a better knowledge of the facts. Success cannot be claimed for the existing procedure. The defendants are acquitted in nine-tenths of the cases of petty hurt, assault, and trespass, that are instituted before the magistrates; and, even so, the chances of erroneous conviction are sufficiently great to encourage persons to submit an enormous number of complaints that are obviously false or unfounded, and are summarily rejected. Nor are the results satisfactory, if we consider petty cases that are initiated, not by petition, but by the police after police inquiry. Of the persons who are thus charged with theft or attempts at theft, nearly half are acquitted. Some tentative steps are being taken to transfer petty criminal cases to village authorities. The difficulty lies in the matter of punishment. There is little objection to investing a panchayet with powers of fining. But very many offenders cannot pay a fine, or will not pay a fine, unless a severer punishment is imposed as an alternative. It is very undesirable that persons sentenced by panchayets should be confined in our district jails where they would become contaminated by association with professional criminals. It might be possible to revive the use of the stocks which, in former days, were as familiar to Indian as to English villagers. There are those to whom public exposure in the stocks seems an indignity which should not be offered to humanity. But in its indignity lies its deterrent value: and surely it is better that a man should suffer public ridicule than that he should be subjected to the demoralising influences of a prison.

It costs much more to enter the civil than the criminal courts. A criminal petition, which will raise indirectly the right to use a field-path, requires a stamp of eightpence only. A civil plaint for the value of a couple of pounds would be five times as expensive, and there are heavy charges for the summoning of witnesses. At the headquarters of a country district of Bengal, amidst a group of unpretentious, low-roofed offices and bungalows, there rises a handsome, double-storied building of decorated brickwork. This is the Civil Court-house —or (cynically regarded) the Casino — of the district, built out of the abundant revenue yielded by the court fee stamps. Around it is a wide space, dotted with trees, which during business hours is a Vanity Fair of chattering humanity—plaintiffs, defendants, their witnesses and backers, lawyers' touts and petition writers. A visit to these attractions is a pleasure to be eagerly anticipated, and for months after to be minutely discussed. You may meet on the roads little groups of people on their way to the court, the opposite parties and their witnesses in amicable conversation as to the abilities and exactions of the lawyers they employ, dropping in private life, like English politicians, the animosity with which each side will shortly impugn the motives and veracity of the other. In English society a man who has had a lawsuit is something of a curiosity: in India you rarely meet one of any means or position who has not had several. Copies of judgments and decrees are amongst his cherished possessions, to be brought out with pride if you show interest in his affairs. Contracts must be enforced: successions must be regulated, and our civil courts have established a

Civil litigation.

reputation for disinterested, if sometimes unaccountable, decisions. But their services cost the country rather dearly. The people even of backward villages spend extraordinarily large sums in litigation. The fluctuating course of a long-drawn suit excites and satisfies the gambling instinct, and the law courts afford a means of maintaining *amour propre*, and of wreaking vengeance—primordial feelings which in India overpower all prudential considerations, and impel even the poorest to singular extravagance. Thus it comes that the agricultural profits which the State has relinquished to the people are in great measure spent upon law, and that lawyers can enrich themselves in a poor country. They make incomes which are liberal, even according to a European standard, and have increased and multiplied exceedingly. An agricultural district in Bengal will support a bar of forty or fifty advocates, who, by their incomes and intelligence, take the lead in the society of their town. They are, as a rule, capable lawyers, alert in cross-examination and eloquent in address, and their influence has contributed very greatly to the increasing purity of our judicial administration. They are generally hostile critics of the Government, and keep severely aloof from its officials. They hold the threads of the new political activity, which is actuated rather by discontent with things as they are than by thankfulness they are no worse —which has a much livelier perception of the hardships than of the benefits that accompany British rule. Lawyers control the native press, and public opinion, so far as it exists, dances to their piping. They have enjoyed the powerful support of numerous English lawyers to whom India has offered a career, whether as barristers or High Court judges, or members of Council, and who, apart from feelings of professional sympathy, cannot divest themselves of an English suspicion of executive authority. The Indian Government has learnt by experience that legal interests are a force to be reckoned with. Between the Calcutta High Court and the executive authorities of Bengal there has been long-standing antagonism, and within the past three years, decisions of this court have complicated the efforts of the Government to cut back the early shoots of anarchism. Outside Bengal, lawyers have constrained the Government with less bitterness but with no less pertinacity; and in all questions involving legislation, have pressed it towards elaborations of idea and procedure which are not only unsuited to Indian conditions, but are positively harmful to the Indian people. Not merely have the speculative attractions of a lawsuit been enhanced by complexity of procedure and the varying chances of appeal. Lawyers are permitted by interminable speeches and by irrelevant cross-examination to increase the length of proceedings—and the amount of their fees—to an extent which, in England, would be condemned as preposterous. And, especially in Bengal, by steady pressure they have fashioned an idea that no ruling can be obtained, whether in the law courts or from the executive authorities, except on a lawyer's application, and have managed in this way to pose as the sole channel of redress. In popular estimation the Government and its tribunals are becoming a machine which issues orders in automatic response to the filing of court fee stamps. An Indian gentleman of the old school, discussing present-day society, commonly winds up with the remark, 'The lawyer is king to-day.' Things have changed indeed from the times of the Moghals. The French traveller, Bernier, remarked with surprise at the court of Aurangzeb, that lawsuits were seldom heard of, and lawyers never.

XVII.—Schools, Colleges, and the Press.

SEVENTY-FIVE years ago the brilliant self-confidence of Lord Macaulay shed a light upon India which opened to her an entirely new prospect. He was at that time a member of the Viceroy's Council, and it was on his advice, delivered with characteristic vigour and assurance, that the Indian Government decided upon an educational revolution — to substitute English for Oriental studies in the higher courses of instruction. There are those who would describe this policy rather as overshadowing than as illuminating the country, who believe that Western literature and science have unsettled the Indian mind without satisfying it, and that it was a mistake to exhibit the dreams of English romance to those whose lives are fast-bound with prosaic limitations, or to offer liberty as an ideal to men who are not free to choose even the food they would eat. But the change was inevitable. India is a member of the Empire, and could not possibly be denied a share in the Empire's heritage. The new learning would obviously increase the difficulties of Government. But the Anglo-Saxon race has impulses which escape the control of its business instincts. Through our policy there has always run a vein of knight-errantry—of what may be called the sporting spirit—which has led us into strange inconsistencies, but to which the development of our Empire owes most of the interest it possesses from

Lord Macaulay and English education.

the philosophic point of view. Our eastern empire rests upon authority: yet we have not scrupled to teach doctrines which belittle authority as the foundation of Government and exalt in its place a liberty of individual judgment which brings our rule to the bar of a new and uncertain tribunal. The doctrine of liberty has a strange appearance to Oriental minds. Our pupils have been quick to appreciate its bearings; but they have, so far, limited its application to politics, and have not permitted it to influence the customs which despotically regulate their social life. The lessons they have drawn are one-sided, and their conceptions of freedom are so imperfect as to be absurd. But they may gradually widen their conclusions; and, in this case, who shall say that England has been mistaken in a policy which breathes new vigour into the stagnation or decadence of Indian life?

If we judge of India by village society, the influence of English studies is, so far, inconspicuous.

Knowledge of English: how far extended.

Except in some parts of Madras and Bengal, one rarely finds a villager who can speak a word of English—indeed, villages are still not uncommon in which but three or four men can read or write their own vernacular. Those who know English congregate in the towns. There are about 40,000 men in India who have graduated at a university in English, and, judging from the statistical results of the examinations, about ten times this number must have read enough English to carry them to the end of the high school course. At the last census (1901) about a million persons recorded themselves as acquainted with English. The knowledge possessed by at least half of them must be exceedingly small; and their number appears trifling in a population of 232 millions. But if we omit women and children, the proportion of those who know something of English rises to about one in a hundred. In the towns it is about four times as high, and a good deal higher in the presidency towns of Calcutta, Madras, and Bombay, where English speech is gradually finding its way into family life. Schoolboys commonly talk English to one another. But these statistics give one a very imperfect idea of the extent to which English instruction has influenced the country. It has changed the character of our public services, and has affected the life of all who come in contact with them. For some years past a knowledge of English has been an essential qualification for appointment to any but the lowest grades of Government employ. The course of the past generation has had few things more noticeable to offer us than the improvement in the efficiency and the honesty of our native Indian officials. There can be little doubt that by the study, through English literature, of higher standards of morality, Indian minds have acquired conceptions of duty which they could with difficulty have gleaned from the Oriental classics.

Influence of English education on public services.

For many years before the Indian Government decided to patronise Western learning, English missionaries had been acting as its pioneers. By the commencement of last century missionary enterprise had established schools for the teaching of English in Calcutta, Bombay, and Madras, and the Government was learning by experience the value of their pupils in the public service. These schools have since grown into large colleges:

Early developments.

other mission schools and colleges have been established in numbers; and until comparatively recent times, missions have led the van in teaching to the youth of India the secular knowledge of Europe. A large proportion of our present officials have been educated under mission auspices, and it is hardly too much to say that India has received education as the gift, not of England, but of Christianity. Mission institutions receive, of course, grants-in-aid from the Government under the general rules in force. Religious instruction is not compulsory, and very few indeed of their pupils have accepted the Christian faith.

Popularity of English instruction.

At the outset no very eager desire was manifested for English courses of instruction. In 1860—a quarter of a century after the Indian Government had formally decided for their adoption —only 30,000 pupils were studying in classes above the primary stage. There are now over 600,000: so rapidly has the new learning grown in popular favour. A powerful stimulus was given by the establishment, in 1860, of the universities of Calcutta, Bombay, and Madras, to which have since been added universities at Lahore and Allahabad. It must not be imagined that these universities in any way resemble those with which we are most familiar —the association of a number of teaching colleges under the control of a central authority, which not only determines the courses of instruction and examines in them, but is concerned in the discipline and morality of the students, is interested in their religion, and itself takes part in instructing them. The Indian universities have been actuated by a narrower ambition—that of examining students and of determining by the examinations the course of high school and college instruction. The colleges which train for the university degrees are scattered over the country, and have no organic connection with one another, except by the fact that they are 'affiliated' to the university. The Indian universities are in fact examining boards, and resemble in this respect the University of London. Three examinations were instituted—one for matriculation (which represents the end of the high school course), a second intermediate between matriculation and the degree, and a third for the degree. They became exceedingly popular. Success in each of them was accepted by the Government as qualifying for admission to certain grades of the public service: to matriculate, or to pass the 'intermediate,' represented not merely a stage in the university curriculum, but the securing of an asset which could be turned to immediate practical advantage. Moreover, the examinations offered an occasion for winning social distinction, which appealed very strongly to the emulative instincts of youths and their families. In conversing with the father of a family, you will find that no subject interests him so keenly as the examination prospects of his sons. In Bengal, where the unfortunate father of girls has practically to purchase husbands for his daughters, the price of a bridegroom depends very greatly indeed on the examination he has passed, and each of his successes is reflected in a direct increase in his realisable value. The most convincing proof the principal of an engineering college could give me of the growing popularity of technical instruction was the rising value in the marriage market of diplomas

University examinations: their effects.

of engineering. Indian youths throw themselves into their studies with a nervous self-abandonment which in England we rarely find displayed except by girls. Their horizon is limited by thoughts of the examination-room. Failure is a disgrace which will even drive a sensitive boy to suicide. I was called one morning before sunrise to receive a visitor who asked to see me on urgent business. He was a Brahmin gentleman of position. I found him in the deepest distress. He handed me a letter addressed to him by his son, who had just returned home after learning of his failure to matriculate. The boy said that his failure had disgraced his family as well as himself, and was more than he could bear. He had determined to poison himself, and wrote these lines of apology and of farewell. Some pathetic words in a postscript asked that bad handwriting might be excused 'as I write this by moonlight.' The father had received this letter from the dead body of his son. He had come to entreat my assistance to save him from the trials of a police inquiry and a public inquest.

Judged by English comparisons, the standard of these examinations is decidedly low. It is not that

Leniency of the examination test.

the examination papers are easy: it is that the examiners are satisfied with a very small degree of success in answering their questions. Generally, candidates can pass if they secure a trifle over one-third of the full marks. The successful candidates exhibit therefore great diversity of talent. At the head of the list are youths of great, often of brilliant, capacity: but the majority are aiming too high for their strength, fail at the outset, or succeed in one examination only to fail in the next. In the absence of an oral examination it is almost impossible to check cramming, and boys frequently matriculate who cannot write or even spell two lines of English correctly. The question papers are ambitious—sometimes too ambitious for the country: but no sooner are the subjects for the following year prescribed than keys issue by the hundred to enable students to memorise replies to all likely questions. It is saddening to find youths who can hardly comprehend simple English prose, condemned to take up such a poem as *Lycidas*. They simply learn by heart an English paraphrase, trusting that when the time comes they will be able to connect the paraphrase with the original. Liberal as is the marking, the examinations result in a deplorable wastage of hopes and aspirations. Of the thousands who annually offer themselves for matriculation, more than half fail, although many of the candidates go up two or three times. Of those who succeed and pursue their studies half again are eliminated by the intermediate examination, and of those who are again successful less than half manage to secure a degree. Amongst the graduates—and especially the few who graduate in honours—are young men of very conspicuous ability. Their admission to Government employ has regenerated the public service: those that turn to the bar make acute and eloquent lawyers. But the fact remains that of about 23,000 students who annually endeavour to matriculate less than 1800 will win through to a degree. The vast majority will slip and fall at the gates of the arena. As some sort of consolation to the thousands who fail, to have failed is itself accepted as a minor qualification. Applicants for employment commonly urge that they are 'failed

It encourages failure.

matriculates' or 'failed B.A.'s.' A considerable number secure subordinate posts in the Government service. But very many are left adrift: they subsist in depressing dependence upon their relations, and fall easily into the net of seditious agitation. They have lived to be examined and have failed; and are the more to be pitied, as their labours for the examination-room are of but little assistance to life outside it.

Greater strictness desirable.

It is earnestly to be desired that, by greater strictness in marking, the university course should be limited to those who are really capable of following it, and that its examinations should not act as a temptation to failure. But it is difficult to reverse a strong current, and there are serious obstacles in the path of this reform. It is extremely distasteful to those who are interested pecuniarily or professionally in the success of schools and colleges, since it would diminish the number of their students, and the receipts from school fees. The universities would also suffer. They derive most of their incomes from examination fees, and would lose in resources if they discouraged candidates. Popular feeling is much against strictness: even now, should an unusually large proportion of candidates be rejected, a vigorous outcry is raised in the native press, which has gone so far as to demand a revision of results by the addition of 'grace marks.' Indian students labour under special difficulties, and it is impossible to deny all sympathy to leniency in examining them. They have to use a foreign language for proving their capacity: it is as if an English youth was obliged to answer science questions in French. Not only are there difficulties of expression: it is not easy for a boy to comprehend lessons that are given in a foreign tongue, and he is tempted to trust to his memory only. There has been a tendency (which the Government is now endeavouring to check) to use English as the language of instruction from almost the beginning of school-life, and one finds quite little boys learning Indian history and geography in English. Consequently examiners not infrequently receive glimpses of ignorance which show that the candidates have no understanding of their subjects, though they may be able to pass in them. Boys who can easily find their way about a globe will show, when pressed, that they still conceive of the world as a plane supported upon the tusk of a monstrous boar, which itself rests upon other chimerical animals.

Such difficulties as these can only be met by great efficiency in instruction. But the teaching is not generally zealous or intelligent. Until recently it has been the policy of the Government to extend education, not so much by the establishment of institutions of its own, as by assisting societies or individuals to establish them—by offering grants in aid to supplement the fees that can be secured from students. This policy was in accord with the English ideas of the day: it appeared, moreover, to provide for the foundation of schools and colleges which would teach religious as well as secular subjects, and thus would offer what the religious neutrality of the State is compelled to deny. But the results have been disappointing. Speaking generally, the aided schools and colleges have taught secular subjects indifferently (and only with an eye to the examination-room), and religious subjects not

Superficiality of instruction.

at all, unless they are in the hands of Christian missions or Muhammadan associations. Of recent years the Government has reconsidered the position, and has aimed at establishing more institutions of its own. But at the present time four-fifths of the high schools and three-fourths of the colleges are under private management. The schools are periodically visited by Government inspectors, but the inspecting staff is too weak for its duties. Some of these institutions, and especially those in mission hands, are supplied with fairly adequate funds by contributions and by students' fees: a few, in private hands, are a source of profit to their proprietors. But generally their existence is a struggle over ways and means. The Government grants are not large, and the fees they can realise from their students are very small. There are many colleges which can be attended for less than £3 per annum. The teachers are underpaid and have no prospects in their profession, and the most capable of them regard their teacherships merely as stepping-stones to other employment. A high school teacher is fortunate if he receives £25 a year.

Laxity of discipline.

The universities have not concerned themselves with discipline or morality. Nor has the management of schools and colleges generally been more regardful of these matters. In old days the pupil was the disciple—the servant of his teacher: the class masters of the present day do not look for much respect and do not receive it. Parents bitterly complain of the bad manners that their boys bring home from their class-rooms. Students who come from some distance (and this is the case with great numbers) have had to find such shelter as they can in the towns. They have drifted not infrequently into disreputable surroundings: indeed it has before now been discovered that lodgings used by students were kept by prostitutes. In Bengal especially they have suffered much from associations of this kind. The connection is not strongly reprobated by public opinion: you may find houses of ill-fame in the close vicinity of college buildings; and the leading Bengali newspaper of Calcutta, in describing the political escapades of some students, mentioned without disapproval that the boys were escorted in their procession by the women of the town. Students at the mediæval universities of Europe also lived in squalid independence. But they were animated by higher hopes than of success in the examination-room. When we offered India an education that was strange and unsettling, we should have safeguarded the reform by a care for morality and discipline. It is a just criticism that our policy has been too ambitious for the means at our disposal.

Schemes of improvement.

The evils of the present system have long been recognised, and during the viceroyalty of Lord Curzon, earnest endeavours were made to place education on a more wholesome footing. In the face of much popular clamour, the constitutions of the university senates were reorganised so as to increase the weight of expert authority and to weaken the predominance of influences that had been harmful in the past. Universities were drawn into closer connection with the colleges that were affiliated to them and to the high schools that led up to the colleges: they were authorised to prescribe rules for management and discipline, and to satisfy themselves by inspection that their rules were observed. Funds were granted them to assist the prosecution of these reforms. It was decided that the staff of Government school inspectors should be largely strengthened, and that the State should not shrink from establishing educational institutions of its own if they were required by special needs or to serve as models. A more practical turn was to be given to science teaching and to teaching generally, and technical instruction was to be specially encouraged. The necessity was realised of providing for the shelter of students who come from distant homes, by the establishment of boarding-houses or hostels under proper control. Special grants were made for this purpose, and satisfactory progress is already evident. But it will be some years before we rid ourselves from the consequences of over-hastiness in the past. And it remains to be seen whether the universities will be able to set the needs of the people above popular wishes, and by excluding from the examination-room those who cannot suitably enter it, will check a craze which has degraded education and caused much unhappiness.

Exclusion of religious teaching.

In India morality is based upon religion, and to banish religion from school-life is to invite a revolution of ideas. In other countries, where the State has decided to foster no religion, churches or associations have stepped into its place. There have been no such agencies in India to counteract the solvent effect of modern science, and the majority of Hindu students see their old beliefs crumble with nothing to replace them but the morality which is enjoined by the criminal law or is supported by calculation. Loyalty to the King, obedience to the teacher, respect for authority, are judged from a purely logical standpoint, and are regarded, not as obligations, but as courses of action which it may or may not be advantageous to adopt. In fact they are dissected into profit and loss accounts. An attitude of religious neutrality was imposed upon us by the political situation, and India has watched a remarkable contrast—one body of Englishmen, the missionaries, striving earnestly to evangelise, while another body, the officials, are careful to display no practical sympathy with them. It is certain that the people would have acutely resented any attempts of the State to proselytise them. Their sons attend missionary colleges and schools in very large numbers; but their actual contact with Christianity is limited to, at most, half an hour's scripture reading a day. An insignificant proportion of the students are Christians, and any conversions to Christianity arouse very bitter feelings. On one occasion the students of one of the oldest established Christian colleges in India struck work and held a meeting of angry protest because one of their number became a Christian. A State which favours no one religion does not abandon its neutrality by assisting all of them; and the Government might, for example, have subsidised the teaching of Hindu and Muhammadan beliefs to Hindu and Muhammadan children, paying the religious teachers in proportion to the number of their pupils. Such a policy would probably not have been unpopular, and would have conciliated influences that can usefully support the State. The Indian Government upholds very large grants from the public revenue that were made by its predecessors to Hindu and Muhammadan religious foundations. But by making fresh grants for religious purposes it would have given an endorsement to alien faiths which would have been very distasteful to Christian opinion, even although Christian teachers were entitled to like assistance in respect of Christian pupils. So it has come about that, amidst the differences of its professors, religion has lain apart, too thorny to be touched.

Muhammadan views.

To the dogmatic ideas of the Muhammadan faith, education without religion seemed wholly mischievous, and until recently Muhammadans have been as distrustful of secular schools as the Catholics of France. Moreover, they viewed with natural suspicion an educational policy which dethroned in favour of English the Persian which had, for generations, been the official language of the State. They preferred to maintain schools and colleges of their own, in which teaching was given on Oriental lines. Instruction commenced with the study of the Korán, and, aiming at scholarship rather than science, led its students to the masterpieces of Persian and Arabic literature. It has suffered from the lack of competent teachers, and was doomed to failure by being out of accord with the times. English learning was the qualification that was required for State employ, and by neglecting it the Muhammadans have lost much of their share in the public service. They have for some time past realised this, and Muhammadan students now attend Government high schools and colleges in increasing numbers. Their objections to purely secular education are being met by the establishment of Muhammadan hostels, which do not remove their boarders from religious influences. The Anglo-Muhammadan college at Aligarh, which was founded forty years ago by Sir Syed Ahmad, has led the van in this reformation of ideas.

Education to be given a more practical turn.

It will easily be perceived that our education has been of too literary a character. In its highest efforts it has turned out men who are excellently well qualified to serve the State in executive and judicial capacities. But its typical product is the clerk. To meet the needs of the State for engineers, doctors, and veterinary surgeons, special colleges for engineering, medicine, and veterinary science have been maintained by Government. Outside State service, men of these professions can still hardly find a livelihood, though of recent years medical practitioners have begun to attract clients. There are special classes for law which are well attended, since they are the doorways of admission to the most lucrative profession of the day. Efforts have been made to train youths in mechanical handicrafts. But a country which is devoted to the producing of raw material, and imports manufactures, does not offer a promising field for acquirements of this kind. There are, however, signs of an industrial awakening: a demand for skilled mechanics is arising, and courses of instruction in mining have been well attended, and have opened a way to profitable employ. Endeavours have been made to develop practical as opposed to literary ability by the offer in high schools of an alternative course, which includes practical training in wood and iron work, and leads to a higher course in engineering instead of in arts. In some provinces it has attracted a large number of students. Its success reflects in some measure the popular movement in favour of encouraging home industries which, under political influences, developed into a boycott of British goods. But it also indicates a growing distrust of purely literary training as an equipment for the struggles of adult life.

Village schools.

It is only within the last generation that the Government has concerned itself very actively with the elementary education of village children. Those who belong to the priestly and trading classes have always endeavoured to give their children some teaching. The Brahmin teacher was also the master of his pupils; learning was a kind of apprenticeship, of which discipline and obedience were essential features. Brahmin boys occupied themselves largely in committing to memory texts of scripture, and each day's lessons commenced with an invocation addressed to the divine patron of learning. To the lower castes, books were mysteries which they had no desire to unveil. Muhammadan parents liked their children—girls as well as boys—to memorise some chapters of the Korán, and sent them, when they could, to classes that were opened for this purpose in the village mosque. Some of the boys picked up a little reading and writing by the way. University examinations had little charm for villagers, and the generality of the people saw no reason to value learning for its own sake. There were no such aspirations as filled the class-rooms in towns; and the task before the Government was not merely to provide schools, but to impel the people to use them. Enthusiastic officials have been known to employ the village watchman to collect the children and take them, in mock custody, to school. But pains have not been spared to alleviate the irksomeness of sedentary instruction. In some provinces little gardens of flowers and vegetables are attached to the school-houses. The boys take some pleasure in maintaining them. They show zeal in practising (to the great interest of their parents) indigenous exercises in combined gymnastics. Boys who are of use to their parents can attend for half the time only, and holidays are liberally given during the busy times of field work. This is in provinces where the schools are State institutions. Where they are managed on the 'aided' system, less is done for the pupils. But, generally, progress has been encouraging. Within the last generation the attendance of boys at primary schools has increased eightfold, and now exceeds four millions. Nevertheless, taking the country as a whole, this is only a sixth of the boys of school-going age. The interest taken by the village people in education varies remarkably from province to province. It is keenest in Bengal and the Maratha country, where one boy in four attends school. It is least in the Panjáb and United Provinces, where the proportion is only one in nine. Curiously enough, these are the provinces where the admixture of Aryan blood is largest. For seven boys, only one girl attends school, and the instruction she receives is generally trifling. So far, female education has affected the country very little. It is a development that has still to come.

Need of village schooling.

It may be inquired why the Indian Government should be at pains to disturb the current of village life by urging new experiences upon the people. To lessen, for one reason, the harassing effect of a still greater disturbance. The time has passed when the cultivator was secure in his field because no one coveted it. To the risk of losses by drought or blight there is added a new and more insidious danger. Land is in great request, and those who hold it are surrounded by men who are anxious to dispossess them, and are only too willing to offer them loans—will indeed force loans upon them. The cultivator stands between his landlord and the money-lender, beset by both of them, and has his only chance of escape in increasing intelligence. Those who have dealings with village people know very well how different are the methods that are employed with an ignorant rustic and with one who is lettered.

From schools to the press may seem an abrupt transition. But Indian newspapers look to students for much of their circulation. There are English schoolmasters who regret that boys take such little interest in the news of the day. In India they would be thankful for their English experiences, for the reading of newspapers has become a feature—and a demoralising feature—of schoolboys' self-instruction. You may see class-room tables littered with journals.

The Indian press.

The first English schools were established by missionaries, and missionaries also started the vernacular press. The newspapers they issued or supported were, like those now appearing in the Khasi hills, mainly concerned with religious subjects; and it was not till some time after the Mutiny that the native press began to cater for its readers by purveying the news of the day, or by discussing politics. It must not, however, be imagined that in the absence of newspapers the more intelligent Indians were ignorant of current events. News flies across India with extraordinary rapidity;

Its early history.

the character of officials in authority is minutely discussed and weighed with accuracy, and it may perhaps be maintained that a people of critical instincts can learn more of things as they are by word of mouth, than when they put their trust in the news that is distilled for them by journalists. But during the last half-century the native press has grown very rapidly in soil that has been prepared for it by education. Omitting from consideration the journals that address themselves to the European population, there are now issued from Indian presses eight or nine newspapers that are written in English, which is quite as idiomatic and picturesque as is employed by most English leader-writers, and is enlivened by even more imaginative ability. The number of newspapers that are issued in vernacular is very large—approaching a thousand: they are more numerous than is supposed, for in eastern Bengal I discovered between twenty and thirty that had apparently not come to official notice.

Freedom of the press.

The confident optimism of the English people has never been more audacious than when it conceded a free press to an alien dominion—a dominion, moreover, which half a century after annexation had exhibited the perils of the Indian Mutiny. It is generally supposed that the gift was Lord William Bentinck's: but the concession which was made by him in 1835 affected Europeans, not Indians, and merely secured adventurous English journalists against the summary expulsion to which unwelcome non-officials were at that time liable. In those days the native press was still in early infancy. In 1878 Lord Lytton, convinced of growing danger, attempted to bridle journalistic licence. An Act was passed under which the proprietors of vernacular newspapers who published seditious or scurrilous matter were required to furnish security, or were given a formal warning. A repetition of the offence entailed forfeiture of the security, or confiscation of the press. They might protect themselves by accepting a press censorship. This Act was much resented by the Indian press: it was only partially effective, since it did not apply to newspapers, however virulent, that were published in English: it was distasteful to Liberal feelings in England, and four years later it was repealed by Lord Ripon. The leading provisions have now been re-enacted, with application to English as well as to vernacular newspapers, and endorsed by a Liberal ministry: but forfeitures or confiscations that are ordered under the new law can be questioned on appeal to a special bench of the High Court.

Attitude of the Indian press.

The spirit of the Indian press has passed through two phases. Until recent years the editor's object has been mainly commercial—to sell his newspayer: lately it has become very largely propagandist — to breed discontent with British rule. If a newspaper is to sell it must be interesting to its readers: no one wishes to hear praises of the Government, unless he is himself connected with it. Accordingly, Indian editors have always criticised Government measures as caustically as they were able. They did not, in those days, venture upon abuse of British rule as such; but they attacked with much violence (and sometimes with good cause) particular officers of Government: they occasionally libelled very grossly Indian gentlemen of position, creating apprehensions which were in some cases used for blackmailing; and by a certain (very disgraceful) character of advertisement, they made open appeal to the proclivities of youth. They were an annoyance to the official world, but not more than an annoyance. Indeed, they were not averse from confidential relations with officials. Only six years ago the editor of one of the most powerful Indian papers, who now is unable to see any merit in British rule, sent to me on three occasions proofs of articles that attacked Englishmen serving under my orders, and offered to withhold publication if I would myself make inquiries and act upon the result.[1] Editors who knew that their papers were read by the head of their Government not infrequently appealed to him directly in their leading articles.

Its increasing hostility.

The Indian editor has now very generally been tempted to change his chair for the pulpit: his profession has become a mission, and the mission is to infect the country with a ferment of hatred for British rule. Of recent years no calumny of our actions has been too outrageous for publication. To the intelligent we have been described as draining the country of its resources, as stifling its development, degrading its arts and emasculating its spirit: for old-fashioned readers we are attempting to destroy caste, and to pervert Hindus from their religion: to the ignorant we are actually shown as poisoning wells to spread the plague: the sentimental—and sentiment pervades the East—are stirred by pathetic references to the India of epic time, which, in deep distress, but with undying

[1] I accepted the offers: in one of the cases the allegations were well founded, and proper notice was taken.

spirit, lies bound at the feet of a nation of shop keepers. To rescue her no act is immoral; and many editors in parables, and not a few in open language, have been exhorting the youth of the country to assassinate Europeans. We are too apt to judge our rule with egotistical complacency. We are so convinced of its benefits as to ignore its distastefulness, and to expect gratitude for work which, to others, may appear to be the fruit of individual ambition. A Nemesis has indeed fallen upon us.

The development of sedition.

The high-priests of this hostility are the Brahmins of the west coast, who cannot forget that only a century has passed since they were the moving spirit of the Maratha confederacy. It was first openly displayed by them thirty years ago in the publication of newspapers which opposed the Government with a seditious virulence that was elsewhere unknown. The people noted with amazement that these attacks were not suppressed—nay, that the man who inspired them was actually permitted to take a seat on the Legislative Council of his province. Naturally they respected him and were inclined to believe him. Bengali sympathy was dexterously enlisted, and was actually attracted to the cult of Sivaji—the national hero of the Marathas—though Bengalis had suffered most grievously from the depredations of his followers. But elsewhere than in the Maratha country the patriotic outpourings of the press were accepted as interesting displays of histrionic ability, until an impression gained root that they could actually move the Government from its purposes. The East is impressed by things, not words. Editors who could do, as well as speak, commanded attention. Their words were listened to with consideration, and found amongst the impressionable youths of the country hands to commit the outrages which they darkly suggested. Their revolutionary sentiments do not, as yet, find practical sympathy amongst the mass of the people. It is true that no assistance is given to the Government in the arrest of anarchical offenders. But this is because, to the Indian, life outside his own family appears to be a drama in which he is not concerned to take a part. From his place in the audience he watches the struggle between the officers of Government and the stalwarts of the extremist party, reprobating in his heart their outrages, yet not without some feeling of pride in the exploits of his young men, and with (for Bengalis) the comforting assurance that his nation can no longer be reproached with lack of courage.

xviii.—England's achievements.

Benefits of British rule.

We pride ourselves on the work we have achieved in India—and with justice. Only a century ago the country was as a field that is ravaged by locusts. There was no government, if we understand by the term an organisation which exists for the benefit of mankind. Such rulers as held their own, exercised their authority for military purposes only, with armed forces constantly turned one way or the other. But over fully half of the country there was no established authority; and the people thought with terror of the next raid of the Marathas and Pindaris. Their only chance of relief was to take a hand with the plunderers. Little beyond a lifetime has passed since Maratha domination was ended. In this short period we have established throughout a continent a rule that in efficiency can be judged by a European standard, and in active benevolence surpasses many European governments. This is no small achievement.

Peace.

We have established peace. In present-day comfort we can hardly appreciate the greatness of this blessing. One must travel in the Near East to learn how industry fades if its fruits are not secured to it—how a land can be sterilised by the fear of armed violence. We have safeguarded India from the incursions of the Afghans and Nepalese, we have allayed the hostile jealousies of chiefs within her borders, and, during years now past, we have built up a protection for her against the ambitions of a European power. In the repression of crime we may have attempted too much for our powers, and may have added in some degree to harassments which we intended to relieve. But we have given security to person and property. If we exclude petty cases of assault and trespass, breaches of municipal bye-laws and the like, only two crimes are annually committed per 1000 of population. There is, proportionately, less criminality than in the United Kingdom.

To restore peace and maintain it, a large army has been required, and the Indian Government maintains a force of 230,000 men. A third of its rank and file are Englishmen, and since, according to present counsels, it is desirable that they should form part and parcel of the English army, regiments are frequently interchanged between England and India at a heavy expenditure to the State. The military charges now amount to £20 millions a year. They are undoubtedly high for a poor country. But the finances have stood the strain. If we credit the Indian Government with the value of its commercial assets, that is to say, with the value of the railways and canals which belong to the State and produce revenue for it, its public debt is but £22 millions —only half the amount which the repression of the Mutiny cost the country. With all its military expenditure the Government is economical for its aims and its efficiency. It may fairly be compared with that of Egypt. In both countries an Oriental race is governed on European methods. It cannot truthfully be asserted that the Government of Egypt does more for the people than that of India. But in proportion to population it is five times more expensive.

Material wealth has greatly increased. There are critics who are so ill-informed as to deny this. Their contention is absurd. At the commencement of British rule land had hardly any commercial value. It is now worth over £300 millions, and those who hold it have been enriched by this amount. From irrigation-works maintained by the State 17 million acres are irrigated—an area half the size of England—and the lowest possible estimate of the increase in produce thus obtained is £30 millions a year. Railways have not only increased the money value of produce: they have stimulated land reclamation, and by facilitating transport have secured the famine-stricken against the possibility of any actual shortage of food. During the last half-century the value of the Indian export and import trade has increased from £40 millions to £200 millions. The commercial classes have profited greatly. Millionaires are not unknown, and the prosperous appearance of the large commercial towns is a visible proof of the substantial incomes that are now derived from trade. The legal profession is flourishing: it is a creation of our own. Our army and public services afford a decent livelihood to hundreds of thousands. Half a million are employed in factories, and another half-million on tea estates. It is not so easy to demonstrate that the poorer classes of villagers are better off than they were. Statistics help us but little: they deal with averages, and we are concerned with the bottom of the scale. Official experience is limited by the frequent transfers of officers and their early retirement from service. But

Material prosperity.

if you will question men who know the country intimately, a European planter who has spent most of his life in India, or an Indian pensioner who grew old in service, they will laugh at the notion that poverty is now as great as ever, and will appeal convincingly to rises in servants' and coolies' wages, and, above all, to the immense improvement that is evident in the people's clothing. Nor must we forget that for two generations India has been absorbing treasure at the rate of £15 to £20 millions a year.

The so-called 'economic drain.'

There are, however, critics who refuse to be convinced by evidences of advancing prosperity. They insist that India *must* have been impoverished by the 'economic drain' she suffers in having annually to provide some £18 millions to meet the 'home charges'—the expenditure which is incurred in England by the Secretary of State on behalf of the Indian Government. The use of the term 'economic drain,' of course, begs the question. India renders no tribute to England, and the payments that she makes in England are for value received or for services rendered. Of the £18 millions thus expended, £6¾ millions represent the interest that is due to those who have lent money for the construction of the Indian railways, £3 millions are the interest on India's public debt, and £1½ million is the price of Government stores which could not be purchased locally of equal quality and as cheaply. These all represent payments for actual value received. The railways fully pay their way; and their interest charges are obviously met, not by the tax-payer as such, but by those who use railway transport for their own profit or convenience. It would, no doubt, be to India's advantage, if the shareholders, and the State creditors, were resident in India, and spent in the country the money they received. But Indian capitalists have not found railway undertakings an attractive investment; and had the lines not been constructed with English capital they would, for the most part, have remained unmade. In this matter India is no worse off than many other countries which are compelled to look to foreign capital for their development, and would be thankful to attract it upon the terms that India can secure. Home military charges amount to £2 millions, and civil administration (including the maintenance of the India Office) to a quarter of a million. A further three-quarters of a million is spent in giving absentee allowances to civil and military officers of the Indian Services who are in England on furlough or sick-leave, and £4 millions in providing pensions for civil and military officers who have retired from active service. The last two charges are of a peculiar character, and would not appear, in anything approaching these proportions, in the accounts of a European State. They are unavoidable incidents in the enterprise of governing a tropical country by European officers, who are unable to work hard in a hot climate without periodical rest and change, who frequently break down from ill-health, and who lose vitality and energy far more rapidly than in their native country. In the still more unhealthy conditions of West Africa it has been found necessary to offer still more liberal furlough rules. The expenditure upon pensions may appear to be surprisingly high. Pensions are of the nature of deferred pay, and experience has shown that any diminution of the existing privileges is followed by a decline in the number and quality of the candidates for the Indian services. The existing conditions have, in fact, been determined by demand and supply.

If we accept the doctrine that the State is responsible for securing (as far as may be) the fair distribution of wealth between man and man, the Indian Government may be charged by the cultivators with having sacrificed, in some degree, the poor to the rich. Proprietorship in land is, speaking generally, of our own creation. Politically, it has advantages. But by creating landlords we relegated the cultivators to the position of their tenants, and, as tenants, they became liable to landlords' aggressions. We realised the position some years after we had created it, and have since striven diligently by legislation to secure tenants in possession of their holdings at a fair rent. We have succeeded pretty well, except in Bengal, where, strengthened by a permanent settlement, the landlords were much more powerful and influential than elsewhere. Protective legislation has not rescued the Bengal tenant from degradation. The remedies it offers must be sought through the civil courts, and on the initiative of the tenant; and men who have long suffered oppression have not the means nor the courage to fight their landlords in the courts, and can only be protected by a summary procedure. The cadastral surveys which are now in progress have disclosed that, directly or indirectly, the landlords of Bengal commonly exact as much as double the rent to which the law entitles them. We may, perhaps, console ourselves with the reflection that a Bengali

Justice.

tenant whose rent is low very frequently sublets his land and retires from farming, and that, in these conditions, the men who actually cultivate the soil can hardly be otherwise than rack-rented and poverty-stricken.

If we understand by justice the decisions of the civil courts, we have established a judicial machinery and procedure which is as elaborate as that of any European country. It is more complicated than India requires; it remedies many evils, but it produces some. It upholds, however, with fair efficacy the sanctity of contracts, it gives redress for damages, and it regulates the succession to property. The decisions of the civil courts are sometimes so unaccountable as to encourage speculative litigation. But the people have confidence, at any rate, in the purity of their intentions. The High Courts in particular are the most popular institutions the country possesses. They appear to stand between the people and the hastiness of the State; and the elaborations of law and of procedure which they have favoured in Bengal are appreciated by a race so quick-witted as to be a nation of lawyers.

Comparisons between the moral standards of different races are invidious and unfruitful. Most

Morality.

nations of intelligence have framed for themselves rules of high ideal morality: all nations are alike in not completely observing them. But it is undeniable that the provisions of the Indian Penal Code have educated as well as disciplined. It is true that the actions which they proscribe are for the most part condemned, for Muhammadans by the Korán, and for Hindus by the caste rules that are enforced by caste committees. But by its punishments the criminal law has reinforced the dictates of religion and of society, and by its pressure has done much to convert maxims into habits. Such crimes as murder and dacoity are regarded more seriously than before. In some notable cases the law has expanded the moral code of the country: it has put an end to slavery, to widow burning, and to human sacrifices, and it has nearly, if not quite, checked infanticide, though it is by no means certain that, if its pressure were relaxed, these practices would be found contrary to the public conscience. In some provinces relations between masters and servants survive which resemble those of domestic slavery. From time to time there are attempts at *sati*, which indicate that its prohibition is unpopular, and that, if we abandoned the country, it would probably revive. But in one important matter the criminal law has produced a habit of mind as well as of conduct. Its denunciation of official corruption has transformed the public services, which have begun to regard the taking of bribes as disgraceful. This is an immense step in advance.

Intelligence.

The severest critics of British rule will not deny that its influence has increased the intelligence of the people. As the result of its educational efforts the number of college students has risen during the past half-century from about 1000 to 26,000, and the number of pupils at school from half a million to nearly six millions. Newspapers are eagerly read and are published in large numbers. The writing of letters is becoming a matter of ordinary life: 700 millions annually pass through the post office—equivalent to nearly three per head of population. If we include only those who can read and write, the average number of letters per head is 50, which is considerably more than half the English average. Postal communication is evidently appreciated. Railway travelling does much to sharpen the wits. In India it is cheap and popular. The number of passengers annually carried exceeds 320 millions. By enabling the people to travel freely, and to correspond through the post, we have not only stimulated their intelligence: we have added very greatly to their general happiness.

Active philanthropy.

It is in India a novel idea that the State should expend its resources on the organised relief of distress. Until recent years famines seemed to be as uncontrollable as cholera or malaria, disasters whose effects were best passed over in silence. The Indian Government has undertaken to combat the forces of nature, and if many perish, many more are kept alive. We have ventured to press vaccination on the people in opposition to their wishes. Smallpox is regarded as a visitation from the 'Great Mother,' whose branding it is impious to resist. These scruples have given way before our perseverance, and now eight millions of children are annually vaccinated. In these days it is only old people that are commonly disfigured by this disease. We have established hospitals and dispensaries throughout the country which give relief each year to 25 million patients. When outbreaks of cholera occur, medical relief parties are organised and sent out to fight the disease by sanitary as well as remedial measures. A sustained campaign against the more insidious and destructive attacks of malaria has hitherto seemed too expensive and uncertain an enterprise; but, forlorn hope though it may be, an attempt is now to be made to lead it. For some time past the Government has distributed through the post office millions of packets of quinine at less than cost price.

On a general survey, then, it must be conceded that we can give a good account of our stewardship. The well-to-do owe their prosperity to British rule: to the poor it has at all events given the blessings of peace. They can give their labour where and when they please. By using their freedom they have secured higher wages, and they have no fear of being despoiled of their earnings.

Openings afforded for ambition.

We have increased material prosperity and have stimulated intelligence. How far have we satisfied the legitimate ambitions of an advancing community? What field have we provided in public affairs for the exercise of the talents which we have done our best to develop?

State service.

The service of the State offers to the educated youth of India a career which, till comparatively recent times, was wide enough to admit all of them. In England the possibilities of Government employ hardly present themselves to a father who is considering how to put his sons out into the world: State appointments are few in number in proportion to the population. Things are different in France; and in India it is not too much to say that the chances of Government employ occupy the horizon of every youth of ability, and provide his family with an engrossing subject for speculation. The most prominent of Bengali politicians, the most animated and eloquent critic of British rule, began his life in the Indian Civil Service, and owes to his dismissal his success in politics. In former days few young men completed their university course who did not secure appointments under Government, and this is still the case in the smaller provinces. But, generally, the universities now turn out graduates much more rapidly than vacancies occur in the public service, and an increasing proportion turn to the bar, to journalism, or to educational work. But the State still attracts the cream of youthful talent, and there are but few young men who deliberately elect for independence. The prospects offered by State employ are not unattractive. A salary of £60 a year in India is certainly equivalent to double this amount in England: there are over 22,000 Indians in the service of Government who enjoy at least this remuneration. The higher posts in the service are, of course, much more highly paid. There are over 2000 Indian magistrates or judges whose salaries, ranging from £200 to £800 a year, provide very liberally indeed for the domestic expenditure of Indian households, and would indeed be envied by officers of similar position in most countries of Europe. More than three times this number in other departments of the Government draw pay between £120 and £400 a year as surgeons, engineers, police and education officers, post and telegraph employés. In filling all these appointments, so exclusively has the State regarded the claims of educational attainments as to have given a fictitious value to education. It can then claim to have provided a career for intellectual ability. It is true that the superior appointments of control (which form the imperial as opposed to the provincial branch of the State service) are filled by the Secretary of State under arrangements that recognise the superior qualifications of Europeans. But natives of India can compete for these appointments in the examinations that are held in London, and have secured some footing in the Indian Civil Service and in the Indian Medical Service. Moreover, a certain number of appointments on the superior staff have been definitely reserved for Indians who have shown conspicuous ability in the Provincial service. Indians hold many judgeships on the High Court benches. Two Indian gentlemen have recently been appointed to the Secretary of State's Council, three others to the Executive Councils of the Viceroy and of the Governors of Bombay and Madras, and a sixth to the King's Privy Council.

As honorary magistrates.

But these, it will be said, are official openings. What scope is afforded to those who own land, or live by a private calling, but desire to take a hand in public business? There are no less than 3000 justices of the peace, or honorary magistrates, as they are called in India. Their powers are as extensive as those of English justices, and any who possess special qualifications, or manifest special aptitude, are invested with still wider authority, and are privileged to sit alone, and not on a bench with others, according to the general practice in India as in England. These honorary magistrates dispose of many thousands of cases annually, and can pride themselves upon being a very substantial force in the public life of the community.

In local government.

Still wider is the arena which local self-government affords for the public spirit of individuals. We have already described the completeness of the organisation which has endowed every town—even to places of 5000 inhabitants—with a municipal board, and has divided up the country into rural areas, each of which in local matters is administered by a board of similar character. Admission to these boards goes very largely by election. There are 1800 of them, offering seats to 13,000 non-official members. Very many of them elect their own chairmen, and have wider authority than is enjoyed by similar bodies in some of the most advanced countries of Europe. It may safely be asserted that outside the presidency towns, where competition for election is keen, there are few Indian gentlemen of intelligence and public spirit to whom these boards do not offer a means of winning local distinction by serving the public.

Pride in distinctive nationality.

In developing a national spirit we have been less successful. The divisions and cross-divisions which split up Indian society, and isolate its sections, are directly opposed to ideas of nationality. A political party has been formed which has taken the style of 'Nationalist.' But it is united merely by a knowledge of the English language and by its jealousy of British authority: its objects are purely negative: it has no constructive political programme: it offers no practical alternative to British rule: it has shrunk from touching questions of social reform—from attempting to remedy abuses and dissipate prejudices which are fatal to the growth of an enlightened national sentiment. In their private lives its members are divided by differences of thought and custom, which would drive them into violent discord were British rule, by effacing itself, no longer to offer a mark for the feelings of antipathy which are their bond of union. The nearest approach to a national sentiment in India is that which springs from a similarity of dress and language. Based on this similarity there are feelings which tend to draw together the heterogeneous tribes and castes of one tract, and to place them in rivalry with the inhabitants of another. The people of Bihar and Assam, at opposite extremities of the country inhabited by Bengalis, claim their land for themselves, and strongly resent the intrusion of their neighbours. The people of Orissa, another outlying province of Bengal, exhibit a similar feeling. The province of Oudh, which, under a separate administration, had gained an individuality of its own, resented its amalgamation a generation ago with the United Provinces. The Bengalis and the Marathas each manifest a unity of sentiment which, with the educated classes of the population, counteracts in some degree the separative effect of caste distinctions. The growth of such collective feelings is to the advantage of the people, since they probably offer the only possible solvent to the antipathies of caste. It would have been well for the country had its division into provinces for the purposes of government followed the lines marked by race and language, so as to reinforce the sympathy which arises from similarity in these matters, by feelings of pride in the local government. The existing administrative divisions of the country are so heterogeneous as to have a directly contrary effect. The presidencies of Madras and Bombay, for instance, each include three distinct peoples, speaking entirely different languages. The population of the province of Bengal, as has already been indicated, is still more diverse. Not only are the existing administrative divisions heterogeneous collections of different peoples: in some cases their limits actually break up national identity. The

Uriyas, the Marathas, and the Canarese are each distributed between two local governments. Provinces were formed, as chance befell, of areas unassorted from the jumble of conquest, and no better arrangement could have been devised for the atrophy of a feeling of affection for the homeland. Aspirations which, if focussed, might have stimulated the pride that leads to self-improvement, have in vague diffusion hurled themselves against the British supremacy. Other advantages would have been gained had it been possible to divide the country between governments that were smaller and much more numerous than the existing administrative provinces. There would have been closer inspection and greater intimacy between the people and the head of their government. Those who have had experience of the administration of large provinces under a Lieutenant-Governor, and of the smaller provinces which have been administered by Chief Commissioners, are generally of opinion that the latter are better suited to the wishes of the people, and to the exigencies of Indian government. And with smaller provinces it would be easier than at present to regulate the employment of Indians in high office to the circumstances of the locality. It is probable that some of them, did they exist, might, at no distant date, be committed very largely to Indian hands. The rendition of Mysore to Indian control has not been a disappointing experiment.

Loyalty to Empire.

What have we done to foster a broader spirit of loyalty—to the Head of the Empire, and to the English Government? Very little, it must be confessed. The authority of a King appeals very strongly to Oriental feelings:

indeed, according to Hindu ideas, devotion to him is a religious sentiment. Indians from the highest to the lowest can also appreciate the dignity of such an institution as the House of Lords, which represents hereditary rank and includes men with whose names as viceroys, governors or military commanders, they have become familiar. But the trend of English politics has been to bring the House of Commons into stronger relief at the expense of the other elements of our constitution. It is from the House of Commons that the Secretary of State derives his authority: it is the House of Commons that he seeks to satisfy: it is in the House of Commons that questions are asked which can embarrass or strengthen the Indian Government. It is unreasonable to suppose that the natives of India should regard with feelings of affection or loyalty a body of men who hold temporary appointments from the hands of the English democracy, and whose authority over India is not based upon representation, or knowledge, or hereditary rank. Why should Indians owe allegiance to Englishmen who are chosen without any reference to Indian affairs by the electors of English constituencies? Because, it may be replied, British electors maintain the navy, which is the ultimate bond of the Empire. But the people of India will be more apt to discover in the authority of the British democracy an assumption of racial superiority which cannot be expected to conciliate their sentiments. Members of the House of Commons who travel in India meet, no doubt, with a good deal of deferential attention. But this seldom springs from any other feeling than a desire to gain some political advantages. To Greater Britain across the seas the supremacy of the House of Commons seems equally unreasonable. The dominions that are self-governing have practically shaken themselves free from its control. Such interference as was recently defeated by the resignation of the Natal ministry is not likely to recur. The fact is that we have accepted the glories and responsibilities of Empire, but have not recognised them officially in our system of government. We are as a man who has added a large estate to his garden, but endeavours to make a shift with his garden establishment. The council of the Secretary of State for India represents an endeavour to give India a voice in the policy of Government. But it has been unable to hold its own against the authority of the Cabinet: its interference is limited to matters of administrative detail, and ir questions of high policy it is rarely even consulted. Nothing is easier than to devise constitutional changes: nothing is more difficult than to carry them out. But we should not feel surprised if India and our dominions across the sea are disposed to resent an authority which does not appeal to their sentiments and does not represent their interests. Many of us have been attracted by the idea of an Imperial Council—a council in the appointment of which the King, the Lords and the Commons, India and our overseas dominions would all share. It would be essential that the Secretaries of State for India and the Colonies should belong to the Council: so long as the United Kingdom maintains the imperial navy, it would be essential that they should also be members of the British Cabinet. There would inevitably ensue such a clash of opinions as has limited the usefulness of the Secretary of State's

Council: the views of the Cabinet would prevail, and difficulties would be increased by the superior dignity of the authority which they would overrule. An alternative proposal is to include in the House of Lords some representatives of India and the oversea dominions. It is not necessary that they should have authority to vote upon questions of British domestic policy, or to pledge the overseas governments that they represent. Their function would be to advise. But to give life to this reform it would be essential that both Secretaries of State should be members of the Upper House, and that members of this House should alone possess the right of interpellating the Government upon Indian and Colonial affairs. Can we venture to hope that, for the Empire's sake, the House of Commons would agree to diminution of its powers, to an act of self-abnegation in the cause of wider interests? If so, we should secure for our Empire a basis of sentiment which is now lacking. A Senate which represented wisdom and experience, as well as birth, which included, moreover, representatives of their own, would for the people of India (and of Greater Britain) command a respect, evoke a sympathy, which can never be accorded to an assembly, however talented and zealous, that is born of the strife of our party politics.

xix.—India's feelings.

It is with many misgivings that an Englishman can attempt to analyse the feelings of an Oriental people. He must not trust too implicitly to their words. For, in the first place, their consciousness of the grievances that annoy them is often hardly so clear as to be expressed: they are as children that are in pain but cannot describe their feelings. And, in the second place, they are disinclined to be expansive in conversation: partly from motives of courtesy, partly from caution, they avoid direct statement, and trust to the intelligence of their listeners to gather their meaning from implication—rather, indeed, from what is left unsaid than from what is expressed. They delight in parables which to a European are not always significant. Their ideas are to be gathered rather from the incidents that come to notice during a long residence in the country than from any study of speeches or newspapers. It is difficult for an Englishman to enter into their feelings. But upon our success in comprehending them depends very greatly our influence in India.

Difficulty of analysis.

We are impressed with the material benefits that British rule has conferred upon India. In our home politics a profit and loss account determines our adherence to one political party or the other, and we are surprised that India should be so inappreciative of her advantages. But

An alien rule must expect some antipathy.

we must realise that we are foreigners in the country, and that a foreign Government cannot, in the nature of things, command much popular sympathy. It must always be on its defence against a spirit of hostility, more or less extended, which is essentially irreconcilable, which desires the expulsion of an alien rule, and will be content with nothing less. It gathers strength from a natural feeling of restlessness. Having slept for some time on one side, we turn over to the other: it is a change, though it may not be so comfortable. In years now past this feeling of hostility exercised itself in underground intrigue with Russian influences. It then aspired to popularity under the symbol of the cow: it was actively propagandist against kine-killing, and fomented in Upper India disturbances which threw large districts into confusion, and were only checked by parading through them regiments of British troops. Its citadel is naturally in the Maratha country, for it was with the Marathas that the British disputed the supremacy of India. For a similar reason we must suspect its influences in the Panjáb, where there are memories of the victorious exploits of the Sikh Confederacy.

The Indian Congress.

It made use of, and has finally devoured, that curious movement known as the Congress, which, started by an Englishman of means and ability, who had retired in disappointment from the service of Government, has for the last thirty years provided India with an amateur parliament. It annually held a sessions in one or other of the large towns, which was attended by two or three hundred delegates from all parts of the country, and, in thousands, by the students and schoolboys of the locality. There was no formal organisation for the selection of delegates: they were indeed self-elected, and without question many of them attended these meetings for change and recreation, and for the pleasure of travelling free of expense. The Congress frequently paid their railway fares. Lawyers were, naturally, the protagonists of these meetings. The debates were conducted with eloquence, and as a general rule without the manifestation of acute anti-British feeling. They annually concluded with the approval of a large number of resolutions, many of which showed no grasp of practical expediency, as, for instance, that the population should be allowed the unrestricted possession of arms. The Congress represented the educated middle classes, and its influence has induced the non-official members of the Legislative Councils strenuously to oppose legislation which aimed at, and has succeeded in, the beneficent purpose of checking the transfer of land from agriculturists to money-lenders. From time to time movements have been started in favour of urgent measures of social reform. The Congress party would have none of them: it relied upon reactionary as well as upon progressive feeling, and was careful to avoid implying that it favoured in social life the liberty it demanded in politics. Its resolutions were politely ignored by the Government: its existence was threatened from time to time by acute internal dissension: its influence declined, and it was not till five years ago that, under an Englishman as president, it gained a fresh accession of popularity, and that its debates were again thought worthy of notice in the English press. The roots of the Congress movement were watered by persons who were bitterly hostile to British rule: but its early popularity represented nothing more serious than the annoyance which was felt by educated non-officials at not being consulted by the Government in regard to its measures. The enlarged constitution of the Legislative Councils has removed all ground for this complaint.

The Congress has now given place to the 'Nationalist' movement, the development of which marks the increasing ascendency of uncompromising opinions. It is not concerned with the improvement of existing methods of Government: its object is to shake off British rule. Like the Irish party, whose title it has adopted, it would rather see grievances continue than seek the assistance of Government for their removal. For the encouragement of Indian industry it prefers the disturbing and evanescent expedient of a boycott to an agitation which would force upon the Government the desirability of changes in the tariff. Its hostility to British rule is supported by no programme of its own. It can discover as an alternative no form of government which could protect India from the violence of the Afghans and Nepalese, or from fierce and sanguinary internal conflict.

The Indian 'Nationalists.'

We must then accept it, that below the surface of Indian society a pulse of hostility will always be throbbing. The waves of its influence will extend, or be thrown back, according as the general sentiment of the country is for or against us. This brings us to the difficulty of the position—the inability of the English race to understand the influence which sentiment exercises over an Eastern people. We reckon up advantages: they, more imaginative, are swayed by feelings. The records of British courage are stirring enough.

Power of sentiment in the East.

But when have we displayed such passionate devotion as has on several occasions moved Rajput garrisons, when hopelessly beleaguered, to complete self-sacrifice? There is a solemn service of consecration: the men dress themselves in yellow—the colour of asceticism: the women assist in preparing an enormous pyre: they ascend it with their children and their property; and their sons and husbands, setting fire to it, rush out of the gates, sword in hand, to meet death among their enemies. To us this appears quixotic: it is not business. This is the difference between East and West.

Disloyalty increased by feelings of wounded pride.

There is nothing which a man of sentiment resents more keenly than behaviour which implies that he is of an inferior race. The Indian gentleman will admit English superiority in particular attributes: these are regarded as accidents. But anything which reflects upon his race as a whole naturally drives him into the camp of our enemies. It is for sentimental reasons that Indians prize so tenaciously the proclamation which was issued by Queen Victoria after the suppression of the Mutiny. Its words breathe a spirit of lofty impartiality:—

'We hold Ourselves bound to the Natives of Our Indian Territories by the same Obligations of Duty which bind Us to all Our other Subjects; and those Obligations, by the Blessing of Almighty God, We shall faithfully and conscientiously fulfil. . . . And it is Our further Will that, so far as may be, Our Subjects, of whatever Race or Creed, be fully and impartially admitted to offices in Our Service, the Duties of which they may be qualified, by their education, ability, and integrity, duly to discharge.'

To Indians our attitude appears not infrequently to be out of accord with these professions. It is not altogether that Englishmen reserve for themselves posts of control in the Government service : Indians will frankly admit that this is necessary for administrative as well as political reasons. It is that the feelings of Indians are wounded by the treatment they sometimes receive in their dealings with Englishmen, and by the assumption of racial superiority that it indicates. The well-intentioned efforts that are made to promote social intercourse between Europeans and Indians are contradicted by unpleasant facts. There are many European clubs which will not admit an Indian within their walls. It may be urged that, as a member, he might introduce friends that might not prove desirable, But he is not admitted even as an honorary member. An Indian when travelling by railway occasionally meets with treatment from Europeans which is inexpressibly galling to his feelings. The influence of English ladies is not always for conciliation. English ladies, it may be objected, lower their position if they meet on social terms men who deny them a like association with their wives and daughters. Not so : there is nothing an Indian appreciates more highly than courtesy from an Englishwoman, and Englishwomen who realise this acquire an influence which their husbands may envy. These social humiliations are all the more irritating as they are unaccountably out of accord with the treatment which Indian visitors receive in England. Racial feeling is born rather of apprehension than of dislike : it is a protest against the consciousness of being outnumbered, and does not arise when there is no question of this. A young Indian who, while reading for the bar, has been received on familiar terms in London houses, finds too often, on returning to his country, that English society there has no place for him. His emotions have been graphically drawn in several recent works of fiction. But it is possible to overdraw them. I have known men who had spent three or four years at Oxford or Cambridge voluntarily return to their old customs, exchanging the dinner-table for the floor, and china and glass for brass or bell-metal. But increasing numbers adhere to English habits: they drift apart from Indian, but find no asylum in European society, and seek consolation in extremist politics. A young Indian's experiences of English life do not generally increase his sentimental respect for England's greatness. Some succeed in the examinations which are the objects of their visit; others fail, drift aimlessly through the shadier phases of English life, and imbibe a spirit of resentfulness towards a nation which speaks to India with so patrician a voice, but is in some respects so very plebeian at home. English officials in India do not always realise the acuteness with which Indians resent indignities which appear trifling to our robuster judgments. Kind though he may be in intentions and in deeds, the Englishman is not infrequently severe in his words. To him facts are facts. In standards of behaviour there is still a gulf between East and West, and hardly a day passes that he does not find something for condemnation, which he often expresses in the directest language. To be reprimanded, however severely, in private by his English superior leaves no tinge of bitterness in an Indian's mind; but to be humiliated before others hurts his feelings intensely, and this is not always remembered. These reflections apply, of course, only to the occasional conduct of a few Englishmen. But the pity of it is that one unthinking man may make for us many enemies.

Rules that appear invidious for admission to State service.

We admit Indians to the higher posts of control, but on a system which can hardly fail to damage their self-esteem, and to withdraw from the concession the grace that recommends it. A limited number of Indian officials who have distinguished themselves in the Provincial branch of the service are appointed to posts that ordinarily are reserved for Europeans. But they are permitted to draw very much less pay than would be received by European incumbents. As has already been observed, economy affords a reason for this distinction. But economy may be purchased too dearly. The distinction cannot fail to be humiliating, and must bring home to an Indian official a sense of inferiority every time he draws his monthly salary. Indians can and do enter the ranks of the imperial branch of the Civil Service through the competitive examinations held in London. But they compete under circumstances of exceptional difficulty and expense, and must feel if they succeed that they have overcome obstacles that were intended to exclude them. Moreover, it is undesirable to offer inducements to young Indians to break with their homes and home influences while still too young to stand alone, and to subject themselves to the ordeals of life in a strange country amongst associations that are apt to be demoralising. We have admitted in principle that Indians should not be excluded from the imperial branch of the service. Many of them have justified their promotion by conspicuous loyalty and efficiency, but it is necessary for political as well as administrative reasons that their numbers should be carefully limited. We should emphasise the race question less annoyingly if we dealt with their claims more directly, if we settled from time to time the proportion of posts in the imperial service which could be committed to them, and filled these posts by recruitment in India, with no invidious distinction in regard to rates of pay. It would follow, of course, that Indians should be debarred from competing at the examinations in London. Such being the case, it would be most politic to effect the recruitment in India by competitive examination also; but, in order to secure the high standard of character required, candidature should be limited to young men who have already shown their fitness as members of the provincial service. Provincial officers of, say, three years' standing would be permitted to enter themselves for a special examination under such limitations as would safeguard success from becoming a monopoly for certain provinces or classes of the population. The system would generally be similar to that on which officers of the British army are selected for the privileges of the Staff College. The provincial service now attracts the very best of the young Indian talent which does not try its fortune in England, and the arrangement which is suggested is not open to the objection that it would create discontent by adding a speculative value to provincial appointments—by encouraging, that is to say, men to enter that service, not for its own sake, but merely as a stepping-stone to the imperial branch.

It cannot, however, be denied that within the last few years very substantial concessions have been made to Indian sentiment. The increase in the number and authority of non-officials on the Legislative Councils, the appointment of Indians to high office on the Councils of the Viceroy, of the Governors of Bombay and Madras, and of the Secretary of State, and on the Privy Council, redeem very substantially the promises made in Queen Victoria's proclamation. They will not only increase the self-respect of Indians: they will heighten the respect in which Indians are held by Europeans in India.

Recent substantial concessions to sentiment.

If, however, by neglecting the claims of Indian sentiment we expose it to the overtures of anti-British influences, it is essential to realise that a similar danger is incurred by weakness of administration. Our influence in India rests not so much upon our strength as upon prevailing ideas of our strength; and if anything occurs to weaken these ideas, the people of the country prepare themselves for a change of rulers. The traditions of a thousand years are not easily forgotten. During this period no dynasty has maintained itself much beyond the limit of a couple of centuries. For this reason a policy of concession, of compromise, is exceedingly dangerous. We must do justice, but because it is justice, and not because we are afraid of consequences. The idea of give and take, which influences so materially the course of English politics, is foreign to Indian notions of government. It does not conciliate our opponents: it merely strengthens their hold upon the imagination of the people.

Disloyalty popularised by weakness of administration.

On the other hand, efficiency of administration is a force that draws popular feeling towards us and weakens the armoury of the anti-British crusade.

There is a tendency amongst English politicians to consider that we may overvalue efficiency in our government of India. It should certainly not lead us to vexatious interference with the customs of the people in matters that are not of real importance. But it should never be forgotten that to a philosopher—and every Indian of intelligence is given to philosophise—it is the strenuous benevolence of our administration that justifies our presence in the country—that makes it worth India's while to accept our authority; and if, by intervening on behalf of the poorer classes, we cause some annoyance to those who might otherwise exploit them, so long as justice is on our side, we command a feeling which few men will repudiate, even though their personal interests may suffer. And if the masses of the people do not show active gratitude for our intervention, they none the less appreciate it in their hearts; and, when invited to condemn our administration, they have something to appeal to for a judgment in favour of it.

Loyalty popularised by efficiency of administration.

Strength and efficiency of administration appeal to the imagination, and it is by their display that we retain the allegiance of conservative forces that are disposed actively to assist us—the Indian princes, the commercial community, the Muhammadans and the Indian staff of our public services. Those who have invested money in trade or industry are naturally on the side of constituted authority: but they will only combine to its assistance when they can trust it determinately to check revolutionary propaganda. The Muhammadans are in a minority and look to us for protection: they

Conservative influences.

will expect it, however, only when they receive it. By their religion and their political ideas they are less disposed than the Hindus to dissent from the assumptions which lie at the root of Imperial authority. It is difficult to overrate the influence of our public services if they remain confident in their loyalty. They include thousands of employés whose relationships ramify throughout every class in the population. They are proud of their position. To an Oriental enrolled in a club, a service, or a regiment, *esprit de corps* is a sentiment possessing the strength of a patriotic, even of a religious, fervour. When supported by the Government, they exhibit, as a rule, courageous independence of the feelings that may be agitating the country around them, and, in spite of every kind of social pressure, will manfully enforce the law against their countrymen and caste-fellows. But their efficiency depends upon their prestige, upon the influence they exert over the imagination of others. If an idea should gain currency that the Government is not prepared to uphold them, that it regards zeal as inconvenient, and will sometimes even sacrifice them to conciliate opposition, their hearts fail them, loyal enthusiasm deserts them, and they may even endeavour to make terms with revolutionaries. And why not? Few men can stand alone.

Conciliatory effect of personal influence.

But of all the forces that work for our credit, few can rank with the influence of individual British officers, and it is the tragedy of our rule that the conditions of service in India limit so narrowly the profit we can draw from it. In the East official relations are transfigured by a personal devotion which we can hardly appreciate.

It lies at the root of that fidelity which, amongst Orientals, shares with courage and generosity the esteem with which mankind regards its noblest attributes. It is from Orientals that we have borrowed its picturesque description as 'faithfulness to the salt.' In troublous times the influence of individual Englishmen has enabled them to preserve little oases of tranquillity in the midst of confusion. The name of John Nicholson at once occurs to us: he was actually worshipped after his death. The personal loyalty which was exhibited in the Mutiny is at least as surprising as the wave of disaffection that it ineffectually opposed. Few Englishmen of any character can have served in India who are not able to illustrate from their own experiences the unquestioning devotion, not only of their Indian subordinates, but of private individuals—landholders, merchants, and lawyers—whose friendship they have made in the course of their duties. Few have no memories of crowds assembled to bid them farewell on their transfer from their districts, even of tears shed, or who on their retirement from service do not receive letters from Indians who are anxious to be remembered by them. A popular officer, on returning to India from leave, will be met at the railway station by a host of friends and admirers who will travel long distances to catch sight of him. Nor do memories fade very rapidly. The son of an Indian officer on reaching India will receive warm greetings from his father's old friends. Personal feelings of regard can withstand the fever of political excitement, and not a few of those who are now in the hostile camp maintain a cordial correspondence with British ex-officials whose acquaintance they have made in earlier days. These feelings can be of immense assistance to us in counteracting the effects of seditious agitation, but unfortunately we turn them to little advantage. Officers are transferred with deplorable frequency. It is exceptional that a man should remain four years in a district, and it happens not infrequently that the people find their interests committed to a stranger two or three times in the course of a year. They are greatly perturbed by these changes: for weeks together the character and disposition of their new chief is a subject of anxious speculation. Much of this shifting is inevitable. Europeans serving in a hot climate require leave at frequent intervals: sudden failures of health are not uncommon: the drift of promotion carries men from office to office, and it seems hard to deny a man advancement because his local influence is useful. But undoubtedly there would be less waste of influence were it not customary to recognise merit or to show favour by transferring officers from one district to another—from a district that, owing to climate or other reasons, is not liked, to one that is a more agreeable charge. Districts differ, of course, very greatly in pleasantness and importance. It is difficult to deny a senior meritorious officer—especially on his return from leave—a transfer which to him has the same effect as promotion. But the practice is carried too far, and would be less general were the value of personal influence more clearly realised. In the past we have set but little store by it—perhaps because we have felt that we could dispense with its assistance Even when an officer is being selected for such high administrative posts as those of Lieutenant-Governor or Chief Commissioner, his personal influence in the country has seldom entered into the balance. The most serviceable passport to high executive responsibility has been success, as a secretary, in an office.

Gratitude.

But, it will be asked, apart from feelings of esteem for individual officers, are the people not grateful to the British Government for what it has done for them? This is the question invariably put by an Englishman who has listened to an account of official endeavours. The mass of the people are conscious of benefit and value it. But it does not move them beyond a feeling of acquiescent appreciation. They may be convinced that under British rule they enjoy advantages which it alone can offer them. But they are accustomed to analyse very strictly the motives of human conduct, and, finding no reason to suppose that the British do not receive an adequate recompense for their labours, they are inclined to attribute to self-interest the zeal and industry from which they profit. They observe that individual officers win promotion and honour by good work, and they can hardly believe that the work is disinterested. Accordingly they see no cause to be particularly grateful for it. One finds traces of this feeling everywhere. Coolies who are paid in a famine relief camp for work that is in itself quite useless, are convinced that the State receives good value for its money, and show little gratitude. This they reserve for relief that is granted quite gratuitously; and even then they will speculate whether in keeping children alive the Government has not an eye to the cultivation of the land and its future land revenue. Men of intelligence will look doubtful if we claim for our Government that it is disinterested, and will think of our deference to the interests of Lancashire in favouring it so unfairly in the taxation of cotton goods: they are perfectly well aware of such facts as that the Colonial Office is maintained at England's expense, whereas India has to pay for the very generous upkeep of the India Office. We appeal with all the pride of philanthropy to our railways and canals: the Indian people understand that they are a source of profit. Women of northern India on their way to the railway station will sometimes sing a little song having this refrain:—

'See how the English
Covet our pennies
And haul us about in a smoke-car.'

But let me not be misunderstood. The Indian people are not enthusiastic over our efforts for them, not because they are unappreciative of self-denial, but because, to them, the self-denial is not apparent. There is no country in the world which sets so high a value upon renunciation of self: with the Hindus, in particular, it is the very summit of virtue. Accordingly, when they notice generosity or self-sacrifice which expects no reward and is not even displayed, they honour it from their hearts, and the most popular officers are undoubtedly those who are generous, free-handed in private charity, and who will privately put themselves to inconvenience in assisting their Indian clients out of difficulties. A man who possesses these merits may even be as hot-tempered as he pleases: the two most popular officers I have known were on occasions remarkably vigorous in expressing displeasure. Things are changing even in the East; but I think there still lingers an admiration for the man who possesses the 'kingly disposition' of the well-known Persian couplet :—

> 'There are days when your humble salaams
> He requites with a frown,
> But your hate he's as like to repay
> With a broidered gown.'[1]

Loyalty.

And what of loyalty to the Empire—to the King? We must look at things as they are, and must not expect that the idea of Imperial unity should appeal to men who are denied admission to the Empire's oversea territories. To us the Empire means union : to the Indians it has not this significance. It is no more than reasonable that Indians should resent the treatment of their fellow-countrymen in South Africa. The position may be one of insoluble difficulty. Indians of intelligence will appreciate its complications. But we should at least secure that the enforcement of the law is not accompanied by the offer of unnecessary indignity. Fortunately, the King-Emperor stands above these troubles, on the eminence to which an hereditary monarch is exalted by the religion as well as the sentiment of the East. But from the West come impressions which may perhaps blur the figure of royalty. An Indian nobleman of enlightened intelligence has recently expressed in the Legislative Council of the Viceroy the astonishment with which he compared the high importance that in his country was set upon respect to the Crown, with statements that were tolerated in England, such as that recently made by a Member of Parliament that the Crown must soon come into the melting-pot. No one,

[1] The *khillat*, which is commonly given in durbar as a reward of merit.

however, can have witnessed the enormous concourse of people who assembled to greet the Prince of Wales on his arrival in Calcutta but must have felt that royalty appeals to India with a force that is possessed by no other of our institutions. The loyal feelings with which Queen Victoria was regarded by the people of India were tinged with real affection. It mattered not that she was distant from them and personally unknown. For them she manifested the gracious, sympathetic queenliness of heroic legend; and their feelings were deeply touched by actions which to us appeared of no great significance, such as the pains she took to gain some acquaintance with their language. Her death evoked genuine sorrow throughout the land. By the unlearned, indeed, she was invested with the attributes of a female deity, and embodied a conception that has at all times appealed to the sentiment of mankind.

Index.